# THE WORLD CUP'S
# STRANGEST
## MOMENTS

*Other titles in this series*

# THE WORLD CUP'S
# STRANGEST
## MOMENTS

Extraordinary but true tales from 80 years of
World Cup football

## Peter Seddon

**PORTICO**

To the next England side to bring the World Cup
home again.

First published in Great Britain in 2005

This revised edition published in 2010 by
Portico
10 Southcombe Street
London
W14 0RA

An imprint of Anova Books Company Ltd.

Copyright © 2005, 2009 Peter Seddon

The moral right of the author has been asserted.

The author has made every reasonable effort to contact all copyright holders.
Any errors that may have occurred are inadvertent and anyone who for any
reason has not been contacted is invited to write to the publishers so that a full
acknowledgement may be made in subsequent editions of the work.

A CIP catalogue record for this book is available from the
British Library.

10 9 8 7 6 5 4 3 2

ISBN 978-1-90603-291-3

Typeset by SX composing DTP, Rayleigh, Essex
Printed and bound by L.E.G.O SpA, Trento, Italy

This book can be ordered direct from the publisher at
www.anovabooks.com

# *ACKNOWLEDGEMENTS*

I would like to thank all the journalists and authors who have chronicled the World Cup since its inception. Their articles and publications have been an entertaining and valuable reference source during the writing of this book.

To friends and colleagues who chipped in with their own favourite stories or read the preliminary text I also say a big thank you – particularly to my partner Kate Ibbitson.

In addition I wish to thank the team at Anova Books for embracing the initial idea and bringing the manuscript to publication, in particular Matthew Jones and Malcolm Croft.

Finally, I must express gratitude to all the players, fans and sundry fringe characters without whom the World Cup would never have been labelled 'the greatest show on earth'.

# Contents

# *INTRODUCTION*

When the first FIFA World Cup kicked off in Uruguay in 1930 it was by way of a bold experiment. Organisers, competitors and spectators alike entered a strange new domain, where anything might happen. The entire event could prove an almighty flop never to be staged again. Or it might catch on.

My overview of that inaugural World Cup ('The Die is Cast') leaves little in the balance. The novel event caught on. Eighty years later, the glittering spectacle continues its four-yearly cycle as millions of football fans around the globe anticipate, then enjoy – or endure, depending on the fortunes of their favoured teams – another *mondial*. They can't all be wrong. No wonder the World Cup has been dubbed 'the greatest show on earth'.

If the next World Cup follows the pattern of its predecessors, it will serve up all the ingredients that any great show would crave – drama, excitement, passion, colour, emotion, comedy, tragedy and breathtaking twists. Grand stages are guaranteed; so too are moments of unscripted genius. And of course the occasional clown. It wouldn't do to forget referees.

It's that heady mix that I have set out to present in *The World Cup's Strangest Moments*. This isn't a history of the World Cup. That's been done. What I aim to do is to capture the tournament's flavour, and above all to entertain. As for what I regard as 'strange', the stories that made the cut all have one thing in common: their theme is 'uncommon', a departure from the expected.

I have included events both on and off the field. And I decided very early on to embrace the qualifying competition. Such is the desperation of teams to be part of the World Cup finals that the very pursuit of 'getting there' has produced some odd moments indeed.

Spectacular failures in that category include some not particularly famous Belgians ('A Famously Unlucky XI'), a very famous Frenchman ('He Wasn't Worth It') and a famously comedic Englishman with a manic aversion to root vegetables, the colour orange and all things vaguely Dutch ('Did We Not Like That'). Never offer to cook carrots in hollandaise sauce for Graham Taylor.

Sometimes the boot is on the other foot. A number of nations have qualified for the World Cup when they patently weren't ready for the experience. 'The Wheels Came Off' explains how West Germany '74 made a laughing stock of poor Zaïre and a skinflint of their country's President. El Salvador were the fall guys at Spain '82 ('Kissed Goodbye'), while once was enough for the Dutch East Indies at France '38 ('No Second Chance').

For one hapless nation the boot wasn't on either foot. The bizarre 'bootless' debate in 'No Passage for India' is the sole story of its kind. But it's not the only tale from the ever-mysterious east. Pakistan's bold attempt to reach USA '94 was ruined by a schoolboy error ('Please, Sir'). Iraq's failure to clinch a place at France '98 rendered Saddam Hussein's son even more unpleasant than usual ('A Terrible Loser'). Nor was there much delight in Turkey when the Spanish got the luck of the draw en route to Switzerland '54 ('Luigi with the Bandaged Eyes').

But making strange news isn't always a team effort. The individual scoring feats of Just Fontaine ('Just Magnifique') and Paolo Rossi ('Vintage Rossi') couldn't be ignored. Nor could the endearing antics of a veteran 'supersub' ('Roger and Out') and the eccentric acrobatics of a flamboyant goalkeeper ('Clown Prince of Poland'). Nor does individual 'strangeness' always confine itself to the field. No balls were kicked in the 'Bobby Moore is Innocent' story, although the British prime minister, Harold Wilson, did his best with those belonging to the Colombian ambassador to London.

That bizarre affair from 1970 was irritating and unexpected, but never 'tragic'. That overused tag has been reserved for the desperate story of Andrés Escobar ('Truly Tragic') and the heartbreaking accidents that befell the Italians ('Taken at their Peak') and the Zambians ('An Aerial Nightmare') just when their hopes had been so high.

At times in my research the spectre of death seemed almost to stalk me, not least when I strayed into Africa. 'A Stiff Decision' and 'Back from the Dead' are both stories with a peculiarly African twist. But even they didn't match the South Korean fan who took his own life in a way no football fan had emulated before or since ('The Twelfth Man'). It is truly odd what the mania surrounding a World Cup can lead to. Far too often it has been the grave.

So I've balanced the dark side with incidents of a lighter hue. Man's best friend is always good for a humorous tale – both 'Cheers and Pickles' and 'Greavsie's Famous Dribble' are far more than shaggy-dog stories.

Mascots too are generally game for a laugh. 'We All Knew his Name' lifts the lid on the proud but incestuous conception of World Cup Willie. And 'Beyond Our Ken' pays homage to his human counterpart Ken Baily, whose cheery character and faintly eerie grin made him 'the most famous man in Bournemouth'!

It's but a short step from naturally fun characters to those who manage to be comic accidentally. Football's world governing body, FIFA, seems often to be the butt of irreverent humour, and I saw no reason to stray from that path. 'Not Down Mexico Way' is one of several tales of organisational incompetence that show football's 'bigwigs' in a typically ludicrous light.

At which point I must mention Arthur Ellis, Ken Aston, Clive Thomas and Graham Poll, all of which British 'men in black' have used their position as referee to facilitate mayhem where serene calm once reigned. Jack Taylor made a pretty good job of it too ('The Butcher of Wolverhampton').

Coaches pop up at the oddest moments. I didn't intend to mention the England manager Alf Ramsey in the same sentence as *petits pois* ('RIP, Sir Alf'). Like the only unguarded moment in Alf's entire life, it just happened. And I'm still not sure how I came to write a piece on Glenn Hoddle without the blessing of his controlling guru Eileen Drewery ('No Way Back').

When such personalities became all too tiresome, I took refuge in linguistic curiosities such as 'The Odd Couple' and 'Lessons in Japanese'. And a drinking pal named 'Big Jim' introduced me to a neat but spectacularly futile numerical conundrum which he called 'The X Factor'. It didn't help David Batty.

Other stories defy categorisation. The nearest I can get is 'having fun at Scotland's expense'. 'Archie Steals the Show' and 'Up the Existentialists' are both shot through with north-of-the-border absurdity. And of course there are the Germans. An episode I particlarly enjoyed writing was 'Fantasy Football', which charts a rare victory that restored pride to a great nation – not Germany.

The book contains more than a hundred stories in chronological order. But they can be dipped into and out of at random. I am grateful to the personalities who made their telling possible and to all the writers whose own accounts of 'the greatest show on earth' have proved invaluable in my research.

Finally may I wish the very best of luck to all future World Cup participants, while being certain in the knowledge that further oddities will befall the hapless few. As far as *The World Cup's Strangest Moments* is concerned, that's the best news since Germany 1 England 5.

Peter Seddon
Derbyshire, May 2010

# WE ARE THE CHAMPIONS

## GLASGOW, 19 MAY 1888

A strange myth endures in Scotland that says the first World Cup was held in Glasgow in 1888 and won by the host nation. The first World Cup was indeed won by the host nation, but that happened to be Uruguay. And the date was 1930. Someone north of the border is guilty of artistic licence.

The fantasy merchants were Renton FC, a once-powerful small village club from Dunbartonshire. In 1888 Renton won the Scottish FA Cup and West Bromwich Albion lifted the English Cup. An end-of-season 'friendly' between the two victors was duly arranged.

It was by no means the first such game. Scottish Cup Winners versus English Cup Winners had been a regular fixture for some years. They were little more than novelty matches, but Renton had other ideas. Ones way above their station.

The game was played at Hampden Park on 19 May 1888. Having already overcome mighty Preston North End in the English Cup final at Kennington Oval, Albion arrived in Scotland with a proud reputation. But it was a filthy day in Glasgow, and 'The Throstles' failed dismally to adapt to the soggy conditions. Renton romped home winners by four goals to one.

That should have been it. A meaningless game on a dreary Scottish Saturday. There was no trophy and no title at stake. But Renton put their publicity machine on full power. Their logic was simple. British football was king. The Continentals were nowhere. So Renton were not only 'Champions of the United Kingdom' but by definition the best team on the entire planet.

After informing the press of their self-proclaimed international supremacy, they erected a sign over their clubhouse door: CHAMPIONS OF THE WORLD. All they needed now was a trophy.

1

So they had one made. Visitors to the Scottish Football Museum at the new Hampden Park can still gaze upon the grandly inscribed silverware: RENTON FC – CHAMPIONS OF THE UNITED KINGDOM AND THE WORLD.

As an exercise in self-publicity, no other team has matched it. Although Renton were never deprived of their lofty title, the team itself fell on hard times. After five games of the 1898–99 season they dropped out of the Scottish League, and subsequently folded completely in 1922.

So never be fooled by a Scotsman who tells you the first World Cup was in Glasgow in 1888. That soaring fantasy was the nearest a Scottish eleven ever came to global domination. Unfortunately for them (but to the lasting amusement of many), the tartan challenge had peaked 42 years before the real World Cup began.

# ENGLAND'S PRETENDERS

## TURIN, 12 APRIL 1909

Imagine being in the hot seat on television's *Who Wants to be a Millionaire*. The £1 million question looks simple enough. In which year was the first World Cup tournament held? And then the doubts set in. 1930 leaps to the fore. But 1888, 1909 and 1911 are also showing. So be prepared.

Renton's dubious 1888 claim (see 'We are the Champions') has already been scotched, so it's only fair that a team of English pretenders should also have their card marked. Followers of West Auckland Town insist it was *their* boys who won the first World Cup in 1909. What's more, they reckon they retained it two years later.

The astonishing tale began when the millionaire grocery baron Sir Thomas Lipton (of tea fame) was made a Knight of the Grand Order of Italy for his business achievements there. Lipton, a keen sports fan, expressed the desire to reciprocate the honour. The Italians suggested he organise a 'world football tournament' to be held in Turin.

The idea came to fruition in 1909. Lipton approached the FA about sending a team of British representatives, but with typical insularity they refused to sanction the release of professional players. It was left to one of Lipton's employees to come to the rescue. He had contacts with a lowly amateur club in County Durham. That's how West Auckland Town became the unlikely British representatives in what countless sources have dubbed 'the first World Cup'.

The tiny pit village team lay third from bottom of the Northern Amateur League. Most of the players were poverty-stricken miners, but full of determination and hard as nails. Jobs and possessions were sacrificed to finance the journey. And the origins of the anonymous minnows were kept quiet. Rumours circulated in Italy that WAFC stood for Woolwich Arsenal Football Club. No one from West Auckland troubled to deny them.

Only four teams competed in a knockout format. In Round One West Auckland beat Stuttgarter Sportfreunde of Germany 2–0, while the Swiss side FC Winterthur overcame the hosts Torino 2–1. The final was staged on 12 April 1909 at the Torino ground. West Auckland took no prisoners. Their left-back Hogg, known as 'Dirty Hoggy', seemed especially keen to live up to his name. The artistry of the Swiss stood little chance in the face of true Durham grit. West Auckland scored twice in the first ten minutes and Winterthur rolled over without reply. The pit lads lifted the trophy known as the 'Crown of Italy World Cup'.

Lipton decided to repeat the tournament in 1911. West Auckland were invited back to Italy as holders, with the promise that they could keep the trophy for ever if they won it again. Once more the lowly miners obliged, beating Red-Star Zurich of Switzerland 2–0 and inflicting a humbling 6–1 defeat on Juventus in the final. The 32-inch solid-silver cup returned to West Auckland for good.

At least until it was stolen. In January 1994, true to established World Cup tradition, the coveted trophy disappeared from the West Auckland Working Men's Club in the dead of night. Although it was never recovered, a replica now stands in its place. West Auckland Football Club guards its prize with pride.

The remarkable story of 'the first World Cup' was made into a 90-minute drama by Tyne Tees television in 1982. Dennis Waterman played the title role of Bob Jones in *A Captain's Tale*. Some liberties were taken with the plot, but the core story is perfectly true and much stranger than fiction.

Sir Thomas Lipton's 'World Cup' wasn't the global tournament now labelled 'the greatest show on earth', but the series of games didn't go unnoticed by the influential body of men at the Fédération Internationale de Football Association – or FIFA.

Should the £1 million question ever come your way, stick with 1930. That's when the real deal known as the 'FIFA World Cup' began in earnest.

# THE DIE IS CAST

## MONTEVIDEO, 13 JULY 1930

When FIFA was formed in May 1904 it reserved the exclusive right to organise a world championship. The first 'FIFA World Cup' duly began in Uruguay on 13 July 1930. Twenty-six years getting its act together seems about right for football's world governing body. Nobody knew whether the tournament would be a huge success or a lame one-off experiment. The entire event embraced the concept of 'strangeness', for neither fans nor players nor officials had ever experienced anything like it before. What sort of tone did it set? Cue edited highlights.

FIFA's selection of the Olympic Champions Uruguay as hosts condemned sides from Europe to a fifteen-day Atlantic crossing just to get there. Little wonder only France, Romania, Yugoslavia and Belgium bothered to travel. The Americas supplied all the other participants – Uruguay, Argentina, Brazil, Chile, Bolivia, Peru, Paraguay, Mexico and the United States. That made 13 teams. FIFA's first major cock-up was complete.

Both France against Mexico and USA versus Belgium were the 'first game'. They kicked off simultaneously in Montevideo, where all the matches were played. Minor stadiums were used for the opening fixtures because the prestigious new Estadio Centenário wasn't finished on time. It was winter in Uruguay. Snow fell the night before kick-off. A strangely symmetrical crowd of 4,444 saw France's Lucien Laurent score the first ever World Cup goal.

Elsewhere, players and officials queued up to clinch an early place in *The World Cup's Strangest Moments*. The Argentine captain Manuel Ferreira missed their game against Mexico because he returned to Buenos Aires to sit a vital law exam. The referee for that match was Ulrico Saucedo, better known as the manager of Bolivia. He awarded three penalties and still didn't notice that the spot was sixteen yards (it should be twelve) from goal. His linesman was the manager of Romania, whose squad had been chosen by their king (see 'By Royal Appointment'). One of the Bolivians played in a beret. The Uruguayan forward Hector Castro was missing his right hand, carelessly severed in a 'carpentry accident'.

Belgium's star player Raymond Braine got himself suspended from the entire tournament by the Belgian FA – for the heinous crime of opening a café. The Brazilian referee, Gilberto Rêgo, lost all track of time (see 'An Absolute Stinker'). Only 300 fans watched Romania beat Peru. The official crowd for Paraguay versus Belgium was 25,466. The unofficial figure was 9,000, which some statisticians believe to be a misprint for '900'. So the crowd was somewhere between 900 and 25,466.

Uruguay's first-choice goalkeeper, Andrés Mazali, was dropped shortly before their opening game for breaking a curfew. In the World Cup's first sex scandal, he was caught sneaking out of the hotel for a 'conjugal visit'. Who could blame him? The squad had been incarcerated for nearly eight weeks.

The Bolivian side each played with a large single letter on their shirts. When they first ran out, Englishmen wondered why their message spelled AIR GUY UVAVU. It proved to be a generous gesture to the hosts. Once they were lined up correctly, all became clear: VIVA URUGUAY.

The full range of standard 'firsts' were quickly established – penalty, own goal, saved penalty, hat trick, glaring miss, fractured jaw, broken leg, sending-off and mass brawl involving Argentina and Chile (thirty officials and police on the pitch). But other individuals established more bizarre records.

In the Argentina-versus-USA semifinal (6–1 to Argentina), the American trainer Jack Coll ran on to tend to a stricken player but had to be helped off the field semiconscious. An untimely trip caused him to inhale the contents of a bottle of chloroform, which spilled in his bag. In the Uruguay-versus-Yugoslavia semifinal (6–1 to Uruguay), the host's third goal was scored after the ball went out of play and was deftly kicked back on by a uniformed policeman. All the officials pretended not to notice.

So to the final between Uruguay and Argentina. The Argentine captain, Luis Monti (see 'Double Monti'), received a death threat before the game. Both sides wanted to use their own ball. They compromised by swapping at half-time. A moat surrounded the pitch. All Argentine spectators were searched for weapons. The Belgian referee, John Langenus, wearing a cap and plus-fours, insisted on police protection. Thousands of Argentine fans failed to arrive for the game because their boats across the Rio de la Plata were delayed by thick fog.

The hosts Uruguay employed '*tactica robusto*' to prevail 4–2 against their bitter rivals. A national holiday was declared. Each of the Uruguayan players was given a house. Someone died in the celebrations. The Uruguayan embassy in Buenos Aires was stoned by a mob of angry Argentines. The two FAs broke off relations. Eighty years later, dewy-eyed accounts of the 'sporting spirit' and 'genteel atmosphere' of the 'golden age' of 1930s football are common.

So there you have it. The 1930 tournament was a perfectly normal World Cup. It was exactly what we have come to expect. The crowds loved it. FIFA decided to do it again. The unique die labelled '*le mondial*' was cast.

# BY ROYAL APPOINTMENT
## MONTEVIDEO, 14 JULY 1930

Two months before the first World Cup began, not a single European country had entered. England, Scotland, Wales and Northern Ireland had rendered themselves ineligible by withdrawing from FIFA over a dispute concerning payment to 'amateur' players. The disappointed would-be hosts, Holland, Italy, Spain and Sweden, all got the sulks. Austria, Hungary, Czechoslovakia, Germany and Switzerland didn't fancy the sea crossing.

Clearly, for credibility's sake, a swift injection of European enthusiasm was paramount. Blessedly, but half-heartedly, France, Belgium and Yugoslavia did agree to enter. But the most enthusiastic response came from the fourth European participant, Romania, the only team in World Cup history to appear 'By Royal Appointment'.

King Carol II of Romania was a fast mover. Thirty-six days before kick-off, he wasn't even king. With two broken marriages and a string of scandalous affairs behind him, the disgraced 'Prince' Carol had been leapfrogged to the seat of power by his better-behaved son, Michael. But Carol was a man on a mission. On 8 June 1930 the 37-year-old 'Playboy Prince' forcibly reclaimed the throne.

His priorities soon became clear. His first act as reigning monarch was to grant an amnesty to all Romanian players serving suspensions for football offences. That cleared the way. No matter that Romania's international debut was as recent as 1922, or that their first professional club was barely two years old. Upstarts or not, football-mad King Carol set his sights on the 1930 World Cup.

With only days to spare, he lodged Romania's entry with FIFA and selected the squad personally. Then he hit a stumbling block.

His best players worked at an English oil company, whose management refused to grant them paid leave. Worse still, any man travelling without permission would be immediately sacked. Carol countered as only a kingly football manager can. He telephoned the chairman and threatened to close the company down. The management swiftly relented.

Romania's players sailed from the South of France on 21 June aboard the liner *Conte Verde* and arrived in Montevideo two weeks later. In their opening game against Peru on 14 July, they scored after fifty seconds and won 3–1. The paltry crowd of three hundred inside the Pocitos Stadium were underwhelmed by the dream start of the rank outsiders. The 'Royals' evidently weren't box office.

Their next opponents Uruguay certainly were. Before over 70,000 in the Estadio Centenário ('Centenary Stadium'), Romania succumbed to both stage fright and superior skill as the hosts swept them aside 4–0. With only one side per group qualifying for the next stage, Romania were left with nothing but the boat fare home after just two games.

But the taking part proved to be everything. King Carol died in exile in Portugal in 1953 after further scandals of the flesh, but Romania's historians still credit him with kick-starting the nation's ongoing passion for football. 'Carol', by the way, is the English equivalent of Charles, but the current heir to the British throne is not thought to be pursuing his FA Coaching Badge.

# *AN ABSOLUTE STINKER*

## MONTEVIDEO, 15 JULY 1930

Brian Clough's celebrated assertion that 'It only takes a second to score a goal' recognises 'time' as football's most valuable commodity. That's why the game needs competent officials to administer it. And why the Brazilian Gilberto de Almeida Rêgo is remembered for a World Cup refereeing debut that proved the most untimely on record.

FIFA seemed nervous about the officials from the start. They appointed fifteen referees for only thirteen competing nations. And all attended a pre-tournament symposium aimed at minimising the error count. Unfortunately, 'how to tell the time' had been missed off the agenda.

Rêgo was given Argentina versus France as his opening fixture. Argentina were considered the main threat to the hosts and favourites Uruguay, so most of the locals inside the Parque Central were firmly behind France. Making life difficult for Argentinians is a popular hobby in Montevideo.

France made a good fist of it, holding out until the 81st minute, when the referee permitted Argentina's hatchet man, Luisito Monti, to take a quick free kick of the type more recently favoured by France's Thierry Henry. The fast-thinking Monti more or less passed the ball into an untended net.

But France weren't dead. With six minutes to go (remember that's 360 scoring opportunities in Clough terms), their flying left winger Marcel Langiller broke away and bore down on the Argentine goal. But whether he crossed, passed, scored a screaming equaliser or meekly fluffed remains entirely academic, because referee Rêgo blew for time – in the 84th minute.

All hell let loose. The Argentine players celebrated wildly. Some even wept with relief. Their exuberant fans scaled the perimeter fencing to invade the pitch. But, even as the dubious 'victors' leaped for joy, the French players were surrounding the referee. And their manager Raoul Caudron, the Alex Ferguson of his day, launched into a manic wrist-tapping routine.

Uruguayans in the crowd soon joined the on-pitch mêlée to lobby for France. Then on came the mounted police. Only slowly was order restored as the French players trooped disconsolately to the dressing room. But Rêgo wasn't finished.

After repeatedly examining his watch and then consulting a linesman, he dramatically admitted to a mistake. With his arms raised to the heavens as witness, he cried in perfect French, '*Marquez que je me suis trompé de bonne foi!*' (something like 'I have dropped a large part of a bull's anatomy'), as he frantically raced to recall the retreating 'losers', who were already heading for the showers.

Now all that remained was to tell the Argentinians, still revelling on the pitch.

This he bravely did while armed police cleared the field of straggling fans. It was all too much for Argentina's inside-left, Cierro, who was said to have fainted with rage during the fracas and was unable to continue for 'the lost six minutes' when the flustered Rêgo restarted the game.

To paraphrase Kevin Keegan, I would really love it (love it, I tell you) if I could say the French scored two to win the game. Alas, their momentum knocked sideways by the referee's dreadful timekeeping error, they failed to score any.

FIFA allotted Rêgo two more games to atone for his absolute stinker and to appease the unimpressed locals. Conveniently, both involved Uruguay. This time he kept going for the full ninety minutes in both matches as scores of 4–0 and 6–1 kept the hosts happy en route to beating Argentina in the final.

Several World Cup referees have since been involved in timing controversies, but none has fallen so far short in his professional duties as the 84-minute Brazilian.

# *NOT DOWN MEXICO WAY*

## ROME, 24 MAY 1934

When FIFA granted the second World Cup to Italy, none of the prospective participants seemed in the least concerned that a bullying dictator held power there. They knew Benito Mussolini would use the tournament to showcase his 'modern Fascist state', but all agreed that the sinister fanaticism of 'Il Duce' shouldn't affect the football itself.

So this time FIFA were spared the indignity of begging for entrants. Thirty-two countries applied for just sixteen places in the finals. After only one tournament, the World Cup had officially 'caught on'. And that signalled the introduction of the first qualifying competition.

It was a perfect opportunity for FIFA to demonstrate their organisational skills, but it was a chance they failed miserably to take. In truth, football's world governing body scored a hat trick of spectacular own goals.

Their first big mistake was insisting Italy must qualify. Mussolini wasn't the sort of host it paid to upset. Luckily for FIFA, they got away with it, as Italy swept aside Greece 4–0 in the first leg of their qualifier in Milan and then 'persuaded' their opponents that a second leg wasn't necessary.

A Greek insider later told a German investigator (who received a death threat from the terrorist group Fiamme Nere – the 'Black Flames' – for his nosiness) that the Italians 'built a property in Athens for the Greek FA in exchange for conceding the game.' FIFA's top brass sighed with relief, turned a blind eye and learned a lesson. The game remains the only qualifier played by a host country.

Major gaffe number two was their decision to make the finals themselves a straight knockout tournament. That meant half the teams who had successfully negotiated the qualifiers would have to return home after a solitary game. Romania, Belgium, France, Holland and Egypt all suffered that fate, but at least hadn't journeyed too far. Not so the other 'one-gamers', the USA, Argentina and Brazil. Asking South America's big two to cross the Atlantic twice for ninety minutes' football (that's ninety miles per minute) was bordering on insult.

But Mexico were the victims of the crassest error of all. Never believe that the Scots are the unsurpassed masters of fruitless World Cup travel. Their 'back before the postcards' reputation is nothing compared with Mexico's sorry fate at Italia '34.

On paper the Mexicans' passage to Italy looked easy. All it entailed was seeing off their sole opponent, Cuba, in a three-game series. No problem. Victories of 3–2, 5–0 and 4–1 represented a comprehensive qualifying campaign by any standards. Their finals place was assured.

Or should have been. But that reckoned without the USA, who arrogantly submitted a late application for the qualifying competition after the groups had already been decided. FIFA should have told them where to get off, but were apparently ignorant of the time-honoured English phrase 'hard cheese'. Instead, they bent over backwards to accommodate the super-powerful latecomers.

And it was poor little Mexico that got shafted. FIFA bizarrely ordered them to meet the USA in a sudden-death play-off on 24 May, just three days before the World Cup began. It ended 4–2 in America's favour. Apart from being abjectly unfair, the game is also noted in the record books because all four USA goals were scored by Aldo T 'Buff' Donelli, an Italian-American whose odd nickname referred to his peculiar obsession with the Wild West legend 'Buffalo Bill' Cody. Understandably, the USA's eleventh-hour qualification for the finals after just a single victory left Mexico mightily unimpressed.

But their shameful dismissal via the qualifying game from nowhere isn't the strangest part of the story. That belongs to the venue. Last time I looked, Mexico and USA were neighbours on the far side of the Atlantic to Europe. So where did FIFA order the play-off to be staged? The Stadio Nazionale del Partito Nazionale Fascista – in Rome.

'Il Duce' himself was one of ten thousand spectators who witnessed Mexico's unjust exclusion from the tournament, but by the time he saw Italy kick off the finals three days later (poetic justice: they beat the USA 7–1), the Mexicans were already going home sooner than any nation in World Cup history.

They had made a round trip of eight thousand miles to play 'at' the World Cup but not 'in' it, and remain the only country to suffer that fate. So Scotland still have one hard-luck story to match after all.

# APPOINTMENT WITH DEATH

## ROME, 27 MAY 1934

An individual's probability of meeting death through murder, suicide or 'mysterious circumstances' is said to be 1 in 5,000. Fewer than 250 men participated in the 1934 World Cup in Italy. Yet three of them involved in games on the opening day met their maker in one of the above ways. According to the laws of chance, that's the most unlikely hat trick of all time.

The second World Cup began in Rome on 27 May 1934 with the hosts Italy playing the USA. The United States team manager Elmer Schroeder saw his side crumble 7–1 and go out of the tournament after a single game. But Schroeder recovered to forge a great career in soccer, managing the USA side to the 1936 Olympics under politically strained circumstances and becoming president of both the United States Football Association and the American League. After his induction into the Soccer Hall of Fame in 1951, Schroeder had every reason to be a proud, upstanding American citizen.

All of which made it bizarre that he was found dead, hanging by his own window blind cord, just two years later. The strange death has never been explained. Neither tangerines nor fishnet stockings were believed to have been involved.

Death number two featured a player from the Austria-versus-France game in Turin. Austria's centre-forward was the brilliant Matthias Sindelar, known as 'Der Papierene' (The Paper Man) because of his delicate physique and elusive style. He scored Austria's first goal in their 3–2 win.

But he wasn't celebrating five years later. On 23 January 1939 he was found dead in his flat above the coffee house he ran in Vienna. Beside him was the body of Camilla Castagnola, a girl he had met only a few days previously. The inquest concluded that 'carbon monoxide poisoning' was the cause of death, which the police hastily blamed on a faulty flue. But many thought Sindelar, who was Jewish, had been driven to suicide in the face of Nazi oppression.

The Viennese newspaper *Kronen-Zeitung* went a step further: 'All the evidence suggests that this model sportsman was deliberately poisoned by his supposed "girlfriend".' But the truth remains locked in the past. Police investigations were forcibly cancelled by the Nazis after a few months, and all the case documents were reported 'lost' at the end of the war.

The third death is odder still. Again, 27 May 1934 provides the link, since all eight first-round fixtures were played on the opening day. Sweden beat Argentina 3–2 in Bologna. Argentina's second goal was scored by Alberto Galateo after a mazy dribble and incisive finish. But the finish 27 years later was even more spectacular. In 1961 Galateo, by then an alcoholic, was murdered by his own son. It remains the only case of World Cup patricide on record.

So three men involved in three different games in three different cities on the opening day of the 1934 World Cup all met a 1-in-5,000 end. Astrologists would doubtless say their destiny was written in the stars. Whatever the truth, their ill-fated appointment with death certainly made a grim hat trick.

# *DOUBLE MONTI*

## ROME, 10 JUNE 1934

Argentina's 4–2 defeat by Uruguay in the 1930 World Cup final had left no man more devastated than their tough *centromedio* (advanced 'centre-half') Luisito Monti. The Buenos Aires-born hatchet man was blamed by his own fans for a loss that plunged the Argentinian nation into deep despair.

Monti's 'crime' was that his infamous style (he once feigned to shake hands with a Chelsea player in a 'friendly' before kicking him) had annoyed the fanatical Uruguay following so much that he received several death threats: 'You upset the mood in the camp, which is why we lost,' said the unsympathetic Argentine fans. Luis Monti was an outcast in his own land, with nothing more than a World Cup loser's medal for comfort.

With his chances of playing for Argentina at the 1934 tournament seemingly remote, his dream of lifting the World Cup in his nation's colours lay in tatters. But Monti lived life as he played football. Shirking a challenge wasn't an option. As one pen picture so charmingly put it, 'Monti had a robust and dirty fame of obtaining what he wanted at any cost.'

If he'd been a jockey he'd have changed horses. As it was, he changed countries. Having an Italian father made Monti an *oriundi*, a foreign player of Italian descent. And Italian clubs love *oriundi* if the price is right and the talent plentiful. Sure enough, shortly after the 1930 World Cup final, Luis Monti signed for Juventus. And after helping them win the coveted *scudetto* (Championship 'shield') in four of the next five seasons, the villain of Argentina became the hero of Turin. They dubbed him *quello che commina* ('the one who walks'), an ironic *double entendre* that paid humorous tribute to both his ambling style and the crippling fate suffered by many of his opponents.

17

As Italy prepared to stage the 1934 World Cup, the national team manager, Vittorio Pozzo, looked longingly at Luis Monti. Rumours suggested Italy's fascist leader, Benito Mussolini, had issued an (only half-joking) ultimatum to the Italian squad, which bade them 'win or die'. So Pozzo acted decisively.

Knowing that the player's parentage made him liable to be called up to serve in the Italian forces, Pozzo shrewdly drafted Monti and several other Argentine *oriundi* straight into Italy's side. FIFA's rules permitted such double-representation, and Pozzo's thinking was clear: 'If they can die for Italy, they can play football for Italy.' Luisito Monti did die for Italy, but only in a figurative sense.

Victories over the United States and Spain took Pozzo's *azzurri* (the Italian national team, 'The Blues') to a semifinal clash with the highly fancied Austrian 'Wunderteam', whose artistic centre-forward Matthias Sindelar was a potential match winner. But Monti crumpled 'The Paper Man' to nothing as Italy eased through to the final with a single goal.

So to Rome on 10 June 1934. Both Italy and Monti lay on the threshold of a dream. Only their Cup final opponents, Czechoslovakia, could spoil the party. But again Monti played a blinder as Italy triumphed 2–1 after extra time to win their first World Cup.

Vittorio Pozzo raised his arms aloft. The broad-shouldered, barrel-chested Luis Monti clutched the winner's medal that had seemed an impossible dream four years earlier. And Benito Mussolini permitted himself a faintly sinister smile as he pondered the winning effect of his 'win or die' motivational slogan.

Many years later, the irony of the occasion was still not lost on Monti. In an interview he gave late in life to an Italian magazine, he reflected ruefully, 'I had to win that game. If I had won in the 1930 final the Uruguayans would have killed me. And if I had not won in the 1934 final the Italians would have killed me!'

'The one who walks' took his last steps in 1983, aged 82. By then, few associated the quiet old gentleman with the 'robust and dirty fame' (to quote the article again) of the football star who 'got what he wanted at any cost'. Luisito Monti is the only man to have played in two World Cup finals for different countries.

# *A NAZI SURPRISE*

## LINZ, 13 MARCH 1938

Not wishing to glorify dictatorships more than is necessary, I'd rather hoped to leave Adolf Hitler out of things after Benito Mussolini's bullying incursion into the narrative for 1934. After all, the Führer detested *fussball*. The only recorded instance of Hitler's attending a match was on 7 August 1936 at the Post Stadium in Berlin for the Olympic Games clash between hot favourites Germany and outsiders Norway. Even then he stormed out early when Norway went 2–0 up with four minutes left. The hosts fell, and the propaganda minister Joseph Goebbels wrote in his diary, 'The Führer is very agitated.'

But my professional duty as a World Cup strangeologist compels me to give the Nazi leader some space, since he's responsible for the sole appearance of FORFEIT in a World Cup finals results chart.

Sixteen countries qualified to take part in the 1938 World Cup in France, but only fifteen turned up. Despite earning their place fair and square, the highly talented Austrian side withdrew two months before the tournament began. As excuses go, theirs wasn't bad. The Austrian Football Federation had ceased to exist. More to the point, Austria had ceased to exist.

On 12 March 1938, German troops had crossed into Austria. The next day, from the balcony of the town hall in the Austrian town of Linz, where Hitler spent his teenage years, der Führer announced the 'incorporation' of Austria into Nazi Germany by the dictate known as 'Anschluss' ('Union').

In the absence of a replacement (FIFA begged England to fill in, but the FA maintained their 'splendid isolation') Austria's first-round opponents Sweden advanced without playing. Thanks to Herr Hitler, the results chart read, SWEDEN BYE. AUSTRIA

FORFEIT. ANSCHLUSS. Several teams have failed to show up for qualification games, but absenting themselves from the finals is an unwanted record that poor Austria have all to themselves.

Nor did Hitler's influence on the oddities of World Cup history cease there. When the 1934 winners Italy retained the trophy in 1938, they became 'holders' for a record sixteen years. That curiosity was entirely of Hitler's making, since the tournaments scheduled for 1942 and 1946 were cancelled due to national clashes outside the arena of football.

That sealed an unhealthy link between Nazism and the World Cup that has periodically surfaced since. In 1944, Alex Villaplane, captain of France at Uruguay '30, was executed by the French Resistance for collaborating with the Nazis. And in April 1998, the Hong Kong newspaper *Apple Daily* had to issue a public apology after bizarrely illustrating a tribute to Germany's World Cup team with a picture of Adolf Hitler wearing a swastika armband.

Even England's David Beckham (a quarter Jewish on his mother's side and once quoted as saying 'I sometimes wore one of those skull cap things when I was young') was ensnared in the web. At his 26th-birthday photocall on 2 May 2001 he wore a hooded top with a picture of a face on it. Unbeknown to David (and his wife Victoria hadn't sussed it either), it was Adolf Eichmann, the Gestapo chief responsible for the murder of millions of Jews in World War Two concentration camps. The *Sun* newspaper ran the headline BECKS' NAZI OWN GOAL as the England captain apologised and made a very convincing job of pleading ignorance.

And who would bet against more Nazi surprises making the news in future? Germany's powerful presence in the World Cup arena seems unlikely to subside. Journalists continue to revisit the past for dramatic effect. The football-hating Führer may be long dead, but his misdeeds are very much alive.

# NO SECOND CHANCE
## REIMS, 5 JUNE 1938

Whether they're labelled minnows, underdogs, rank outsiders or no-hopers, teams who don't stand an earthly are an endearing part of the World Cup's heritage. None typifies the breed better than the Dutch East Indies, whose fleeting appearance in the 1938 finals set a record that no side will ever match.

It was a freak that they got to France '38 in the first place. They should have played (and almost certainly lost to) Japan in a two-team qualifying group, but the Japanese team withdrew when their country invaded China and precipitated the Second Sino-Japanese war.

Keen to improve the quality of participants in their burgeoning 'world showcase' tournament, a dismayed FIFA tried to head off the Dutch East Indies by pitting them against the United States in a hastily arranged qualifying play-off. The USA were already veterans of both the 1930 and 1934 finals, but this time a guilty conscience swayed their decision. They refused the unseemly back-door play-off option they had controversially taken in 1934 (see 'Not Down Mexico Way'). Like it or not, FIFA were stuck with the Dutch East Indies.

They made their finals debut on 5 June 1938 against Hungary at the Stade Vélodrome Municipal in Reims. The French press made good use of the usual platitudes reserved for small fry. The Southeast Asians were all 'diminutive' ('*bien trop petits*') but some were '*tres brilliants dribbleurs*'. Nine of them were winning their first caps. Most were students. Their defence lacked the rudiments of organisation. One of their wingers was nippy. Their captain played in glasses.

It was neither a surprise nor a disgrace that they lost the game 6–0. But what put them in the record books was the finality of their departure. The straight knockout format of the tournament denied them the chance to bounce back that later minnows would enjoy. They returned home after a single game and none of their players was ever capped again.

After seventeen tournaments, a cumulative total of 69 countries had played 1,288 matches in the seventeen finals, but the Dutch East Indies remain the only team to have played a measly ninety minutes. No other country will ever match it, since even the lowliest finalists are now guaranteed several games. Only the 'one-gamers' themselves can expunge their own unique record. After securing their independence from Holland in 1947, the Dutch East Indies became Indonesia. Their national sport is badminton. They have tried to qualify again but consistently failed.

Until they put their shuttlecocks away nothing looks likely to change. So let's hear it one more time for the team trapped in a World Cup vacuum:

Tan Mo Heng, Frans Hu Kom, Jack Samuels, Achmad Nawir, Frans Meeng, Anwar Sutan, Tan Hong Dijen, Suvarte Soedarmadji, Hendrikus Zomers, Isaac Pattiwael, Hans Taihuttu. For them, there was no second chance.

# THE RUBBER MAN MYSTERY
## STRASBOURG, 5 JUNE 1938

The Round One meeting of Brazil and Poland at France '38 has been called 'the greatest World Cup game of all time'. But the accomplishments of the two men who supposedly 'made history' on 5 June 1938 at the Stade de la Meinau divide football statisticians to this day. So I'll tell it straight down the middle.

First the irrefutable facts. This was one of only five World Cup games in which the total goals tally reached double figures. But don't expect a Hungary 10 El Salvador 1 (see 'Kissed Goodbye'). This one finished Brazil 6 Poland 5 after extra time. It was the closest double-digit game in World Cup history.

It's also undisputed that Poland's rangy blond inside-left Ernst Willimowski scored four in the game, one of only a handful of players to achieve that rare feat at a World Cup. His first three came in the shape of a dramatic second-half hat trick (53, 59, 89), which clawed Poland back to 4–4 at full-time after they trailed 3–1 at the interval. His fourth came in the 28th minute of extra time, but too late to save Poland from a heroic defeat, which sent them out of the tournament.

FIFA's official records honour the Pole's magnificent achievement, confirming Willimowski as the first player to bag four (known by the shooting metaphor *a double brace*) in a World Cup match. But there's the mystery. For countless other sources say he was beaten to that record by a matter of minutes. According to these alternative versions, the Brazilian Leonidas da Silva (the 'Forest Man') also helped himself to four in the very same game.

The revisionist stories have assumed a copybook appearance. Leonidas was the coal-black centre-forward with the pencil moustache and loose-limbed acrobatic style. They called him the

'Black Diamond' or the 'Rubber Man'. He is noted for 'inventing' (perfecting would be better) the *chute de bicicleta*, known in English as the bicycle kick. He was tricky, with quick feet, was diminutive in stature and had an unerring instinct for goal. It's perfect prose for 'the first player to score four goals in a World Cup game'. By comparison, the jug-eared Willimowski was really rather dull.

So is this an urban myth perpetuated for the sake of colouring up the record books? Leonidas certainly did score three (one of which was definitely in extra time), but where does the phantom fourth come from?

In *World Cup* (1958), Brian Glanville unequivocally gives the Brazilian four: 'Brazil took a 3–1 half-time lead thanks to a hat trick from centre-forward Leonidas, who later scored his fourth in extra-time'. Then again, Glanville also says that 'like some forest animal, Leonidas was as fast as a greyhound and agile as a cat, seeming not to be made of flesh and bones at all, but entirely of rubber.' Might a hint of artistic licence be detected?

While John Robinson concurs entirely with Glanville in *Soccer – The World Cup* (2002), Cris Freddi dares to spoil the story. His *Complete Book of the World Cup* (2002) claims to be 'the most accurate and meticulously researched on the market', and he credits Leonidas's 'missing goal' to Romeu. Furthermore, according to Freddi, the 'Rubber Man' scored only once in the first half and completed his hat trick with two in extra-time! And FIFA agree to the letter.

Nor does the confusion end there. Some reports say the 'Forest Man' nabbed one of his goals barefoot after he petulantly tossed aside his heavy mud-caked boots to 'go native'. And going back to the original newspaper reports for an 'accurate picture' is futile. Pressmen in 1938 were just as prone to 'creativity' as they are today.

In reality, the only man who might (how many strikers really tell the truth about goals?) have given the definitive account is no longer with us. Leonidas da Silva died aged 90 on 24 January 2004. Even then, Alzheimer's disease had long since wiped his memory of his famous football deeds.

So the remarkable 6–5 game between Brazil and Poland remains shrouded in mystery. The only cast-iron certainty is that poor Ernst Willimowski is the only man to score four in a World Cup match and still end up on the losing side.

# KEEPER'S CRYSTAL BALL

## TOULOUSE, 5 JUNE 1938

No one but a clairvoyant could have predicted that the baseball-mad island of Cuba would make it to the 1938 World Cup to become the first Caribbean country to play at the finals. In which case, one man not surprised that they got there must have been their goalkeeper Benito Carvajales, whose apparent gift of second sight enabled him to make the best pre-match prediction in World Cup history.

Cuba were mere fledglings at international level. Their first ever game was in 1924 and their attempt to qualify for the 1934 World Cup in Italy had ended in humiliation at the hands of Mexico. On that occasion, a bizarre FIFA ruling condemned them to play the Mexicans no fewer than three times (see 'Not Down Mexico Way'), resulting in an aggregate 12–3 hammering.

Now Cuba were again placed in Mexico's pool for the 1938 qualifying tournament, along with the mighty Brazil. Things didn't look good, but Mexico obligingly withdrew even before the fixtures were drawn up. So both Cuba and Brazil got a bye to the finals in France.

Not that hopes were high. Only the presence of the Dutch East Indies (see 'No Second Chance') relieved Cuba of the 'tournament whipping boys' label they had anticipated. Those who had seen the Cubans in training were ambivalent at best: 'They look like miniature copies of the Brazilians,' mused one journalist, before acidly adding the rider, 'but with an alarming tendency to be rather disorderly.'

All the forecasts predicted 'no cigar' for Cuba, despite the expected presence of Benito Carvajales between the sticks. He had let in only nine goals in the Cuban championship that season and was said by one observer to have 'the virtuosity, courage and theatrics' of the great Spanish custodian Zamora.

The 1938 tournament was a straight knockout. Cuba's first opponents were Romania (yet another side who 'qualified' via a bye, after Egypt withdrew), who were an experienced and stronger outfit altogether. But the Cubans excelled themselves to earn a 3–3 draw after extra time in a thrilling encounter. Despite being beaten three times, Carvajales played a blinder.

If he had shown 'virtuosity and courage' in the first game, the 'theatrics' were reserved for the replay. The Cuban coach José Tápia perversely decided that three goals were too many. Carvajales was sensationally dropped in favour of Juan Ayra, renowned as 'a fantastic acrobat'.

Carvajales might have sulked, but didn't. Instead, he dramatically called the press to a private conference on the eve of the game, announcing he had something to reveal: 'Gentlemen, I shall not be playing, but we shall win the replay, that's certain. The Romanian game has no more secrets for us. I say to you that we shall score twice, they will score only once. Adios, Caballeros.'

And, on 5 June 1938 in Toulouse, that's exactly what happened. Romania led 1–0 at half-time before Cuba claimed a famous 2–1 victory with a winning goal that was flagged offside by a linesman but mysteriously allowed by the German referee. Maybe he was under a Carvajales hex, because he later disallowed what looked like a perfectly legitimate Romanian equaliser. The 'fantastic acrobat' Ayra, by the way, didn't hang upside down from the crossbar but did have an excellent game.

The theatrical Carvajales had accurately predicted the first real World Cup shock. Three days later, though, it was the keeper himself who was in shock. Recalled for the quarter-final against Sweden in Antibes, Carvajales was deceived badly by his crystal ball – and by the eight shots that flew past him into the net.

The Cuban camp put the 8–0 defeat down to unforeseen circumstances. More predictably, despite fourteen further attempts to qualify, Cuba have never played in a World Cup again.

# TAKEN AT THEIR PEAK

## TURIN, 4 MAY 1949

Guided by the 'Father of Italian Football', Vittorio Pozzo, Italy won the World Cup in 1934 and 1938. Despite Pozzo's retirement as manager in 1948, Italy were fully expected to retain the trophy in 1950, when the competition resumed in Brazil after its enforced wartime break. Yet they flopped completely, victims of a tragedy arguably even worse than the Munich Air Disaster of 1958, which claimed the lives of eight Manchester United players.

The heart of the Italian side for 1950 was to have been supplied by Torino. Eight of their players were regular internationals. In 1947 Pozzo had picked ten of 'La Granata' (Garnet Reds) for a match against Hungary. No wonder their side of the 1940s was dubbed 'Il Grand Torino'. With four games of the 1948–49 Italian Championship remaining, they were top and gunning for their fifth *scudetto* in a row. And they hadn't been beaten at home since 17 January 1943.

The 'Festa de Homenagem' (testimonial) against Benfica in Lisbon on 3 May 1949 had been arranged as a favour. Torino flew back on 4 May to resume the real business of retaining the Championship. But the players never made it. Minutes after 5 p.m., and just a few miles from Turin airport, their propeller-powered Fiat aircraft plunged into the rear wall of the Basilica di Superga atop a hill just outside the city.

The majestic Basilica still stands, often eerily shrouded in mist just as it was that fateful day. Thousands of faithful pilgrims visit each year to marvel at 'The Room of Popes' and 'The Tombs of the Royals', but most are moved even more by the simple and touching monument to 'Il Grand Torino'. All thirty-one on board were killed, including the entire eighteen-man squad of 'La

Granata'. In a country where religious faith and football are so close in spirit, how ironic that a holy place should have robbed Italian football of its very heart.

By sheer coincidence, Vittorio Pozzo was one of the first on the scene. A police officer asked him if he could identify the bodies: 'What a question,' said Pozzo. 'These were my boys. Boys I had seen off to sleep before great international victories. Now they slept again. They looked so peaceful. Their faces were unmarked. But what I found terrible was that some had lost their feet.'

A crowd of 500,000 massed in Turin for the collective funeral. For the last four games of the *scudetto*, Torino played their youth team. So did their opponents. Torino won all four to clinch their fifth Championship in a row.

The Italian side that travelled (this time by boat) to Brazil '50 was a shadow of what it should have been. No Valentino Mazzola, their inspirational captain, whose son Sandro was to play in the 1970 final. No Bacigalupo in goal. No Ballarin, Rigamonte, Castigliano or Menti. All six of them had played in the last international before Superga.

On 25 June 1950, Italy lost 3–2 to Sweden in São Paulo in their opening game of the tournament. They became the first holders ever to be beaten. It would be thirty-two years before they would lift the World Cup again.

No tragedy has had a bigger impact on top-level international football. A book chronicling the Superga disaster was published in 2000. Few followers of 'Il Grand Torino' would argue with the choice of title: *The Day Italian Football Died.*

# NO PASSAGE FOR INDIA

## RIO DE JANEIRO, 24 JUNE 1950

The fourth World Cup, the first since World War Two, began in Brazil on 24 June 1950. Everybody present at the opening game in the (not quite finished!) 200,000-capacity Maracana Stadium was left in no doubt that international football had truly entered the modern age.

Hosts Brazil took the field against Mexico to a 21-gun salute, a thunderous cacophony of fireworks and a mass of colourful balloons. Troops released five thousand pigeons and an aircraft dropped a snowstorm of leaflets. When Brazil opened the scoring, fifteen radio commentators and dozens of reporters invaded the pitch to grab on-the-spot interviews.

Elsewhere in this brave new world, surgeons were performing the first liver transplant, Russia announced it had an atom bomb, Diners' Club issued the first credit cards, Andy Pandy took *Watch with Mother* by storm and India withdrew from the World Cup because FIFA would not allow them to play barefoot.

The standard response to that final astonishing oddity is one of disbelief. In the annals of World Cup trivia, the Indian no-boot trick is seldom more than an unsubstantiated one-liner. So what's the truth?

Common sense dictated that footballers should play in boots right from the game's organised beginnings in the mid-nineteenth century. But India's players were made of sterner stuff. In the 1948 London Olympics their team of bootless 'leatherfoots' caused a sensation when they lost to France at Wembley by only two goals to one. So why change things for the World Cup?

But first they had to qualify. No problem. Group 10 was the easiest of all time. Burma, the Philippines and Indonesia all withdrew, leaving India a free passage. According to midfielder

T Shanmugham, their preparations went well: 'We were all very excited about going to the 1950 World Cup. Boots hadn't been compulsory for the Olympics and most of our players went without. We played five forwards and were a very good attacking side. In our warm-up tour we went to Singapore, Malaysia, Sri Lanka and Hong Kong. We were very ready.'

But not ready enough. FIFA's 'compulsory footwear' bombshell, which was dropped at the eleventh hour, denied India their one moment of World Cup glory. Hampered, too, by a chronic shortage of funds, India opted to pull out of the tournament rather than pull on the footwear.

Over fifty years later, in a 2002 interview for *The Hindu Sportstar*, poor Shanmugham was still misty-eyed: 'We got to know very late. And our captain Sailen Manna was such a good defender. I suppose we didn't know the rules. Perhaps that has always been the bane of Indian football.'

After a severe bout of frozen tootsies afflicted the team at the 1952 Helsinki Olympics, the All Indian Football Federation finally made footwear compulsory. The Indian side's ambitions were quickly rebooted, but their studs have yet to make an impression at a single World Cup.

# *THE GAME OF THEIR LIVES*

## BELO HORIZONTE, 29 JUNE 1950

The country that invented association football finally conde-
scended to compete in the World Cup in 1950. A running dispute
with FIFA had kept England away until then. That and a superior
attitude. They *were* the best in the world. Why should they have
to prove it? Little did England anticipate the monumental banana
skin that awaited them in Brazil.

They started well enough, beating Chile 2–0 in their opening
game. But they found the humid conditions and thin air difficult.
Other things were unfamiliar too. Most of the sides wore brief
shorts and light boots. They looked like athletes. England seemed
cumbersome and lumpy by comparison. They looked like men
from prewar cigarette cards. Even their manager, Walter
Winterbottom, sounded like a batty character from a boys'
comic. Could the rest of the world be catching England up?

Their next game was against the USA in Belo Horizonte, a
rundown mining town three hundred miles north of Rio. The
Estadio Mineiro was a ramshackle affair with an arid bumpy
pitch. But an England side who included some of the world's top
names were fully expected to overcome such difficulties against
America's mere amateurs.

England had Billy Wright and their future manager Alf Ramsey
in defence. Tom Finney, Stan Mortensen and Wilf Mannion were
all star forwards. Stanley Matthews couldn't even get in the side.
The American team included only one professional, their
Glaswegian captain Eddie McIlvenny, later to play for
Manchester United. Among the others were a teacher, a hearse
driver, a stray Belgian and a Haitian named Joe Gaetjens, who was
a failed accountancy student who worked as a dishwasher in a
German restaurant in New York. The line-ups said it all.

A cable sent home by the Arsenal manager Tom Whittaker encapsulated England's confidence: 'The United States, 500–1 to win the tournament, should give England much-needed match practice.' The England players believed their own publicity. They spurned the rudimentary dressing rooms at the Estadio Mineiro, decamping to a nearby hotel to get changed. They cockily arrived at the ground only minutes prior to kick-off as the USA manager Bill Jeffrey, another exiled Scot, nervously joked about doing his best to 'avoid a cricket score'.

United States 1 England 0 still rates as the biggest shock result of any World Cup. England had chances galore but couldn't find the net. America had fewer, but breached England's defence in the 37th minute when a misdirected shot from Walter Bahr (the teacher) was headed in by Joe Gaetjens (the dishwasher) to give USA their greatest ever victory.

Back in England the scoreline was greeted with disbelief. One newspaper editor assumed it was a misprint and went to press with the result England 10 USA 1. When the horrible truth dawned, the *Daily Express* bordered their report of 'the death of English football' in funerary black. England lost their next game against Spain by another 1–0 scoreline and returned home utterly humbled. Scotland fans embraced America's triumph like a home victory.

Another strange aspect of the story was the reaction in America. The editor of the *New York Times* at first dismissed the result as a wind-up and refused to report it. Only one American journalist, Dent McSkimming of the *St Louis Post-Despatch*, was present at the game. Quite frankly, nobody cared. In the absence of decent film footage and press photographs, the game in Belo Horizonte was largely forgotten. That was fine with England.

But in April 2005 a feature film was released to tell the whole story. In the midst of the publicity, the truth emerged about what happened to the game's goal hero. Joe Gaetjens played for Racing Club Paris before returning to Haiti in 1954 to run a dry-cleaning business. Members of his family became opponents of the repressive regime of François 'Papa Doc' Duvalier. In July

1964 Joe was shot dead by the Tontons Macoutes, Papa Doc's brutal gangster militia.

England lived another day. After spiralling into an alarming decline they began the rebuilding that led to their 1966 World Cup triumph. So without the USA's canny Scots manager, they might never have reached that pinnacle.

One final touch of strangeness concerned the film itself – the American-made 'limited-release' *The Game of Their Lives*. Emanating from the land of 'soccer' it naturally departed from the genuine script. Having qualified by 'residency', the U.S. captain against England had been the Greenock-born Scotsman Ed McIlvenny, who later played a handful of games for Manchester United. But in the film the triumphal captaincy was handed to Walter Bahr – no prizes for guessing he was born in the United States.

When Ed McIlvenny's widow Sheila was informed of the judicious re-write (some might say a downright snub) she delivered a pithy reply: 'It's disappointing – but what do you expect from Hollywood?'

# DROPPING LIKE FLIES

## BELO HORIZONTE, 2 JULY 1950

After the disruption of an enforced wartime break, it was no easy task garnering a full complement of teams for the 1950 World Cup. It was to FIFA's credit that they somehow managed to scrape together a nice round sixteen coming into the finals. But, when sides began to pull out willy-nilly, the organisers seemed to lose all sense of reason. And the 'group stage' shambles that followed gave Uruguay the easiest passage of all time to the latter stages of a World Cup.

A year ahead of the tournament, everything had seemed so straightforward. FIFA's blueprint was for sixteen nations to begin the 1950 finals in four equal groups (then known as 'pools'). Previous World Cups had been straight knockouts, which were always apt to produce shocks. FIFA didn't favour shocks. The pool system would make things fairer. All that remained was to gather together the teams.

Germany fancied the trip but was quite reasonably barred. Japan, still under occupation, was equally unwelcome. All the eastern European countries behind the new 'iron curtain' refused point blank to enter. The Austrians felt their team was too immature. Argentina, locked in a petty dispute with the Brazilian Football Federation, slunk away during the qualifiers.

More encouraging was the news that England, Scotland, Ireland and Wales were all eligible to compete after reconciling their earlier differences with FIFA, who generously decided to 'soften' the qualification process as a sweetener. They designated the 1949–50 Home International Championship a qualifying group in itself. The top two from this (now defunct) annually contested British mini-league would travel to Brazil. That hardly helped Ireland and Wales, but made it a breeze for England and

Scotland, who both secured their World Cup qualification even before they met each other in the final fixture.

Qualification elsewhere was similarly 'facilitated'. There were so many withdrawals from the South American zone that Uruguay, Bolivia, Chile and Paraguay all secured their passage to Brazil without playing a single game. Turkey played only one, a 7–0 thrashing of Syria.

Three months ahead of the tournament, it looked as if FIFA had miraculously pulled it off. By a combination of generosity and luck they had sixteen teams in place. They made the draw for the finals. What a great relief to have four pools of four. Symmetry had won the day.

But then things began to go pear-shaped. India withdrew from Pool 3 (see 'No Passage for India'). Burma was invited instead, but politely declined. Then Turkey withdrew from Pool 4 because they were strapped for cash. But France, who had lost out in the qualifiers to Yugoslavia, blessedly stepped in.

The most unexpected nail in the coffin was hammered home by Scotland. On 15 April they met England at Hampden Park in the 'meaningless' World Cup qualifier. Both sides had already secured places in Brazil, but, when Scotland lost the game 1–0 to finish second behind England in the Home Championship, they came over all high and mighty: 'Qualifying by finishing second doesn't seem right,' said a Scottish FA spokesman. 'We're withdrawing from the World Cup.'

That left FIFA scrambling for substitutes afresh. Portugal were invited to replace Scotland in Pool 4, but refused. Then France, already a Pool 4 replacement, dealt the hammer blow. Sensing the tournament organisation lacked 'va va voom', they pulled out altogether. That left only thirteen countries, with the original Pool 4 depleted to just Uruguay and Bolivia.

Why FIFA didn't make a redraw for the finals only they will know. But instead they did absolutely nothing. So it was that the 'Pool of Two' was decided in Belo Horizonte on 2 July. Uruguay were one of the tournament favourites. Bolivia were arguably the worst side in the tournament. There was no upset. Uruguay hammered their South American rivals 8–0 to go straight into the last four. No team has ever had an easier passage.

And how it showed. Feeling wonderfully fresh, Uruguay progressed smoothly to a final showdown against the hosts Brazil. Naturally, in honour of FIFA's thin grasp of organising an equitable pool system, this story can have only one ending. In front of a record crowd of 199,854 in the Maracana Stadium in Rio, Brazil were beaten 2–1.

The distasteful defeat plunged the home nation into a state of utter despair as their bitter rivals Uruguay lifted the 1950 World Cup with undisguised glee. It had been the most disorganised tournament on record. But, while other countries were dropping like flies, the grateful winners issued a hearty thank-you to FIFA for the nice easy ride.

# WHO ARE YA?

## OSLO, 24 JUNE 1953

The significance of Norway's home qualifying fixture on 24 June 1953 is closer to absolute zero than any other game in World Cup history. Nothing remarkable happened during the match, which ended in a 3–2 victory for the away side. Neither team advanced to the 1954 finals in Switzerland, since West Germany ultimately clinched a place at both their expense.

So what's the game doing in *The World Cup's Strangest Moments*? It's there, if I'm honest, because there's little more satisfying than tripping up a bumptious trivia buff with a question they can't answer. And this match provides a sporting chance of experiencing that sublime moment.

You'll notice I haven't mentioned Norway's opponents. That's the challenge.

After 43 countries initially entered the qualifying tournament, 10 withdrew to leave 33 fighting it out. To narrow it down a bit, I can confirm that only 23 of those were European. And Norway's opponents were European. So name that team.

I'm not for a moment suggesting you're the bumptious trivia buff. This is one to keep up your sleeve for the right occasion. Part-time aficionados generally plunge in regardless with Liechtenstein, San Marino, Cyprus, Malta, Iceland, Albania, the Faroe Islands, Bosnia-Herzegovina, Macedonia, Armenia, or Andorra. All of them have indeed ploughed a lonely qualification furrow at some time, but none of them are Norway's mystery opponents.

Sooner or later, someone will sagely remind you that the late Pope John Paul II was a useful goalkeeper during his youth in Poland, so illogically the answer must be the Vatican. He was, but it's not.

Only after many incorrect nominations will some former class swot finally remember their school history lessons to deliver the definitive answer: 'It has to be Schleswig-Holstein'. But it isn't. 'The Lofoten Islands then'. Sorry, no. 'The Isle of Man'. Not even warm. 'Cornwall?' Not really a country, I'm afraid. Anyway they prefer rugby.

The true expert will either get the answer (please hit them on my behalf) or remain silent, being just wise enough to know that random naming of minor territories, defunct or otherwise, is the refuge only of the desperate or the inexperienced trainee anorak. Yet they'd be on the right track, for the answer does lie in history.

Cowering nervously between France and Germany once lay a territory that almost routinely changed hands between the two powers. But in 1953 they were enjoying a brief window of independence, which permitted them their one and only tilt at World Cup qualification. Who can blame them for going for it?

Forget the Netherlands Antilles and Vanuatu. For my money our mystery side remain the most unmemorable country ever to compete in a World Cup game.

Of course you will have realised by now that I refer to the Saar.

The who? Well, to be absolutely frank, I'd never heard of them, either.

# LUIGI WITH THE BANDAGED EYES

## ROME, 17 MARCH 1954

Any organisation more hospitable than FIFA might have made a party of the 1954 World Cup in Switzerland. It was, after all, right on the doorstep of their Zurich headquarters, and in the fiftieth anniversary of their existence to boot. The divisive vestiges of war, too, were lessening with each passing year. Exactly the circumstances in which to bump up the guest list.

Yet FIFA permitted a miserly sixteen nations to tread 'their' hallowed turf, which automatically spelled disappointment for some of the record number of countries that entered the qualifying tournament. Of those, none were made to suffer more anxiety than Spain and Turkey.

Spanish chances looked healthy when the qualifiers were drawn. FIFA had decided on a faintly odd system of thirteen worldwide groups, several of which contained only two teams. Spain got lucky, landing a place in one of the 'twos' with rank outsiders Turkey.

After the first leg in Madrid on 6 January 1954, the picture looked even rosier. A crowd of 110,000 saw Spain beat the Turks 4–1. The return leg was in Istanbul on 14 March. Only thirty thousand turned up at the Mithat Pasha Stadium, but the faithful were well rewarded as Turkey went ahead after ten minutes and hung on for a famous 1–0 victory.

Turkey's triumph put FIFA's wisdom to the test. Each side had a home win, but Spain led 4–2 on aggregate. Yet FIFA decided that counted for nothing. The rules had already been written. They decreed that a single play-off would be staged on neutral territory. So, just three days later, both teams reconvened in Rome's Olympic Stadium for one last showdown. Winners to go to Switzerland.

Always up for a big game, the Italians turned out in force to swell the neutral gate to a staggering sixty thousand. But they didn't get a winner. After ninety tense minutes and thirty more of extra time, the score stood at 2–2. Again FIFA's pre-ordained wisdom came under scrutiny.

Over the three games, Spain now led 6–4 on aggregate. Surely that would count in separating the teams at this stage. Not in FIFA's book. The rules stated the solution clearly: 'Lots will be drawn.'

The cruellest and most meaningless decider in football (even penalties, 'Golden Goals', and away goals counting double are surely fairer) took place on the spot. The atmosphere in the stadium was electric. It was like waiting for the emperor to give a thumbs-up or thumbs-down to some gibbering gladiator. But the character now thrust centre stage was not an all-powerful ruler. He was a fourteen-year-old schoolboy.

Subsequent embellishment of this moment of high drama has it that the local youth chosen to draw the lots was blind. But Luigi Franco Gemma could see all right. So they blindfolded him. Not that he would have been tempted to cheat, or indeed that he could. The two lots were put deep in a drum. FIFA knew how volatile the camps of Spain and Turkey could be. Perversely, the cruel act of sudden death had to be made 'fair'.

The most charming account I have seen is an Italian translation into English:

The 17 of March 1954, Turkey that was not group head faced in Rome Spain that yes it was, to determine which of both would happen to Switzerland to voyage. With a victory of both until then, the final party would be decisive, but the encounter finished a tie and a Roman boy Luigi Frank Gemma would solve the dispute. Luigi with the bandaged eyes removed from the big drum the name of Turkey, creating the first surprise of the contest, since Spain was eliminated.

So unfancied Turkey went to Switzerland '54 and Spain

skulked home. As it was, there was an element of poetic justice in Turkey's fate at the finals. Finishing second in their group with a positive goal difference of plus four, they were level on points with West Germany, who were placed third with a negative goal difference of minus two. Only one of the two teams could advance further. Yet, bizarrely but entirely true to form, FIFA ignored the goal difference and ordered a play-off. Germany won it 7–2.

Even so, the demise of the Turks was little comfort to Spain, who had to wait until Chile '62 to appear again in the finals.

Spanish fans still insist they are the unluckiest team in World Cup history, but FIFA seem intent on one day relieving Spain of their dolorous tag.

A year ahead of Germany '06 the incisive brains of football's world governing body got together to address a thorny issue: how to differentiate between teams with deadlocked records in the group stages of a World Cup. The resulting document outlined a complex multistep system in which the final resort had a strangely familiar look to it: 'the drawing of lots'. All of which FIFA-induced nonsense left me with one mischievous thought: could 'Luigi with the bandaged eyes' still be alive?

# GOALS IN THE SUN

## LAUSANNE, 26 JUNE 1954

Outside forces were surely at work in the summer of 1954. Perhaps the crystal-clear air of Switzerland had a bracing effect. Or maybe the introduction of television cameras exerted a galvanising influence, as previously 'faceless' sides felt an increased obligation to entertain. Whatever the explanation, the 1954 World Cup finals provided a goal feast like no other before or since.

In 26 matches there were 140 goals. Hungary alone bagged a net-busting 27 from five games, the sort of rate usually reserved for the qualifying competition, where 'cannon-fodder' opponents roll over on cue.

As the tournament progressed, an 'anything you can do, we can do better' attitude seemed to prevail, as a remarkable series of spiralling scores unfolded. On the opening day, Brazil beat Mexico 5–0 in Geneva. A day later in Zurich, the hot favourites Hungary, with the 'Galloping Major' Ferenc Puskas leading the attack, destroyed a makeweight South Korea 9–0. And three days later in Basle the Hungarians humiliated West Germany by eight goals to three, then an equal record for most goals in a finals game.

Other teams also got in on the act. Turkey conquered South Korea 7–0, then meekly surrendered 7–2 to West Germany. Austria chipped in with five against Czechoslovakia without reply, while England and Belgium restored some balance to the goal-fest with a thrilling 4–4 draw.

Seasoned observers suggested the weather was a factor. Many of the games were played in scorching temperatures as parts of Switzerland enjoyed a brilliant summer. Scotland, making their World Cup debut, were certainly caught out. Despite the 100°F heat in Basle for their first-round game with the world champions Uruguay, the Scottish players wore old-fashioned thick woollen jerseys with long sleeves and heavy buttoned collars. Oh that their defence had been as tightly knit!

Fans back in Scotland had the rare experience of watching the game live on BBC television, and forty years later the team's wing-half Tommy Docherty was still explaining the debacle: 'The Scottish FA assumed Switzerland was cold because it had mountains. You'd have thought we were going on an expedition to the Antarctic. The Uruguayans wore light V-necked shirts with short sleeves. No wonder we lost 7–0.' Superior ability may have played a minor part too.

But all that mayhem was in the pool games. The quarter-finals, devoid of the weak links, were expected to be much tighter – particularly the game between neighbours Austria and Switzerland in Lausanne, since neither side was truly renowned as an attacking force. The Swiss, moreover, were past-masters of the lock-tight defensive system dubbed the *verrou* ('door bolt'), ironically introduced by their Austrian-born manager of the late 1930s, Karl Rappan.

Sure enough, the first fifteen minutes in La Pontaise Stadium on the brilliantly sunny afternoon of 26 June proved duller than watching a yodelling contest and a lederhosen troupe back to back. Just eight minutes later, though, roared on by a partisan home crowd, Switzerland were 3–0 ahead!

Austria, motivated by their imperious captain Ernst 'Clockwork' Ockwirk, were stung to reply. Wagner was first to orchestrate a goal in the 25th minute, and by the 34th the Austrians astonishingly led 5–3. Switzerland's lock had been comprehensively picked by an amazing five goals in nine minutes, but still they stuck at it. Minutes later they pulled one back and staggered in at half-time trailing 5–4.

It remains the most incredible half in World Cup finals history, and one that Swiss officials explained away in Scottish terms. A half-time communiqué distributed in the press box at the Uruguay-versus-England match in Basle made it clear: 'All goals scored against Switzerland owing to the sun.' They certainly couldn't blame the referee. He was faultless – Charles Edward Faultless from Scotland, who wore a nice thick blazer for the occasion.

It was impossible for the second half to match the first. A mere three goals were added as Austria shaded the game 7–5. No other team except Portugal (against North Korea in 1966) has won a finals match from three goals down, and no other finals game has produced as many goals.

Brain Glanville gave an apt summing up in his account of the tournament: 'Austrian superiority had been firmly and irreducibly established. It was a wonderful triumph, a magisterial lesson by a team of thinking artists. It was probably the most extraordinary match in the history of the World Cup.'

I can't possibly disagree, although I must add a postscript. True to the bizarre results sequences of Switzerland '54, the magisterial Austrians lost their semifinal 6–1 to West Germany, who then faced Hungary in the final in Berne. Quite forgetting that the 'Magnificent Magyars' had already hammered them 8–3 in the first round, the Germans regrouped in the Wankdorf Stadium to win by three goals to two. The game is still known to Germans as 'The Miracle of Berne'.

Jimmy Greaves was only fourteen at the time, but he almost certainly said, 'It's a funny old game!'

# IT'S A KNOCKOUT
## BERNE, 27 JUNE 1954

The English referee Arthur Ellis officiated in 74 internationals in 50 different countries in a whistle-blowing career that lasted 30 years. But the game for which he is always remembered is the 1954 World Cup quarter-final between tournament favourites Hungary and second favourites Brazil.

This was the first World Cup bloodbath fully captured on film. Ellis awarded 42 free kicks and two penalties. He cautioned four and sent three off. Many more clandestine offences were committed behind his back, mostly by Brazil. And the violence continued in the dressing rooms after the final whistle. The match was quickly dubbed the 'Battle of Berne.'

Yet no one had predicted the mayhem. Hungary generally relied on talent. In November 1953 they won 6–3 at Wembley to become the first side to beat England on home soil. And they beat them again 7–1 in Budapest six months later. England's Tom Finney labelled them 'the finest team ever to sort out the intricacies of this wonderful game'. The press dubbed them the 'Magnificent Magyars'.

Maybe that riled the proud Brazilians. Five o'clock in the Swiss capital on a rainy Sunday afternoon sounds like a perfect recipe for peace and quiet, but the forty thousand inside the Wankdorf Stadium on 27 June witnessed the exact opposite.

Hungary went ahead in the fourth minute through Nandor Hidegkuti, despite the fact that his shorts were ripped off by a Brazilian as he shot. Moments after he'd changed them, he crossed for Sandor 'Golden Head' Kocsis to score Hungary's second with a trademark header.

Trailing 2–0 with only seven minutes gone, Brazil increasingly resorted to reckless challenges in the wet and muddy conditions.

Nor were Hungary blameless. Their centre-half Lorant was cautioned by Ellis, but openly laughed at the official in the process. An eighteenth-minute penalty for Brazil pulled them back to 2–1 at the interval, but any hopes that it might calm them down were soon dashed by a moment of madness from Ellis.

In the 61st minute he awarded Hungary a highly contentious penalty for an offence that both sides thought had gone the other way. Even the television pictures failed to solve the mystery. Left trailing 3–1, Brazil upped their violence level again. And by now the Hungarian players were retaliating. Arthur Ellis was losing control.

Brazil again pegged one back in the 66th minute through Julinho, and that glimmer of hope seemed only to harden their air of desperation. Five minutes later, Ellis sent off Bozsik and Nilton Santos for brawling. The Brazilian trainer came on to remonstrate. The police came on to remove him. Cameramen and journalists came on to record the drama. Brazil's right-back Djalma Santos went in Keystone Kop-style pursuit of Czibor around the pitch. Arthur Ellis had lost control.

Four minutes from time, when the game had degenerated into open fighting, he sent off Brazil's inside-left Humberto Tozzi for lunging at Kocsis. Tozzi left the field in tears – whether of rage, shame or grief, nobody knows. Hungary secured a 4–2 win with a final goal from Kocsis with two minutes left. Ellis brought the shameful affair to a close and was escorted from the field.

But that wasn't the end of it. No one knows exactly what happened. Some say Hungary's Ferenc Puskas (out injured) smashed a bottle over Pineiro's head in the tunnel. Puskas claimed he was the victim. But there were certainly unseemly scenes, which went far beyond the tame pizza-throwing of today. A photographer attacked a policeman. The lights in Hungary's dressing room went out and the Brazilian players waded in. When the lights came on again, there was blood. Several Hungarians were said to have had their faces slashed. There was talk of an iron bar.

No sanctions were imposed by FIFA. Both sides blamed each other for the most disgraceful scenes in the World Cup so far. As for Arthur Ellis, his life as an arbiter continued for many years, but in a rather surreal vein. He first decided that a foolproof way to avoid controversy was to officiate at games where no players were present – he became a 'pools panel' forecaster. And he followed that by refereeing the pantomimic games on TV's *It's a Knockout* and *Jeux Sans Frontières* as a sidekick to Stuart Hall.

Lumbering giants beat each other about the head. There were ludicrous chases. All the rules were broken. The whole thing degenerated into farce. Everybody who remembered the Switzerland '54 quarter-final agreed Arthur Ellis was perfect for the job.

# A QUITE EXTRAORDINARY SCORELINE
## GOTHENBURG, 11 JUNE 1958

When England met Brazil in the first round of the 1958 World
Cup in Sweden, amateur pundits both sides of the Atlantic were
keen to tell the next man exactly what would happen. And, as any
shrewd punter knows, current form and sound historical statistics
are the most reliable indicators.

As things stood on the eve of the game, Brazil had competed in
every World Cup finals to date, scoring 49 times in seventeen
matches. That's almost three goals a game. What's more, they'd
scored in every single one. They also found the net in both their
qualifiers en route to Sweden. Quite obviously, everything
suggested they'd continue their remarkable scoring streak against
England. Fans in the know said Waldir Pereira, better-known as
'Didi', was the man to watch.

England were playing in only their third finals, but their
record of twelve goals in seven games was creditable. More to
the point, their forwards were enjoying the proverbial 'rich vein
of form'. In their four qualifying games England had notched a
mightily impressive fifteen goals, ten of them coming from the
young Manchester United stars, Tommy Taylor and Duncan
Edwards.

That set the stage perfectly for the night of 11 June 1958. Every
one of the 40,895 spectators inside Gothenburg's Nya Ullevi
Stadium was supremely confident of one thing: they would see
some goals.

But football's fortunes are fickle. Tommy Taylor and Duncan
Edwards were not in the side. Both had tragically perished in the
Munich Air Disaster four months earlier. That put England's
manager Walter Winterbottom in a negative frame of mind. So
when 'The Preston Plumber' Tom Finney was also ruled out of

the Brazil game through injury, Winterbottom studied his forward options ruefully.

Intuition suggested that neither Derek Kevan nor the future England manager Bobby Robson was likely to be a match winner, so the England boss started to believe a draw would be a good result. So too did his assistant, Bill Nicholson, coach at Tottenham Hotspur, who swiftly issued England's captain Billy Wright with one overriding instruction: 'Neutralise Didi.'

The plan worked a treat. As the final whistle sounded, Brazil had failed to score in a finals game for the first time. And neither Kevan nor Robson, nor anybody else for that matter, was on the mark for England.

So a dejected crowd were left pondering the one scoreline that nobody had predicted. Perhaps the only compensation was that the unexpected 0–0 draw prompted Brazil to immediately draft in an unknown seventeen-year-old named Pelé, whose six goals in the next four games helped them land the World Cup for the very first time as they swept aside Sweden 5–2 in the final.

For my money, no result in World Cup history has ever been more curious than Brazil 0 England 0 in 1958. Not that I don't expect a certain amount of reader dissent, for naturally I've anticipated that a pundit of your calibre would be well aware that a goalless draw is among the more common results in football. 'Quite unexpected,' I hear you say, 'but not all that strange, surely.'

Which is why I must confess that there's a garden path in this story. The one you've possibly just followed me up. Brazil versus England was the 105th game in the World Cup's 28-year history, but the very first to end nil–nil. As the commentator David Coleman was inclined to warble, 'Quite extraordinary.'

# JUST MAGNIFIQUE

## GOTHENBURG, 28 JUNE 1958

Third-place play-off tickets were hardly gold dust at Sweden '58, but the 32,482 who saw France beat Germany 6–3 at the Nya Ullevi Stadium in Gothenburg went home buzzing after witnessing a record that no one is likely to break.

The man hoisted shoulder high at the final whistle was France's Just Fontaine. Yet his World Cup journey had started inauspiciously. At the squad's first get-together in Orly in May, the striker turned up with a thick head after spending the previous night celebrating the League and Cup double of his club side, Stade de Reims. Then one of his boots fell apart, so he borrowed a pair from his teammate Stephane Bruey. He was still wearing them in Sweden a month later.

But the Marrakesh-born Fontaine, son of a Spanish mother and French father, hadn't even expected to be in France's line-up. Only a late injury to René Bliard landed him the centre-forward berth alongside the Real Madrid striker Raymond Kopa, formerly Fontaine's teammate at Reims. It proved to be a fruitful reunion. Fontaine and Kopa struck up a telepathic understanding that earned them the nickname 'Le Tandem Terrible'.

France beat Paraguay 7–3 in their opening game, with Fontaine grabbing a hat trick. They then lost 3–2 to Yugoslavia, but Fontaine got both French goals. He scored another in a 2–1 victory over Scotland and two more in the 4–0 quarter-final drubbing of Northern Ireland. Although France's World Cup dream ended in a 5–2 semifinal defeat against Brazil, Fontaine again notched a goal.

That made nine goals in five games, which left him two short of the single-tournament record of eleven set by Hungary's Sandor Kocsis in 1954. Now only the third-place play-off remained.

The consolation game against Germany proved to be an open affair ideally suited to Fontaine's elegant and dashing style. He plundered four in France's 6–3 win to finish his remarkable World Cup on thirteen goals from just six games. Not bad for a third-choice striker in borrowed boots.

It's odd that today's generation of fans know so little about Just Fontaine, while less prolific winners of the 'Golden Boot' have gained legendary status. Brazil's Ronaldo clinched the top-scorer award in 2002 with a modest eight goals. Gary Lineker (1986) and Paolo Rossi (1982) both did it with six. Only Germany's Gerd Müller (ten in 1970) and Portugal's Eusébio (nine in 1966) got anywhere near Fontaine in the modern era. But the 'Marrakesh Express' tops them all.

And his career statistics prove it was no fluke. Fontaine scored 30 goals for France in 21 outings and his overall record of 200 goals in 213 games gives him a scoring rate of 0.93 goals per game. Even the great Pelé could manage only 0.92. And, but for terrible luck with injuries, Fontaine would have scored many more times. On 20 March 1960 he broke his leg in a French League game. Five games into his comeback, he broke it again. It ended his career at the age of 27.

After the 2002 World Cup, the seventy-year-old Fontaine was asked about Ronaldo's eight-goal tally. He gave a congratulatory reply but added a gentle reminder to the modern breed of super-strikers: 'I don't think anyone will beat my thirteen in a tournament. It is a record I will take to my grave.' It will certainly take someone very special to catch the 'Marrakesh Express'.

# TRY, TRY AND TRY AGAIN
## LUXEMBOURG CITY, 8 OCTOBER 1961

Few results sequences presented more intriguing reading than those for Group 6 of the European zone qualifying competition for Chile '62. The table itself looked quite ordinary. Only three teams competed. England came top with seven points. Portugal were second with three. And Luxembourg trailed in last with two points. England duly qualified for the 1962 World Cup.

But Luxembourg's meagre two points stood in strange isolation, for they represented an astonishing oasis of success in a vast desert of defeat. What's more, Luxembourg have a claim to World Cup fame that Brazil, Germany, Italy, England and Argentina can't match. In fact, no one can.

Let's put things in perspective. The Grand Duchy of Luxembourg is not a large country: it's the sixth smallest in the world. It measures 51 miles long by 32 miles wide. It is tucked between Belgium, France and Germany and on most European maps is not even large enough to contain the letters of its own name. It is hardly surprising that football success has generally eluded it.

But Luxembourg has always tried. The team entered the very first World Cup qualifying tournament, held ahead of Italy '34. Their debut promised little. They played only two games, losing 9–1 to Germany and 6–1 to France. Yet they entered again in 1938, this time losing to Belgium and Holland. After the wartime break they were straight back for more. In the 1950 qualifiers they made up a group of only two with Switzerland, but still success eluded them.

The Swiss won home and away by an 8–4 aggregate.

It began to look very much as if Luxembourg were attempting a planned programme of defeat to every nation in Europe. When they tried to qualify again in 1954, they lost to the Republic of Ireland. Then in 1958 they fell to Austria. At each attempt they finished bottom of the group but never once gave up.

The familiar trend continued in the 1962 qualifiers. Their opening game was at home to England on 19 October 1960. England won 9–0 as two youngsters both grabbed hat tricks – both Robert Charlton and James Greaves were suitably lauded in the local press, for the Luxembourgers had by now learned to be gracious in defeat.

Luxembourg then added another 'reverse scalp' to their growing tally by losing 6–0 to Portugal in Lisbon, the ninth European country they'd been generous to. In September 1961 England went easy on them at Wembley, strolling to a 4–1 win. That left only one game remaining, the home tie with Portugal in Luxembourg City.

It was 8 October 1961. Something strange must have possessed Ady Schmidt that day. Stealing the thunder from the prolific 'Black Panther' Eusébio, who was making his international debut, plain old 'Smith' notched a hat trick. Luxembourg won 4–2. It was their first qualifying victory in 27 years. It was certainly a shock, but more notable still was the result's symbolic significance as a reward for sheer perseverance.

Again Luxembourg finished bottom of the group, but again they came back for more. They hit the road to England '66 with all their usual enthusiasm, but soon skidded to another disaster – this time Norway and Yugoslavia joined the list of conquerors. Yet the 'Duchymen' consistently attempted to qualify for every World Cup since – 1970, 1974, 1978, 1982, 1986, 1990, 1994, 1998, 2002, 2006 and 2010 – adding new countries to their lengthening 'hospitality list' as each qualifying tournament passed in customary fashion.

There was an isolated success in October 1972, as Luxembourg managed a 2-0 victory over Turkey during the World Cup qualifying campaign for West Germany '74. They followed this up by recording draws with both Belgium and Iceland, before reverting to type. After a protracted period of ignominy, their luck changed for the better in 1995, as minor successes during qualification for the European Championships included home-and-away victories over Malta and a remarkable home win against the Czech Republic (who went on to reach the final of Euro '96). But another dark period ensued, and from 1995 to 2007 Luxembourg failed to win a single game, slipping down the FIFA world rankings to a low of 195th. Then in February 2007, the team beat Gambia 2-1 in a friendly match. In October of the same year they recorded their first competitive win in 12 years, beating Belarus 1-0 in a Euro 2008 qualifier.

The watershed moment for the national side was arguably the qualifying campaign for the 2010 World Cup. This proved to be their most successful ever, in which Luxembourg finally avoided finishing bottom of their group, thereby consigning their unenviable record to history. A heroic 2-1 win over Switzerland in Zürich in September 2008, followed by home-and-away draws with Moldova saw them amass a total of 5 points, enough for them to finish below Switzerland, Greece, Latvia and Israel, but crucially, ahead of Moldova, who only gained a paltry 3 points (from the two aforementioned draws, with the third point coming from a 1-1 stalemate with Greece).

Perhaps things are looking up at last for Luxembourg, brave minnows of world football. Even if this proves not to be the case, they still have an unassailable claim to fame – the fact remains that they are the only team to have played in every World Cup qualifying tournament to date. If prizes were given for effort alone the persistent little burghers of the Grand Duchy would win every trophy going.

# WELL BOWLED, THAT MAN
## LIVERPOOL, 30 MAY 1962

No sportsman likes to fail. But sometimes it's in the public interest that they do. That's why a County Championship cricket match has somehow forced its way into *The World Cup's Strangest Moments* and why England owe a debt of gratitude to two bowlers, one a legendary off-spinner and the other a long-forgotten fast right-armer.

This is the story of an aspiring sportsman who didn't quite make it in the summer game. When he made his debut for Essex against Lancashire on 30 May 1962, the strapping twenty-year-old was regarded as a highly promising right-hand batsman. The three day County Championship game was played at Aigburth in Liverpool, the ideal minor stage on which to blood a youngster.

There was no real pressure on the debutant. In the first innings he batted at Number Ten. But a cricketing legend well into the twilight of his career denied him the opportunity even to nudge a few singles. The England spin-bowler Jim Laker, famed for taking nineteen Australian wickets in a Test Match at Old Trafford in 1956, should have batted at Eleven. But he declined to go to the crease, nursing a minor injury. As a consequence the disappointed youngster was left stranded on 'Not out 0'.

The second innings gave him the chance for a longer stay. The crestfallen lad was heartened to be elevated to Number Eight in the order. Had he impressed, it might have been the start of a long and fruitful cricket career. As it was, his dreams were cruelly dashed by the Lancashire paceman Colin Hilton, who clean-bowled the hopeful for a duck. Although the debutant took a couple of catches, he entered the annals of cricket statistics as a long-forgotten one-gamer with a batting average of zero. He never played for the Essex First XI again.

A few weeks later he made his debut for the Second XI and there he stayed. Even so, ten games was the sum total of his appearances. The highlight of his career was an innings of 61 against Kent at the Orsett and Thurrock Cricket Club. On 23 July 1964 his brief affair with the leather and willow came to a sorry end at the County Ground in Worcester. Batting at Number Three, he was dismissed for a miserable eleven in the first innings and trapped LBW for seven in the second. The experts said his footwork let him down. Essex lost by 115 runs.

The cricket bible *Wisden* once deigned to give space to this undistinguished career: 'He was an outstanding fielder and occasional wicket keeper. However, his football commitments meant that he was restricted to only one first-class match.' They failed to delineate what the 'football commitments' were. All they gave was his name. Geoffrey Charles Hurst.

Such odd little factoids are manna from heaven to that peculiar breed who run pub quizzes. Geoff Hurst's record seems safe – the only county cricketer to score a hat trick in a FIFA World Cup final. But he isn't the only cricketer-footballer beloved of the quiz fraternity. A popular question is 'Who is the only person to appear in World Cup matches at both cricket and football?' The standard answer is the West Indies cricketing hero Viv Richards, who also played football for Antigua and Barbuda in the 1974 qualifying competition.

But thereby hangs a tale, for the answer has been known to cause disputes. That's why sensible quizmasters substitute 'play in' for 'appear in', because sooner or later someone always comes up with the Jamaican-born umpire Steve Bucknor. The man they call 'Slow Death' because of his lingering finger-raising technique began as a FIFA-qualified referee. On 16 October 1988 he took charge of the 1990 World Cup qualifying game in San Salvador between El Salvador and the Netherlands Antilles. But it was his only game at that level. He was required to retire at age 45 because FIFA consider a man's judgement to be declining by then. So Bucknor took to umpiring and at the last count had stood at four Cricket World Cup finals!

It doesn't do to get too deeply involved in the World Cup's links with the 'double breed', because it can go on a bit. Andy Goram was Scotland's 'keeper' at both football and cricket – his three times behind the stumps were in 1989, including an appearance against Australia. England's Phil Neville played for Lancashire Second XI and has vowed to take up cricket when his football career ends. We all look forward to the day.

And there are more, I promise. But let's reflect on Geoff 'Quack Quack' Hurst for one last time, the only man to have scored more goals in a World Cup final than he managed runs in his entire first-class cricket career. But for Colin Hilton's demon right arm, that's one record that might not have stood. Well bowled, that man!

# THE BATTLE OF SANTIAGO
## SANTIAGO, 2 JUNE 1962

Chile was justly proud to be appointed host for the 1962 World Cup. When the small impoverished nation suffered a devastating earthquake in May 1960, their chance looked to have gone. It claimed five thousand lives and damaged a third of the country's buildings beyond repair. Rival claimants Argentina seemed certain to get FIFA's vote. But the minnows prevailed after an impassioned plea from the Chilean FA president Carlos Dittborn: 'It is *because* we now have nothing that we must have the World Cup'.

When Dittborn died of a heart attack shortly before the tournament began, it only heightened Chilean pride. But two Italian journalists seemed insensitive to the mood. First Antonio Ghirelli cast aspersions on the looks and morals of Santiago's womenfolk, and then Corrado Pizzinelli twisted the knife: 'Chile is a foul country afflicted by every evil – undernourishment, illiteracy, alcoholism, open prostitution and general misery.' The battle lines between Chile and Italy were drawn. Trust them to be in the same opening group!

The grudge match took place in Santiago's Estadio Nacional on 2 June 1962. The Andes mountain range provided a stunning backdrop to the occasion. The BBC's David Coleman provided a stunning introduction to the television highlights: 'Good evening. The game you are about to see is the most stupid, appalling, disgusting and disgraceful exhibition of football, possibly in the history of the game.' Nobody turned off.

Already anticipating a robust encounter, FIFA had hastily appointed the English referee Ken Aston in place of the scheduled official. Aston was a schoolmaster who had served as a lieutenant colonel in India during the war. He had a reputation for stern control. Latin temperaments didn't faze him.

But the game started badly and got worse. Prior to kick-off, the Italians tried to give the Chilean players conciliatory carnations, but were brusquely rebuffed. The first bone-crunching tackle came after only twelve seconds. In the eighth minute Giorgio Ferrini of Italy retaliated after being kicked from behind by Chile's centre-forward Landa. Aston meekly took refuge in the 'homer' approach and ordered Ferrini off. But the Italian refused to go. It took nearly ten minutes before FIFA officials and armed police got the incensed player off the pitch.

The incident further galvanised the tackling, which Chile's players augmented with surreptitious spitting. Five minutes before the interval Chile's Leonel Sanchez reacted to a series of hacking kicks from Mario David by flattening him with a left hook. Amazingly, neither Aston nor his linesmen (Elcaz of Mexico and Goldstein, an Israeli New Yorker) appeared to witness the blow. Chile somehow kept eleven men.

So David sought his own revenge. In the 46th minute he tackled Sanchez somewhere in the region of the jugular. Aston saw that one and sent David off. Italy now had only nine men. And Umberto Maschio had a broken nose from an earlier collision with a Chilean arm thought to belong to that man Sanchez. Yet still there was no score. Both teams seemed to have forgotten the object of the game.

Twice more armed police came onto the field. The jeers and whistles from the 66,000 crowd never stopped. Several spectator incursions occurred. Aston was frequently surrounded and jostled by the players. He considered abandoning the game but feared the consequences. Although Chile were the greater villains, the official must have been relieved when they took the lead in the 74th minute from a Ramirez header.

Two minutes from time a second goal from Toro secured a 2–0 victory for the hosts. The same player should have been sent off in the dying seconds for one last act of fisticuffs, but again Aston bottled it. He added no stoppage time and was escorted from the field by an armed guard. What on earth would have happened if Italy had won? As it was, they got a stoning at their training camp and an early ticket home as the Italian press slated Aston's 'disgraceful arbitrage'.

'The Battle of Santiago' might not have shocked a modern World Cup audience, but by 1962 standards the episode was shameful. FIFA later used television footage for the first time to mete out further punishment. Ferrini was suspended for one game and David and Sanchez received 'severe admonishments'.

As for Aston, he perversely became a top refereeing administrator (see 'Cards for Every Occasion') but never took charge of another World Cup game. A convenient 'Achilles' tendon strain' sustained during his nightmare match prevented him from risking further embarrassment. Lack of experience of the Continental temperament was his real Achilles heel, but he mitigated his performance with a pithy observation: 'It was me against twenty-two. The game was uncontrollable. I wasn't reffing a football match. I was an umpire in military manoeuvres.'

There had been previous World Cup slugfests (see 'It's a Knockout') but 2 June 1962 was when the 'modern' tournament truly kicked off. David 'Ooh I'm really shocked' Coleman didn't know it, but winning at all costs would become par for the course after the brutality of Santiago.

# WE'LL MEET AGAIN

## SANTIAGO, 10 JUNE 1962

The German coach Joseph 'Sepp' Herberger had seen it all. Shortly after Germany flopped at 'Hitler's Olympics' in Berlin in 1936, the former Mannheim forward was appointed *Reichsfussballtrainer* and instructed to 'make Germany great'. He was still at the helm 26 years later for the Chile '62 World Cup. In the back-'em-and-sack-'em world of football management, that's quite remarkable.

As Germany travelled to Chile, Herberger had already taken his sides to France '38, Switzerland '54, and Sweden '58. His finest hour was winning the 1954 final against the mighty Hungarians, a victory that entered German folklore as 'Das Wunder von Bern' ('The Miracle of Berne').

Much of his success was attributed to meticulous preparation in an age when management styles were wont to be somewhat cavalier. Long before Don Revie compiled his infamously detailed (and useless) 'dossiers' for England, Herberger was famed for his trademark notebook, which detailed the opposition's strengths and weaknesses and the outcome of all their previous encounters with Germany.

It probably didn't contain the memorandum 'If it's June it must be a quarter-final victory against Yugoslavia', but it should have done.

On 27 June 1954 West Germany had beaten Yugoslavia 2–0 in the quarter-final in Geneva. On 19 June 1958 West Germany had beaten Yugoslavia 1–0 in the quarter-final in Malmo. And on 10 June 1962 West Germany again faced Yugoslavia in the quarter-final in Santiago.

Only a student of probability could state the exact odds on seeing the same sides meet in the quarter-final at three successive

World Cups, but in my humble back-of-a-matchbox opinion they must be very long indeed. It's the only time it's happened in the tournament's history.

However, alas for Herberger, this time Yugoslavia ruined the symmetry by winning the game 1–0. It presaged the end of the *bergermeister*'s canny reign, as he abdicated in 1964 in favour of his protégé Helmut Schoen. Having deservedly taken the plaudits as 'the founding father of German international football', Sepp Herberger died in 1977 aged eighty.

Yet it was by no means the end of June's most frequent football fixture. On 26 June 1974, West Germany had beaten Yugoslavia 2–0 in Düsseldorf. On 10 June 1990 West Germany beat Yugoslavia 4–1 in Milan. Even the political fragmentation of the old Yugoslavia in 1991 failed to end the sequence. On 21 June 1998 a smaller reincarnation of the same name drew 2–2 with Germany in Lens.

Who would dare bet that the World Cup's most familiar foes won't one day meet again? As the Trinidad and Tobago goalkeeper Shaka Hislop once said (pinching a line first used by the New York Yankees baseball legend Yogi Berra), 'It looks like it's going to be *déjà vu* all over again.'

# *GREAVSIE'S FAMOUS DRIBBLE*
## VIÑA DEL MAR, 10 JUNE 1962

James Peter 'Jimmy' Greaves, affectionately known as 'Greavsie', was one of British football's greatest strikers. Achieving the rare feat of scoring on his debut for England, England under 23s, Chelsea, AC Milan, Spurs and West Ham, he notched 357 goals in 516 League games and scored 44 times for England in 57 appearances.

But the likeable Greaves is almost entirely excluded from the archive of World Cup classics. He scored only once in his seven outings, and in 1966 was cruelly injured in England's first-round game against France. Alf Ramsey brought in Geoff Hurst as a replacement and stuck with him in the celebrated final despite Greaves's recovery. Highly fortuitous for England, truly tragic for Jimmy.

One celebrated incident sums up his World Cup hoodoo more than any other. At Chile '62, England faced the World Cup holders Brazil in the quarter-final. On 10 June, at an eerily mist-shrouded Estadio del Tranque in Viña del Mar, the World Champions cruised to a 3–1 victory and retained the trophy a week later.

Greaves had an ineffective game. The star of the match was Brazil's brilliant outside-right 'Little Bird' Garrincha, who scored two. But it was another of God's creatures who truly stole the show.

Early in the proceedings a stray black dog of indeterminate pedigree entered the arena of play in the manner of a bull released from the holding pen at a *gran corrida*. As most canine intruders do once they find themselves thrust into a midfield holding role, the dog made a series of disoriented runs and led a posse of star footballers and sundry ball boys a merry chase. It even achieved the rare feat of side-stepping the master-dribbler Garrincha.

Only when the quick-thinking Greaves decided to stoop to the pooch's level was order restored. Going down on all fours close to the centre-circle, he eyeballed the cheeky Chilean mutt face to face before scooping him up and delivering the squirming package to a steward.

It can only be assumed that the intruder was relieved to be apprehended, because Greaves felt a steady dribble of something hot and wet soaking into his coveted England shirt. And it wasn't the striker's hard-earned perspiration.

The British public being what they are, this incident was recently voted into Channel 4's '*100 Greatest World Cup Moments*'. The Chilean populace were also much amused, as was Brazil's star player. The dog was quickly named after Garrincha, who in turn adopted it as a lucky mascot. He is said to have called it Jimmy Greaves.

Forty years later the revered England legend still had pungent memories of the occasion: 'For some reason, the dog stopped at me. Maybe he thought, "Here's another poor sod who's in just as desperate straits as I am. I smelt so bad, it was awful. I should have won the game for England, because no Brazilian defenders came near me".'

Every great striker goes through a sticky patch once in his career. Greavsie will never be allowed to forget his.

# THE LITTLE WORLD CUP
## RIO DE JANEIRO, 30 MAY 1964

All right-thinking individuals know in their hearts that a four-yearly cycle is perfect. Every six years would be too long to wait. Every two years would be overkill. The feeling was never better expressed than by the French goalkeeper Lionel Charbonnier, understudy to Fabien Barthez in their victorious squad at France '98: 'The World Cup is like a woman. The longer you wait for one, the more you appreciate it. Four years is fine.'

Without wishing to delve any deeper into the woefully intermittent sex lives of French goalkeepers (no wonder Barthez was crazy and always kicking his posts), it has to be said that he's right. Love it as we may, any more frequent than once every four years would be too much of a good thing. And that's one very good reason why FIFA need watching.

Football's world governing body have never been short of daft concepts. In the late 1980s they genuinely flirted with the idea of splitting World Cup games into four quarters to accommodate more television commercials. The scheme was rejected, but only after fans around the globe had made their feelings clear. Rumours surfaced again prior to USA '94. FIFA were going to make the goals bigger. In truth they never were, but the very idea certainly caused outrage among the fans.

Few appreciate any meddling with football for the sake of it. That's why the tournament dubbed 'The Little World Cup' stayed that way. The innovatory competition held in Brazil in 1964 might have been the thin end of a very thick wedge. FIFA were certainly behind it. Some of their top brass had been advocating two-yearly competitions for some time. This was a chance to see if it might catch on. As it is, the presumptive little pretender has been consigned to the World Cup oddities pile, where only the keenest of statisticians are wont to forage. Here are its remains.

After the 1962 World Cup had been staged in Chile, FIFA had every reason to butter up the winners Brazil. Their great rivals Argentina had very nearly stepped in as hosts after Chile's devastating earthquake. That had put Brazil's nose right out of joint. No one wanted the World Champions sulking, least of all FIFA.

The perfect opportunity arose via historical convenience: 1964 was the Brazilian FA's fiftieth anniversary, so the Brazilian Jubilee Tournament was hastily conceived. Journalists labelled it 'The Little World Cup'. FIFA didn't object. The Brazilians named it the Taça das Nações (Nations' Cup), which seemed a bit overblown, seeing that only three other nations took part.

Portugal agreed to travel to uphold their colonial links with Brazil. Argentina just wanted to upset the party. And the England manager Alf Ramsey, barely two years into his reign, jumped at the chance to test his boys against South American opposition. Things went pretty much to script.

The format was certainly 'little'. The entire tournament spanned a single week. Each team played the others once, which made six games, all played in the Maracana Stadium in Rio de Janeiro. Brazil and England opened the proceedings on 30 May before seventy thousand fans.

Alf Ramsey had rather bulled himself up following his appointment as England manager on 25 October 1962. His opening pronouncement to the press was a bold one: 'England will win the World Cup in 1966.' This was the first chance to put his men fully to the test on hostile foreign soil. Brazil won 5–1. Test failed.

The next day Argentina easily disposed of Portugal 2–0 and on 3 June did exactly what they had set out to do. They beat Brazil 3–0 in their own backyard.

England and Portugal then served up a dull 1–1 draw before England were beaten 1–0 by Argentina. Second test failed. As crowd interest dwindled, Brazil closed the non-event with a minor flourish by giving their colonial cousins Portugal a sound 4–1 thrashing. End of 'Little World Cup'.

Argentina won it, Brazil were second and England came 'joint last' with Portugal. Both sides had an identical goal difference of minus five. The only comfort for Alf Ramsey was that his side were officially placed third on two significant counts. They had lost to the winners Argentina by one goal fewer than Portugal. And alphabetically they were far superior to the Portuguese.

Alf Ramsey and his squad returned home somewhat chastened by the whole experience. And that is the only reason why England fans should be grateful that the 'Little World Cup' took place at all. Ramsey prepared for 1966 with enhanced awareness and renewed vigour. The rest is history.

Once in a while another minor tournament is dubbed the 'Little World Cup', but few genuine football fans are fooled. There is only one World Cup. It is anything but little and comes round every four years. Should FIFA or anyone else suggest otherwise, or should your resolve begin to falter, remember the profound words of an iron-willed French custodian.

# WE ALL KNEW HIS NAME
## LONDON, 12 JULY 1965

The eighth World Cup was still a year away when the Football Association called a press conference on 12 July 1965 to discuss ticket sales. During the meeting they casually introduced a novel promotional idea that changed the face of England '66 and every tournament that followed. The stuffy old FA had conceived the first World Cup mascot. Soon, World Cup Willie mania swept through England.

The shaggy lion with just the right combination of attitude and cuddliness was drawn by Reginald Hoye, an artist for the merchandising agents Walter Tuckwell and Associates. Willie wore a Union Flag shirt, sturdy boots and a determined expression. His square shoulders, clenched fists and strutting gait were a match for any foreigner in town. Those who say England wouldn't have won the World Cup without him may not be wrong. Willie was a tonic to the nation. Alf Ramsey's men couldn't possibly fail.

No item of official merchandise or humble household requisite was safe from the leonine countenance. Nor was Willie hidebound by political correctness. Boxes of 'Wee Willie Cigars' showed him puffing on a cheroot. His bushy mane adorned the most intimate area of ladies' briefs. Watney's 'World Cup Ale' was brewed in his honour. Smith's did the crisps to go with it.

Horse brasses, tea towels, braces, jigsaws, bath mats, bed-spreads, periscopes, playing cards, darts, tumblers, ties, balloons, cufflinks, masks, glove puppets, belts, biscuit tins, money boxes – the list was endless. Months before England's victory, Willie cultists had already founded an official Collectors' Club.

In December 1965 Lonnie Donegan's catchy single record reminded the rest of the world that 'We all know his name'. What a delicious irony that Anthony James Donegan was born in Glasgow. When Scotland narrowly failed to qualify for England '66, the *Daily Express*'s depiction of a kilted Willie in tears was surely a sardonic joke.

Stranger still was the German squad's obliging recording of 'Fussball Willi' in their own language. Adidas later compounded that sublime own goal by kindly supplying Geoff Hurst with boots hand-crafted in Germany. A final goal for each stripe, thank you very much. Now let's hear 'Fussball Willi' one more time.

The real unsung hero of the hour was the long-forgotten chief administrative officer of the 1966 organising committee. Ken Willson was a stocky little chap with square shoulders and a pugnacious jaw. He strutted the FA corridors roaring orders. The office girls nicknamed him World Cup Willie long before the mighty lion was unveiled. When it was, the likeness to Ken was uncanny. The christening was a foregone conclusion.

Without Ken and Willie, the strange procession of subsequent World Cup mascots would never have happened. Who could ever forget 'Juanito', the chirpy lad from Mexico '70? Most people, actually, overshadowed as he was by a ludicrously large sombrero.

West Germany '74 redoubled the cheeky-boy theme with 'Tip' and 'Tap'. Argentina '78 spawned 'Gauchito', yet another cutesy mite. Then things took a bizarre turn towards the organic as 'Naranjito' the orange failed to inspire the Spanish hosts in 1982. They were squeezed out in the quarter-finals. Four years later Mexico suffered the same fate when they failed to warm to 'Pique', the only chilli pepper ever to sport an authentic Zapata moustache.

'Ciao' the cuboid stickman fell apart at Italia '90. 'Striker' the dumb hound (think Deputy Dawg's less intelligent brother) summed up much about USA '94. 'Footix' the blue cockerel came closest to Willie for jauntiness as the hosts France majestically ruled the roost in 1998. But FIFA's ill-advised high-tech trio of Ato, Nik and Kaz ('The Spheriks') bombed completely at Japorea '02. 'Inane', 'repulsive' and 'grotesque' were some of the kinder words that emerged from a fan survey.

For Germany '06, favouring the retro route, the committee decided on a lion named Goleo VI ('Go Leo' and he was the 'sixth' applicant – get it?), who looked uncannily like a Willie for the twenty-first century, except he wore no shorts. Alas, fans of the host nation failed to embrace the exhibitionist lion – the company who had paid a cool £19 million for the Goleo marketing rights went spectacularly bust.

The green-haired leopard 'Zakumi' was created for South Africa 2010 – that's 'ZA' for 'Zuid Afrika' and 'kumi' meaning 'ten'. Where he settles in the mascot pecking order only time will tell. But one thing is certain – generations on from the lion king who started it all, World Cup mascots are here to stay. Who knows what strange creatures are yet to be conceived? In the surreal domain of Willie and his progeny, anything is possible.

# STAMP OF DISAPPROVAL
## WHITEHALL, 24 NOVEMBER 1965

As a student of strange moments I am honour-bound to relate the uplifting story of 'the little North Koreans' and their plucky adventure at the 1966 World Cup. Their qualification for the finals was confirmed on 24 November 1965. It was largely by default. They sneaked in only because sixteen other sides withdrew following a dispute with FIFA about 'unfair structuring' in the Asian and African qualifying groups.

Their finals debut started badly with an expected 3–0 loss to Russia. Then a 1–1 draw with Chile raised eyebrows. But their 1–0 win against Italy via the 'ballerina's foot' of the 'diminutive Pak Doo-ik' was 'true fairytale stuff'. How the press milked those clichés. And how the good citizens of Middlesbrough, where the Koreans' group games were played, lapped it all up. They truly took the 'happy-go-lucky Orientals' to their hearts.

Next was the unforgettable quarter-final clash with Portugal at Everton's Goodison Park. North Korea sensationally led 3–0 after 24 minutes before Eusébio scored four and made another to see Portugal through by five goals to three. Everybody cheered North Korea from the field. All England loved them. Long live the underdog. So that's it. I've done the story.

Except that the fairytale version isn't the one I've chosen to tell. Stranger still is the story exposed thirty years later, when access to 'top secret' government papers was finally enabled. Forget about a hospitable host nation's romantic ideal of 'the sporting spirit' of a quaint outsider. This one's about the underhanded diplomatic skulduggery of a British government that didn't want North Korea in England in the first place.

How much more convenient it would have been if Australia had taken care of North Korea in the two-leg qualifier in

November 1965. Britain could have put the flags out to welcome a nice Commonwealth country. But, when communist North Korea stormed through 9–2 on aggregate, chins were rubbed ruefully in the corridors of Whitehall. The Foreign Office knew all too well that the United Kingdom officially 'failed to recognise' the Democratic People's Republic of Korea. Something would have to be done.

The anonymous 'suits' initially considered a drastic solution. They would deny the North Koreans entry visas. But the FA and Harold Wilson's pro-sport Labour government soon marked their card. If North Korea were simply barred, FIFA might deny England the tournament. That was unthinkable. The compromise that emerged from Whitehall aimed to 'minimise the visual presence' of the North Korean side and 'avoid doing anything where possible which might imply a diplomatic acceptance of the regime'.

It was expressly agreed that the unwelcome visitors must play as 'North Korea' rather than their preferred and FIFA-recognised DPRK. Certain invitations were mysteriously overlooked. When the draw was made in a London hotel on 6 January 1966, North Korea were the only competing nation not represented. Packing the team off to Middlesbrough, as far away from Wembley as possible, was a further means of sanitation. And restricting royal attendance only to the opening ceremony and final was another neat touch.

There was also the thorny question of flags and national anthems. The Foreign Office report of 9 December 1965 – 'North Korean Participation in the finals of the World Cup' – demanded a total ban on their flag and anthem. The FA managed to reverse the flag-flying dictate (only because they had already ordered the flagpoles and committed sponsors!), but on the anthems Whitehall got its way. Unusually, they were played only at the opening game and the final. So the North Korean anthem was never publicly heard.

All this subterfuge was at the time kept entirely from the press and public. It entailed countless hours of discussions between the Foreign Office, the FA, the Department of Education and Science and the British Embassy in Seoul. Even NATO were consulted. And the South Korean ambassador in London chipped in with frequent protestations that North Korea should not be made too welcome.

The final stamp of disapproval came barely six weeks before the finals began. Just when the Foreign Office thought their airbrushing was complete, they discovered that one of the official World Cup stamps about to be issued depicted the North Korean flag. It was hastily pulled and replaced by another design.

It's been said that sport and politics are inseparable, but surely the Foreign Office took the whole thing too seriously. Most sports fans will take satisfaction from the knowledge that this particular Whitehall farce largely bombed. Banishing the Koreans to a northern outpost seemed only to magnify their novelty value and increase their exposure. And the unscheduled advance to the quarter-finals was a worst nightmare for the ministerial killjoys.

This alternative story reveals that not everybody took 'the little Orientals' to their hearts after all. The distasteful sub-agenda to the 1966 World Cup suggests that 'FO' written on a North Korean file might well have stood for something rather less polite than the Foreign Office.

# CHEERS AND PICKLES

## WESTMINSTER, 20 MARCH 1966

On Saturday, 30 July 1966, England's captain Bobby Moore lifted the World Cup after a memorable 4–2 victory over West Germany. But he wasn't the first to do it that year. On Sunday, 20 March, a light-fingered thief had already lifted the trophy after a memorable security boob by the Football Association.

So it was that England shamefully became the only side to have lost and won the Jules Rimet trophy in the same year. And what a valuable piece of history it was! When the French sculptor Abel Lafleur designed it for the first World Cup in 1930 he didn't skimp. Everybody agreed that the solid-silver, gold-plated Goddess of Victory holding aloft an octagonal chalice made a truly handsome trophy to be eternally treasured.

No wonder FIFA guarded the icon jealously. Throughout World War Two it was hidden in a shoe box under the bed of Dr Ottorino Barassi, their Italian vice-president. But would the cup that survived the Nazis be safe in the bumbling hands of England's football hierarchy?

FIFA were certainly nervous about the request to release the trophy for display at the Stanley Gibbons 'Stampex' exhibition at Central Hall in Westminster. Weeks of negotiation preceded their grudging permission, but the FA's 'categorical assurance' in writing that 'every security measure' had been taken finally got them the nod.

The trophy was insured for £30,000 and guards would remain by its side day and night. With £3 million worth of stamps also on show, the FA insisted it would be as safe as the Houses of Parliament just round the corner.

After the FIFA president Sir Stanley Rous finally signed the release papers, the cup was collected on Friday, 18 March, the opening day of the exhibition. Some 48 hours later, on the morning of Sunday, 20 March, a day the exhibition was closed, the loss of the trophy was discovered after the security guards 'came back from their break'. Embarrassment wasn't the word. The 1966 World Cup hosts were faced with having to run the tournament without a trophy.

A ransom telephone call was soon made to J H W Mears, chairman of the FA. The detachable chalice was posted to his home as a carrot. The thief wanted £15,000 for the body of the trophy. Scotland Yard were called in as the World Cup organising committee became frantic.

On 23 March, an officer arranged a rendezvous with a middle man to hand over a stash of fake notes. The ruse worked a treat as the man panicked and was arrested. He was a 47-year-old London dock worker named Ted Betchley. But Betchley was mere small fry. He got two years inside for his part in the theft, but refused to reveal the whereabouts of the cup or the name of the mastermind, whom he referred to simply as 'the Pole'.

If the collective brainpower of Scotland Yard's most senior personnel couldn't recover the trophy, then what could? How about a two-year-old mongrel dog?

On the evening of Sunday, 27 March, one week after the cup's disappearance, a Thames river barge worker, David Corbett, took his inquisitive pooch Pickles for a walk near his south London flat in Beulah Hill. When the mischievous hound started rooting under a holly hedge, his owner went to investigate and pulled out a weighty object wrapped in newspaper. The Jules Rimet trophy had been miraculously saved, and with it the FA's bacon.

David Corbett received the substantial reward of £5,000, five times as much as the bonus paid to each of the England players for winning the World Cup four months later. While Dave bought a house on the strength of it, Pickles became a national hero who made the front pages the world over. The Sherlock Holmes of the dog kingdom was awarded a medal by the National Canine Defence League and given a year's supply of treats by a pet food company. And naturally there was a movie. Pickles starred with two bulldogs and Eric Sykes in the 1966 spoof espionage film *The Spy with the Cold Nose*.

There are three postscripts to this bizarre lost-and-found tale. The Football Association became so paranoid about putting England's victory spoils on display again that they commissioned goldsmith George Bird to make an exact replica, which they passed off for several years as the real thing. FIFA executives and many drooling onlookers were thus fooled. The fake then spent 27 years under George Bird's bed before being auctioned by Sotheby's after his death. At their July 1997 sale it was knocked down for a cool £254,500.

The second oddity is that Brazil later went one worse than England by losing the genuine Jules Rimet trophy for good in 1983 (see 'Anything You Can Do ...'). And, last but not least, the supreme power that rules the animal kingdom showed itself to have a very morbid sense of humour indeed. On 3 August 1971 the plucky Pickles passed away after hanging himself on his own lead. It caught in the lower branches of a tree while he was in merry pursuit of a cat.

What a sad end for the Football Association's best friend.

# *ANIMALS!*

## WEMBLEY, 23 JULY 1966

It takes some doing to single-handedly change the context of a word in the *Oxford English Dictionary*. But, following the 1966 World Cup quarter-final at the Empire Stadium in Wembley, the England manager Alf Ramsey achieved it at a stroke. Before the game, 'animals' was simply the plural for any of God's creatures. After the post-match interviews, no English football fan would ever utter it again without thinking of Argentina.

England always knew the Argentines would be tough. 'We accepted in our guts it was going to be hard. Maybe brutal', said Bobby Moore. England's captain read his entrails just as well as the game. The controversial appointment of the German referee Rudolf Kreitlein didn't help. Having had a man dismissed against West Germany in the group stage, Argentina became convinced of a Teutonic conspiracy to thwart their further progress.

Kreitlein's patience did seem thin right from the start, but not without reason. England's hard man Nobby Stiles was spat at several times. Geoff Hurst was kicked when the ball was nowhere near him. Hair-tugging and eye-poking were established routines. The Argentines constantly moaned at the referee.

Several players, including the towering Argentine captain Antonio Rattin, had already been booked before the 36th minute flashpoint. After spitting in front of the referee, then fouling Bobby Charlton and Roger Hunt in quick succession, Rattin refused to withdraw ten yards from a free kick before remonstrating yet again with Kreitlein over a caution issued to Luis Artime. This time the official snapped and dismissed Rattin from the field.

But the captain refused to go. Some of the Argentines left the pitch in sympathy, and others formed a threatening posse around

Kreitlein. Alf Ramsey frantically waved England's players away as Stiles sniffed around looking to 'get involved'. Rattin later claimed he had been asking for an interpreter. But several of his team could speak German. And which bit of the referee's pointing-to-the-tunnel gesture didn't he understand?

After what seemed like an eternity (eight minutes) Rattin finally allowed himself to be led from the Wembley turf. He then staged a brief sit-down on the touchline before being persuaded by a policeman to reacquaint himself with the changing room. Rattin was a tall, dark, brooding character, straight out of a spaghetti western. The scowl on his face was something to behold and his nostrils all but breathed fire as he dawdled petulantly to his infamous early bath.

Tempers didn't improve as Argentina tried to keep the game goalless. But Hurst headed in a Martin Peters cross in the 77th minute to put England into the semifinals. A ball boy ran onto the field to celebrate the goal. Argentina's Oscar Mas clipped him round the ear!

Rattin alone had been sent off, but Argentina's collective demeanour had been shameful. A terrified-looking Kreitlein (small, bald, hollow-eyed and perspiring profusely) was escorted to the tunnel by the police and former referee Ken Aston (see 'The Battle of Santiago') while Alf Ramsey engaged in a tug-of-war to prevent the England right-back George Cohen exchanging shirts with Alberto Gonzalez. The Argentine promptly swapped with left-back Ray Wilson instead!

Then came Ramsey's famous press conference: 'We have still to produce our best, and this is not possible until we meet the right type of opponents, and that is a team that comes out to play football and *not to act as animals.*'

The statement provoked fury across South America as the Argentine press lambasted the 'shameful English insult'. Englishmen countered by suggesting Ramsey's taunt was an insult to animals. The sides remain opposed to this day.

I should say that this is the anglicised version of the 'animals' affair. All Argentina blamed the German referee and assured the world that Antonio Rattin was as mild-mannered as a baby once you got to know him. More words were written in Argentina about the 1966 quarter-final than anywhere else. In his pre-game build-up, the journalist Osvaldo Ardizzone established a communications record. His cable to Buenos Aires was 20,246 words long and took five hours and forty minutes to transmit. No wonder losing 1–0 was such an anticlimax.

All subsequent England-against-Argentina battles carry something of Wembley '66 with them. But it pays not to delve too deeply. Lost in all the sound and fury surrounding this match was the strangest statistic of all. England committed 33 fouls to Argentina's 19. Nice one Nobby!

# WAS IT ALL OVER?

## WEMBLEY, 30 JULY 1966

When England beat West Germany 4–2 at Wembley to win the 1966 World Cup, eleven footballers became legends at a stroke. But the 'Boys of '66' were joined by another cult hero. The forty-year-old Azerbaijani linesman Tofik Bakhramov became the most unlikely World Cup celebrity of all time.

After ninety minutes' play, the 200th game in World Cup history stood at 2–2 thanks to an 89th-minute equaliser from Germany's Wolfgang Weber. The goal followed a disputed free kick. There was a hint of handball in the build-up. England had had victory cruelly snatched from them at the very death.

But they began extra time with the inspirational words of manager Alf Ramsey still ringing in their ears: 'Look at the Germans. They're flat out. They can't live with you. You've won the World Cup once. Now go out and do it again.'

In the tenth minute of extra time, Geoff Hurst swivelled on a near-post cross from Alan Ball and smacked a rising shot onto the underside of the bar. The ball bounced down 'onto' the line, then spun back into play before it was headed over by Weber for what he hoped would be nothing more than an England corner.

England's players raised their arms to claim a goal, none more convincingly than Roger Hunt, who was racing into the six-yard box with Weber. Hunt later admitted, 'I wouldn't have got to the ball.' But his apparent refusal to go for it suggested at the time that he 'knew' the whole of the ball had crossed the line. That meant a goal. The Germans disagreed. No moment in World Cup history has led to more lasting debate.

The Swiss referee Gottfried Dienst wasn't in a position to see. He consulted linesman Bakhramov, who at the crucial moment had markedly craned his neck to get a better view. Time stood still. The fans held their breath. Then Bakhramov nodded emphatically and raised his arm. Dienst signalled the goal.

The Germans aggressively surrounded the linesman, who cut a rather comedic figure with his drooping black moustache and shorts to match. But the Wembley scoreboard undeniably read 'England 3 Germany W. 2'. Twenty minutes later, Hurst's hat trick goal in the final second of the game made it 4–2: 'They think it's all over. It is now,' said the BBC commentator Kenneth Wolstenholme. It was never intended as a *double entendre* (even Ken wasn't that clever), but it would have fitted Hurst's second goal just as well.

The 'Russian linesman' became an honorary English hero overnight and the sobriquet (although geographically incorrect) entered popular vernacular. 'We could do with a Russian linesman' remains a rally cry in times of dire sporting need. But the cryptic headline in one German newspaper cut a stark contrast: WE LOST 2–2. And they have another phrase again. Anything unfairly earned is still known as a *'Wembley tor'* ('Wembley goal') in everyday German.

The 'was it or wasn't it?' debate has never been resolved conclusively, but significantly no photograph or film has ever proved that the ball *did* cross the line in its entirety. When even sophisticated computer simulations tended to support the German view, most fair-minded Englishmen converted to a neutral stance at best. And in Scotland, discrediting England's victory became a national sport. Only Geoff Hurst remained entirely unfazed, cultivating a standard tongue-in-cheek response to the question he's been asked thousands of times: 'Of course it was over the line. The linesman said so.'

Tofik Bakhramov died in 1993, but his name lives on. The Azerbaijani national stadium in Baku is the Tofik Bakhramov Stadium. When England played a World Cup 2006 qualifier there on 13 October 2004 (England won 1–0) many English fans wore shirts emblazoned BAKHRAMOV '66 – COX SAG ULUN, which means 'Thank you very much'.

Sir Geoff Hurst went one better. Before the game he unveiled a handsome bronze statue of the celebrated Azeri official and delivered a heartfelt speech.

'I can tell you all one hundred per cent that the goal I scored in the World Cup final against Germany in 1966 was a real goal. On behalf of the whole of England I would like to thank the family of Tofik Bakhramov.'

In Germany the collective murmur of '*Wembley tor*' was heard once more. They still thought it wasn't all over. Nearly forty years on, an Englishman's word and the eternally outstretched arm of a bronze statue had finally confirmed that it was!

# BY FAR THE GREATEST TEAM
## WEMBLEY, 15 APRIL 1967

Cock-eyed logic can 'prove' many things. Football fans employ it to show that one team is better than another. City beat United. Argyle beat City. Therefore Argyle would beat United. And so it goes on. Eventually, a Sunday pub team called Real Ale Madrid end up as the World Club Champions.

The World Cup has not been spared this strange treatment. There are those who say that winning the tournament means absolutely nothing in the wider scheme of things. For devotees of 'cumulative logic theory', the true 'best side in the world' is decided by a different formula altogether. The initiators of this desperate-for-success concept hailed from Scotland.

England had become official World Champions when they won the 1966 World Cup. Scottish fans found that hard to stomach. When Scotland arrived at Wembley for a 1968 European Championship qualifier on 15 April 1967, England hadn't been beaten since lifting the Jules Rimet trophy. For Scottish fans that gave the game far more significance than any other previous battle against the 'auld enemy'.

Close to thirty thousand members of the Tartan Army had travelled south, full of beer and wild revisionist theories. All the usual pre-match antics ensued. Kilts were lifted in the faces of blushing ladies doing their weekly shop. The spirit of Bannockburn was invoked. The spirit of the local off-licence was freely imbibed. Flagpoles were climbed. Streets were liberally 'watered'. Genuine belief took hold.

The Scotland side responded. Manchester United's Denis Law put them 1–0 ahead after 27 minutes. England tried desperately to equalize. A Charlton header seemed to cross the line, but the West German referee Gerd Schulenberg (still thinking of '66?)

waved play on. With twenty minutes remaining, Celtic's Bobby Lennox scored Scotland's second. Jack Charlton pulled one back five minutes from time. Jim McCalliog restored Scotland's two-goal cushion, and there was still time for Geoff Hurst to net England's second consolation goal. It really was a thriller.

Scotland had beaten the reigning World Champions 3–2 on the very turf that had witnessed England's glorious coronation just nine months earlier. Hordes of Scottish fans invaded the hallowed playing surface, digging up fistfuls of turf to take back across the border as souvenirs. And on the long journey home there was time for reflection and analysis. By the time the trains pulled in, Scotland's fans had already declared their side the unofficial Football World Champions.

The rest of the world took little notice. And Scotland's cockiness soon subsided when they were beaten 2–0 by the USSR only 25 days later at Hampden Park. Everybody forgot about the unofficial World Championship – until in 2002 a Scottish caller to an English radio show raked up the 1967 saga all over again.

The *Guardian* newspaper quickly picked up the baton and asked for feedback. Within weeks a team of self-confessed anoraks led by Pete Tomlin from Letchworth had begun scanning every full international result in football's history, starting with Scotland versus England in 1872. Once their work was done, the UFWC (Unofficial Football World Championship) was officially launched. It listed every UFWC title holder since that long-forgotten game.

The new 'semi-virtual' competition (the matches themselves are real) received some high-profile press coverage. The first 'title game' (the rules are similar to those in championship boxing) ended Scotland 0 England 0 at the West of Scotland Cricket club near Glasgow on 30 November 1872. In a sense the World Cup itself stems from that very day (but see 'We Are the Champions'). On 8 March 1873 the two sides played again at London's Kennington Oval. This time England prevailed by four goals to two. Little did they know it, but the result made England the first UFWC winners.

Scotland regained the title the following year by beating England. Then, as international football developed, other sides entered the fray blissfully unaware that retrospective glory would one day be bestowed upon them by twenty-first-century nerds. Since the 2002 launch, the competition has flourished. Just like the World Cup, it boasts an astonishing range of statistics and even its own strange moments.

Lowly sides particularly look forward to meetings with the title holder. Such games can end in glory. And any shock result alters the entire course of the title's destiny. Since Scotland's 1967 triumph, it has changed hands more than eighty times.

Even winning the World Cup itself doesn't guarantee the UFWC crown. Uruguay won the First World Cup in 1930, but had never played or beaten England, the UFWC holders. So England remained the unofficial champs – until they were beaten by Scotland in March 1931. Two months later Scotland allowed the title to leave the British Isles for the first time when they lost 5–0 to Austria.

Subsequent unlikely holders of the UFWC have included the Dutch Antilles, Northern Ireland, Wales, Israel, Costa Rica, the Republic of Ireland, Ecuador and Angola. As 2010 dawned, the Netherlands were in possession of the title, but it seldom stays put for long – no rigid four-year cycle for the UFWC.

Pete Tomlin continued to develop the idea, even prising a reluctant blessing from FIFA – 'fans can have fun as long as the competition breaks no FIFA rules'. There is a burgeoning website, and Tomlin also devised an all-time ranking system in which sides are awarded one point for every title match victory. The resulting league table reveals the identity of the all-time international top dogs.

At the last count, England held second place in the table. But few Englishmen would pretend that's significant. The true value of the UFWC is in providing the no-hopers with moments of surrogate glory. Some countries instinctively know they will never lift the real World Cup – the UFWC is all they have.

So perhaps it's fitting that Scotland, the nation that initiated the 'alternative' World Championship back in 1967, should currently top the all-time table by a formidable margin of twelve points – quite simply they have won more UFWC challenge matches than any other nation. Netherlands may be the latest holders of the UFWC title, but Scotland are by far the greatest team the world has ever seen. And that's official – at least unofficially.

# NOW IT'S WAR

## MEXICO CITY, 28 JUNE 1969

On 3 June 1970 El Salvador made their World Cup finals debut in the Azteca Stadium in Mexico City. They lost all their three games at Mexico '70, conceded nine and scored none. What the statistics don't reveal is what El Salvador had endured to get there. They had already played a qualifying game at the Azteca a year earlier. It was a grudge match so highly charged it contributed to an armed conflict dubbed the 'soccer war'.

The antagonists were tiny El Salvador and their bigger neighbour Honduras. Both countries were racked by economic hardships. A decade of tension between them made the area the tinderbox of Central America. By the late sixties about 300,000 Salvadoran peasant farmers were living in Honduras. Their presence was bitterly resented. On 30 April 1969 they were given thirty days to vacate their land.

No two nations of the 71 striving to qualify for Mexico '70 were hotter rivals. The tinderbox needed only a spark. So it was almost inevitable that El Salvador and Honduras would have to play each other in the qualifying tournament. It was a two-leg tie, the loser to be eliminated.

The fixtures from hell took place during June 1969. On the 8th Honduras played host and beat El Salvador 1–0 in Tegucigalpa. Like any good host they supplied all-night music, constant singing and loud fireworks at the visiting players' hotel the night before the game. There was rioting between the rival supporters. And an eighteen-year-old El Salvador fan, Amelia Bolanios, fatally shot herself after watching the game on TV. She received a massive state funeral and immediately became a symbol of El Salvador's ambition to triumph over their neighbours.

88

A week later the return game was played in San Salvador. Goal difference didn't matter. El Salvador needed a win by any score to force a play-off. The Honduras players were treated to a reciprocal pre-match serenade with the added piquancy of rotten eggs and dead rats being thrown into the hotel rooms. During the national anthems prior to kick-off, the Honduran flag was burned and a filthy dishcloth raised in its place. El Salvador triumphed 3–0. Two Honduran fans were seriously hurt and hundreds injured in the rioting that followed.

Newspapers in each country escalated the mutual smear campaign. Nothing was off limits. Honduras claimed that Colgate toothpaste (made in El Salvador) was rotting the teeth of their children. El Salvador insisted that Glostora haircream (made in Honduras) caused dandruff. An already inflamed situation was getting silly. Football and the spectre of war seemed inextricably entwined.

The very day after the second game, paramilitary groups in Honduras forcibly evicted Salvadoran peasants from lands they had cultivated for years. Tens of thousands returned forlornly to their native country with nowhere to live. El Salvador responded on 26 June by breaking off diplomatic relations with Honduras. And on 28 June came the play-off on neutral territory in Mexico City.

The prize for the winners wasn't a direct passage to Mexico '70, since one last play-off against Haiti awaited the victor. But the real prize was the elimination of a hated rival. The 112,000-capacity neutral venue enabled relative calm to reign among rival supporters. Only 15,000 turned up at the Azteca, and there were 1,700 Mexican police. El Salvador triumphed 3–2 after extra time in an atmosphere rendered oddly surreal by the displaced location.

But the football-fuelled time bomb had to go off somewhere. A few days later Honduran and Salvadoran troops began to assemble on border territory as each government claimed military superiority. On 14 July El Salvador broke the deadlock with an aerial attack on Tegucigalpa airport. Honduras replied with bombs. The 'soccer war' had kicked off.

Officially it lasted only four days. But six thousand were killed and an informal period of extra time saw the conflict rumble on for years. The Organisation of American States decreed that El Salvador must withdraw their troops, which they did. But the winners on the field declared themselves moral victors off it as well. Naturally, Honduras disagreed. Their mood was further dampened when El Salvador overcame Haiti (again over three games and only after the El Salvador coach had flattened Haiti's witch doctor) to clinch their place in Mexico.

In *The War of the Dispossessed,* Thomas Anderson argues eloquently that the 'soccer war' was not caused solely by football. He is absolutely right. But it's undeniable that the three qualifying games acted as a catalyst.

In 1946 George Orwell, author of the futuristic *Nineteen Eighty-Four*, warned that sport might one day precipitate national conflict. He labelled football 'war minus the shooting'. It was only 1969 when El Salvador and Honduras kicked the 'minus' violently into touch.

# TO MEXICO THE HARD WAY
## WEMBLEY, 19 APRIL 1970

On 30 July 1966, Wembley had witnessed the end of a remarkable World Cup. Now, four years later, on 19 April 1970, it witnessed the start of another.

Unlike the torch procession that traditionally heralds an Olympic Games, the passing of the baton between one World Cup tournament and the next had always been largely uneventful. But, thanks to a casual remark from a promoter with close links to the England Football Supporters Association, the journey from England '66 to Mexico '70 proved to be an unusual one.

'Lots of England fans will go to Mexico,' said Wylton Dickson one night at a boozy party. 'What say we do it the hard way? Let's drive there.' It was at that jovial stage in the proceedings when he didn't really expect his *Wacky Races* challenge to be taken seriously, but at least one person was sober enough to recall it the next day.

Soon the British motor sport and car industries had risen to the challenge. The *Daily Mirror* came on board as sponsor. And on 19 April 1970 the first ever World Cup Rally Championship set off from Wembley on a 16,241-mile journey that would take in 25 countries and a crossing of the Atlantic.

A crowd of 25,000 turned up to see the 96 cars and 240 drivers embark on their epic trip. England's manager Alf Ramsey waved them off with a sweep of a giant Union Flag watched by his captain Bobby Moore. And both reserved a special nod to one intrepid co-driver in particular.

He'd fallen foul of a canine intruder at Chile '62, been cruelly sidelined at England '66 and was now considered 'too old at 30' to make the squad for Mexico '70. West Ham's Jimmy Greaves was determined to get there somehow.

91

But this was no idle publicity stunt. The race was billed as 'the longest and most ambitious trip in postwar rallying'. Some stages were 650 miles long, which meant driving through the night. Greaves shared the wheel with professional Tony Fall and was greeted like a star even in the remotest of places. Everyone knew the famous J Greaves, but who the heck was that amateur, A Fall?

On a tortuously roundabout route, their finely tuned Ford Escort made it through Vienna, Sofia, Northern Spain and Lisbon, then across the Atlantic to Rio, Montevideo, Buenos Aires, Santiago, La Paz and Panama City. They needed oxygen to traverse the Andes. Greaves hit a horse in Peru. But there were no renewed encounters with ill-mannered Chilean dogs (see 'Greavsie's Famous Dribble').

Sheer determination saw them through. Greaves and Fall arrived in Mexico City on 28 May. It was a toss-up which was more battered, the car or they. Greaves immediately sought out his troubled West Ham teammate Bobby Moore (see 'Bobby Moore is Innocent') to share a few beers. 'That trip was harder than any football match I've ever played in,' Greaves told him.

The World Cup Rally was won by the 'Flying Finn' Hannu Mikkola and his co-driver Gunnar Palm, with Greaves and Fall finishing a remarkable sixth. Escorts took first, third, fifth, sixth and eighth places. The Ford Mexico was launched a few months later.

England's route to Mexico '70 couldn't have been easier. As World Cup holders they were exempt from qualifying. For Greaves it couldn't have been harder. Shame he wasn't playing. Jeff Astle's glaring miss against Brazil was soon to go down in history. Jimmy Greaves would have steered it home like the true finisher he'd proved himself to be.

## BOBBY MOORE IS INNOCENT
### BOGOTÁ, 18 MAY 1970

England's 1966 winners truly believed they could retain the World Cup in 1970. But, with high-altitude stadiums awaiting them in Mexico, the squad needed to acclimatise. So they arranged a warm-up game in Colombia at 8,500 feet. That was 3,300 feet above what they would face in Guadalajara for their opening World Cup game against Romania. A trouble-free preparation was vital. What they got was the exact opposite.

After an arduous flight from London, the England party reached the opulent Tequendama Hotel in Bogotá at 6 p.m. While check-in was attended to, England's 'Golden Boy' captain Bobby Moore and squeaky-clean legend Bobby Charlton ambled into the Fuego Verde (Green Fire) jewellery shop in the foyer to browse for a gift for Charlton's wife Norma.

When they wandered out again, the burglar alarm sounded and Moore was accused by the 21-year-old shop assistant Clara Padilla of pocketing a £600 emerald and diamond bracelet. She identified 'Fingers Charlton' as accomplice. Alf Ramsey rushed to the scene, followed by the hotel manager and Colombian tourist police. Heated exchanges occurred. Moore and Charlton offered to turn out their pockets but were denied the opportunity. Both were questioned, then released. An unfortunate 'misunderstanding' looked to have blown over.

Next day England trounced Colombia 4–0, then flew on to Quito 9,500 feet up in the Andes, where they beat Ecuador 2–0. England's preparations were bang on course. On Monday, 25 May, they flew back to Bogotá for a four-and-a-half-hour stopover before the big flight to Mexico. Being bloody-minded, Ramsey elected for the squad to rest at the ill-fated Tequendama. That proved a grave mistake.

While the players watched a film in the hotel (*Shenandoah*, starring James Stewart) two plain-clothes detectives moved in and removed Bobby Moore for further questioning. He was arrested and formally charged with the theft of the bracelet on the previous Monday. When the story broke in Britain the next day it caused uproar: BOBBY MOORE COURT SHOCK, screamed the *Daily Express*. The 'Bogotá Incident' was under way with a vengeance.

So England flew to Mexico without their inspirational captain. And Bobby Charlton was a nervous wreck. With their opening game just eight days away, everything had gone pear-shaped. The saga was to last only four more days, but it seemed a lifetime: BOBBY MOORE HELD AS THIEF, said the London *Evening News*. All of England was outraged. So too was most of Colombia. Few believed he was guilty.

As a diplomatic crisis developed, only the discreet lobbying of the British prime minister, Harold Wilson, and Foreign Office officials kept Moore out of jail. Instead, he was placed under loose 'house arrest' and a reconstruction of the crime was ordered for the morning of 27 May.

Three hundred people crowded into the lobby around the tiny Fuego Verde. Another witness had emerged. He was 27-year-old Alvaro Suarez, a swarthy antiques dealer straight out of a Bond movie. But the England captain looked cool. His steady features never wavered. His name was Moore. Bobby Moore.

It took ninety minutes for Clara Padilla to make a fatal error: 'I saw him put the bracelet definitely in his left pocket, the same clothes he is wearing now,' she said. With the immaculate timing he generally reserved for tackles, Moore lifted his arms. He had no left pocket.

It took another day of formalities before Moore was released. The shady Suarez was found to be in league with the shop's owner, Danilo Rojas. The whole thing was declared a set-up. Whether for insurance money, extortion or simply to upset England, nobody really knew. Football's elders said this was perfectly normal for Colombia.

Still in the same clothes he had worn for the last four days, Moore boarded a plane for Mexico City on Thursday, 28 May.

On arrival he was mobbed by photographers before snatching a surprise beer with Jimmy Greaves (see 'To Mexico the Hard Way') and going on to Guadalajara the next day.

When he landed, Alf Ramsey greeted him with uncharacteristic emotion: 'How are you, my old son?' Then it was off to the Hilton Hotel (no shopping!) for the inevitable press conference. On 2 June England beat Romania 1–0. Moore was immaculate and went on to play a memorable tournament.

Bizarrely, it took five years for the loose ends of the 'Bogotá Incident' to be tied up. A bracelet *had* gone missing and the Colombian authorities wouldn't let it lie. There was even a suggestion that Moore had been 'covering' for a 'third man'. A senior England official hardly helped by suggesting that 'a prank from one of the younger players may have misfired'. Moore finally got his 'letter of pardon' on 2 December 1975.

No one will ever know the absolute truth surrounding this strange affair. England's greatest captain took the secret to his grave when he died of cancer on 24 February 1993. Only one thing is certain. Bobby Moore was innocent.

## THE ODD COUPLE
### LEÓN, 7 JUNE 1970

Football statisticians had a whole new experience on 7 June 1970. Bulgaria played West Germany at the Guanajuato Stadium in León. It was a first-round game. West Germany won it 5–2. The defeat sealed Bulgaria's fate. Even with one match left to play, they knew they were on their way home from Mexico '70.

But what made the game special for the stats fraternity was the appearance of one man. Making his World Cup debut that day was the Bulgarian defender Milko Gaidarski. He was responsible for the most unusual ending ever experienced in a game involving Bulgaria. Indeed his name would stand alone in the record books for many years to come.

It wasn't until USA '94 that a second Bulgarian matched Gaidarski's unusual claim to fame. On that occasion Bulgaria played Mexico in a second-round game at the Giants Stadium in New Jersey. They won it via a penalty shoot-out. But again it was an unusual ending which stirred keen-eyed statisticians into as near a state of excitement as statisticians ever experience.

This time the man responsible was Petar Mikhtarski, who came on as a substitute towards the end of extra time. Despite being on the pitch for only two minutes, Mikhtarski made his mark in exactly the same way as Gaidarski had done 24 years earlier. And no other Bulgarian international has matched the duo since.

As I write this, Bulgaria have appeared at the finals of seven tournaments. No fewer than 120 players have pulled on the white shirt to appear for their country in a World Cup game. Thirty-four others have sat on the bench without getting on. Famous names such as Hristo Stoichkov and Emil Kostadinov undoubtedly stand out in the list, but no players are as prominent as Gaidarski and Mikhtarski.

Of the 154 Bulgarian World Cup players they are the only two whose surnames don't end in the letter 'v'. My sincere apologies for stringing you along.

# SNIFFER'S RED LETTER DAY
## GUADALAJARA, 11 JUNE 1970

When England faced Czechoslovakia at the Jalisco Stadium, Guadalajara, on 11 June 1970, they knew exactly what they had to do. A 2–0 defeat would condemn them to the farce of a coin toss with Romania for the right to progress to the quarter-finals of Mexico '70. Anything better would see them straight through.

Under a clear blue sky, the temperature reached 98 degrees. England played in unfamiliar pale blue because the Czechs wore white. Several times early in the game, English players passed straight to the opposition because the blinding glare of the sun made distinguishing the teams difficult. It was just the sort of day when things could go horribly wrong.

Hardly the ideal stage for a pale and callow youth from the Black Country. But Alf Ramsey had selected Allan 'Sniffer' Clarke ahead of Geoff Hurst and Francis Lee. Leeds United fans called their predatory striker 'Sniffer' because he had an uncanny nose for goal, but neutrals might easily have guessed the sickly Willenhall lad was consumptive. His sallow complexion, half-lidded eyes, pinched features and painfully thin physique suggested nothing whatsoever of the athlete.

Yet here he was, leading the line in a vital game for the holders of the World Cup. And not just that: this was his full international debut. What's more, he'd volunteered to shoulder the responsibility if England were awarded a penalty.

But the 24-year-old had every reason to be confident. The date 11 June had always been propitious for Sniffer. On 11 June 1966 he married his wife Margaret. On 11 June 1968 he was transferred from Fulham to Leicester City, a move that paved the way for his transfer to Leeds United for the then UK record fee of £165,000. And, lest further reminders were needed, 11 June was also Margaret's birthday.

With the score at 0–0 in the 46th minute, England were awarded a penalty. Those watching on live television back home expected Bobby Charlton to take the spot-kick in an attempt to score his 50th goal on his record-equalling 105th appearance for England. But Clarke knew this was his day.

His mother Alice had already told the Birmingham *Evening Mail* that she'd had a premonition that her son would get the winner. Alf Ramsey wasn't so sure. He turned to the England trainer Les Cocker: 'Will he score, Les?' The reply was as swift and accurate as Clarke's successful conversion: 'Put your mortgage on him.'

England duly celebrated a 1–0 victory, but for the coolest man in the cauldron of Guadalajara it was just like any other eventful 11 June. No player in World Cup history has had a red letter day quite like it.

# 'MONTEZUMA'S REVENGE' OR 'MICKEY FINN'?

## LEÓN, 14 JUNE 1970

English international football has never recovered from Sunday, 14 June 1970.

In the Guanajuato Stadium, León, England ceased to be World Champions. All the supporter angst that's gone since – 'lucky Germans', 'sneaky Argentinians', 'failure to qualify', 'the agony of penalties' – is a direct consequence of that fateful day. The ghost will be laid only when England win the World Cup for a second time.

First the bare facts. England had overcome the trauma of the 'Bogotá Incident' (see 'Bobby Moore is Innocent') to finish second in their group and advance to the quarter-final of Mexico '70. West Germany were the opponents. A record British television audience of 30 million hoped for a repeat performance of the 1966 final.

Tottenham's Alan Mullery put England ahead after 32 minutes. Accomplished lip readers smiled at his 'fucking yeah!' as the ball hit Sepp Maier's net. West Ham United's Martin Peters put England two up after fifty minutes. Everton's Alan Ball verbally taunted the tame opposition. Chelsea's Peter 'The Cat' Bonetti looked feline sharp in goal. England were coasting into the semis.

But no one told 'The Cat' that goalkeepers are not the custodians of nine lives. After 67 minutes, Franz Beckenbauer beat Mullery on the right-hand corner of England's box and released a quick but speculative shot along the ground. Bonetti dived like a sleepy-eyed tabby. The ball went in under his body.

The feeble mistake fired up the Germans and made England nervous. In the 82nd minute the German captain, Uwe Seeler, strained to get a hopeful head to a cross as England's defenders were caught napping. The ball looped freakishly off the side of his bald pate and over a flat-footed Bonetti for the equaliser. It was another body blow, but, as the game entered extra time at 2–2, England were still on course for an exact repeat of 1966.

But this was another time and another place. Gerd 'Der Bomber' Müller hooked the German winner past a shell-shocked Bonetti nineteen minutes into the extra period. At the final whistle, Bobby Moore slumped to the ground. Nineteen sixty-six became a date marooned in time. England were going home from Mexico '70.

Now for the strange bit. The hapless Peter Bonetti wore Number 12 on his shirt that day. England's true 'number one', indeed the world's number one, was in bed at the Motel Estancia just a few hundred yards from the ground.

After his much-vaunted super-save from Pelé in the first round, the Brazilian press had dubbed Gordon Banks 'El Magnifico'. That didn't surprise England fans. 'Safe as the Banks of England' was the truest pun in football. With Gordon between the sticks against Germany, how could England possibly lose?

Instead, he was between the sheets. The first signs of 'Montezuma's Revenge' had emerged (literally) two days before the game. That was nothing unusual. Allan Clarke, Keith Newton and Bobby Charlton had all had similar discomfort and recovered quickly.

Alf Ramsey was so paranoid about 'foreign food' that England had brought all their own provisions with them, but Banks blamed his suffering on 'a dodgy bottle of Mexican beer I'd had a sip of as a treat'. The England keeper suffered a classic attack of 'both enders' and, after the buttock-clenching bus journey from Guadalajara to León he admitted being 'just glad to make it without embarrassing myself'. It didn't bode well that England played in white shorts.

In León he felt better, then worse, then better again. Only two hours before the kick-off against Germany he was 'in'. But then a sudden relapse. The bottom fell out of his world and vice versa. Banks took to bed groaning while Ramsey told a surprised (and possibly startled) Bonetti he'd be playing.

No one knows the truth to this day. In *Banksy*, his 2003 autobiography, the keeper reflected ruefully, 'Why only me? We all ate the same. And it couldn't just have been that one sip of beer. Unless it was spiked.' There's the rub. Many remain convinced that Banks was deliberately nobbled by a surreptitiously administered 'Mickey Finn'. One theory blames Brazilian sympathisers, desperate to avoid a possible final showdown against the only team they genuinely feared.

Would Banks have seen England through? Quite probably he would. And the German defeat arguably did change the course of football history. Alf Ramsey was later sacked when England failed to qualify for West Germany '74. That heralded the arrival of first Don Revie and then Ron Greenwood. When England again failed to qualify for Argentina '78, the traumas had truly begun.

The Labour prime minister, Harold Wilson, even blamed his 1970 general election defeat on the fateful game in León. Four days after Bonetti's nightmare, a woefully depressed British public went to the polls. Labour had been placed 7 per cent ahead just a week before, but Ted Heath swept Wilson aside in the second shock result of a dramatic week.

A World Cup lost. A Conservative prime minister gained. Thirty years of hurt, and rising. All for a Mexican beer.

# CLOWN PRINCE OF POLAND

## WEMBLEY, 17 OCTOBER 1973

Peter Shilton, Norman Hunter, Paul Madeley, Roy McFarland, Emlyn Hughes, Colin Bell, Mick Channon, Martin Chivers, Tony Currie, Martin Peters (captain), Allan Clarke. That was the England team that faced Poland at Wembley on 17 October 1973 in the final qualifying game for the 1974 World Cup.

Seldom had such a weight of expectation fallen on eleven men. Having already lost 2–0 in Poland and been held to a 1–1 draw against Wales at Wembley, England had to beat the Poles to clinch a place at West Germany '74.

Nothing less than victory would do. And the nation expected one. The manager Alf Ramsey, already dogged by heavy criticism, wasn't helped by the refusal of the Football League to cancel the key domestic fixtures on the Saturday before the game. The League secretary, Alan Hardaker, seemed desperately out of touch: 'This is football, not a war. If England do lose, the country won't die. It will be a big thing for six weeks, and then everybody will forget about it.'

Heavyweight pundits assured England's fans that the unthinkable couldn't happen. Brian Clough, who had just resigned as manager of Derby County, was particularly outspoken, likening the lumbering Polish captain Gorgon to 'a boxer in football boots'. But his most outrageous jibe was reserved for Jan Tomasjewski. The straggly-haired goalkeeper generally turned out in a yellow jersey, red shorts and white socks. On the evidence of nothing more than a few clips, Clough labelled him 'a circus clown in gloves'.

But the first keeper to fall flat on his face was Peter Shilton. In the 53rd minute, England's Norman 'Bites Yer Legs' Hunter wafted an uncharacteristic powder-puff challenge at the Polish

103

winger Lato close to the team benches. Lato emerged the stronger and moved the ball swiftly to Domarski, who shot first time. It whistled under Shilton's body at the near post to give Poland the lead. Shilton had hardly touched the ball until then. Tomaszewski had already performed heroics.

Such had been England's domination (fourteen corners in the first half) that the capacity Wembley crowd still expected them to prevail. When the predicted equaliser did arrive through an Allan Clarke penalty there were still 27 minutes to go. The winner would follow as sure as night followed day. But this was a freak night.

Gorgon the pugilist was magnificent. But the star of the show was the 'clown in gloves'. Tomasjewski delivered the most unorthodox but effective performance Wembley had ever known, saving everything that England threw at him with an eccentricity that any circus impresario would have been proud of. Frank Keating of the *Guardian* was incredulous: 'He hurled himself arms, knees, and bumps-a-daisy all over his penalty area like a slackly strung marionette. And all with a half-taunting, half-surprised smile which made one think this might be his first ever game.'

One final cruel twist awaited England. Ramsey decided to replace the struggling Chivers: 'Get stripped, Kevin,' he barked along the bench. Liverpool's Keegan prepared to go on. But he was the wrong Kevin. Ramsey meant Kevin Hector of Derby County. By the time Alf noticed the mix-up, there were only three minutes remaining. When Hector did get on, he had what looked like a certain headed winner cleared off the line by a Polish knee in the ninetieth minute. The 1974 World Cup would proceed without England.

The statistics tell the story. England had 35 goal attempts to Poland's two. The next day's newspaper headlines completely belied the happy-go-lucky naïveté of 'Hardaker of the League'. The *Sun*'s black-edged message was stark: THE END OF THE WORLD. The pro-football peer Lord George Wigg labelled the affair 'The Polish Crisis . . . It's worse than losing a war. It's a national disaster of the highest magnitude.'

The fallout duly followed. Alf Ramsey was relieved of his duties six months later. Brian Clough's ill-judged 'clown' comments put paid to any chance he might have had of taking Ramsey's place. 'Genial Joe' Mercer took temporary charge for seven games and did quite well. But then Leeds United's Don 'Carpet Bowls' Revie was appointed England manager (the sobriquet comes from the fact that making his team play carpet bowls and bingo was his secret weapon in preparing them for big games!). The team failed to qualify for another World Cup until Spain '82.

Far from being forgotten within six weeks, the night of 17 October 1973 is still talked about today as a pivotal moment for English football. Enough clowns were involved in England's demise to form an entire troupe. Hunter, Clough, Shilton and Hardaker all had bright-red faces, but only the 'Clown Prince of Poland' was laughing.

# A FAMOUSLY UNLUCKY XI

## AMSTERDAM, 18 NOVEMBER 1973

The old chestnut about there being 'no famous Belgians' has had its day. Among the 259 celebrities listed on a website to prove it are such giants as Edward de Smedt, 'the inventor of modern asphalt', and the legendary John Massis, who is 'the man with the strongest teeth in the world'.

If that smacks of desperation, let webmaster Marc Tielmans explain: 'Everybody thinks Belgium is second best. They always place us below Holland. Or even think our famous people *are* Dutch. It's so annoying.' Quite simply the Belgian nation craves heroes. That's why they follow their football team so passionately. Hercule Poirot and Tin-Tin are all very well, but real-life World Cup stars are so much better.

All of which faintly chip-on-the-shoulder angst explains why Group 3 of the European Zone qualifying competition for West Germany '74 was fraught with tension from the start. Belgium, Holland, Norway and Iceland made up the group, from which only one could qualify. The rankings suggested Norway and Iceland were no-hopers, so Belgium and Holland were effectively going head to head for a place at the 1974 World Cup.

The Belgian coach Raymond Goethals had no real stars in his squad. Only his captain, Paul van Himst, was really known to the rest of Europe, whereas Holland boasted several players of wider renown. Rudi Krol, Johan Neeskens, Rob Rensenbrink, Johnny Rep and the 'Dutch Master' Johan Cruyff were names that tripped off the tongue so much more easily than Gilbert van Binst and Odilon Polleunis. The Dutch were already ahead on one-upmanship.

But Goethals was no fool. He understood one of the cast-iron tenets of football: 'Don't concede goals and you won't lose matches.' Whatever the French is for 'let's set our stall out and keep a clean sheet', the canny Goethals instructed his players to do exactly that.

Belgium's campaign started in May 1972 with a 4–0 home win over Iceland. That was followed by another 4–0 win in the return in Reykjavík, and a 2–0 victory away to Norway. In November they faced the first big one, at home to Holland in Antwerp, but again the defence stood firm as 54,923 saw the Dutch held to a 0–0 draw. And, on the last day of October 1973, Belgium continued their impressive run of five straight shutouts with a 2–0 home win against Norway. They had scored twelve, conceded none and remained unbeaten. Goethals's plan was working.

That left one game, the away fixture against Holland on 18 November. With both teams locked on nine points, a win for either side would see them qualify at the other's expense. In the event of a draw, goal difference would decide the issue.

A crowd of 60,000 packed the Olympic Stadium in Amsterdam to witness the showdown between two of football's keenest rivals. And, much to their credit, Belgium's superbly drilled defence yet again held firm, as they kept the talented Dutch forwards at bay to complete a remarkable six out of six clean sheets. Only a linesman's flag, which ruled out what seemed a perfectly good Belgian goal, denied them a deserved victory.

So it came to goal difference. But, because the Dutch had scored highly against Norway and Iceland, they nicked it. While Holland's famous names went on to West Germany to showcase their stylish 'Total Football', the famously unlucky Belgian XI were left wondering how they'd somehow managed to disprove the soundest maxim in football.

They are the only side to have kept clean sheets throughout the qualifying competition but still miss out on a trip to the finals.

# A DISAPPEARING ACT

## SANTIAGO, 21 NOVEMBER 1973

Anyone who ever doubted the 'sense of place' inherent in football should read the passionate prose of Simon Inglis, a self-styled 'stadiologist' who vividly captures the soul of what unbelievers would describe as 'mere football grounds'.

Inglis could have a field day with the Estadio Nacional in Chile. On 17 June 1962 it had been a happy place, as Brazil beat Czechoslovakia 3–1 to lift their second World Cup in succession. But eleven years later the stadium in Santiago had become tainted by such dark secrets that the USSR refused to play there.

Russia were already niggled that they had to play Chile at all. FIFA's insistence that only sixteen teams from 95 entrants could qualify for the 1974 World Cup made the qualifying tournament the oddest of all time. Despite winning their European group easily, USSR were forced to enter a play-off against Chile. No wonder the Russians were miffed. It was the first time ever that European and South American sides had been made to meet in a qualifier.

The opening leg in Moscow at the end of September was as uneventful as the 0–0 result suggested. But events away from football had already taken an interesting turn. On 11 September the democratically elected President of Chile, Salvador Allende, had been overthrown in a violent military coup and burned to death in his palace. The perpetrator (with generous assistance from the USA!) was the sinister dictator Augusto Pinochet Ugarte. General Pinochet, as he came to be known, had an uncompromising way with 'opponents': they were either openly murdered or became *los desaparecidos* ('the disappeared'). But, as vanishing acts go, there was little mystery about their true fate.

Pinochet was fanatically anticommunist, and up to three thousand so-called left-wing sympathisers ultimately entered the ranks of the *desaparecidos*. Teachers, students, trade unionists, workers, women and their children – no one was safe. From 11 September to 7 November 1973, no fewer than twelve thousand were taken to the Estadio Nacional, which became a prison camp and torture chamber combined.

And Pinochet's henchmen had a gruesome sense of humour. Where once Brazilian flair had won the World Cup, unspeakable atrocities took place. Talented musicians had their fingers chopped off. Women were raped in front of their husbands, and children cruelly abused while their mothers looked on in horror. The pitch became a hellish holding pen from which many were removed into the bowels of the stands, never to be seen again.

The full facts took time to emerge, but sufficient news filtered through to the USSR to make them think very hard indeed. On 21 November 1973 they were scheduled to play the second leg of their qualifier in that very stadium. Countless countries have abandoned their scruples in pursuit of World Cup glory, but the Soviet Union became one of the few to put conscience above ambition. Four days before the tie, they pulled out. Their Football Federation chief, Valentin Granatkin, was adamant: 'Soviet sportsmen cannot play on a ground stained with the blood of Chilean patriots.'

Chile duly qualified for the 1974 World Cup by default, but still insisted on the bizarre charade of a phantom match. The USSR game went ahead as planned in front of forty thousand spectators, but with only one team. Chile wore their full kit and finished off a neat nine-man move with a close-range tap-in from their captain. Only Scotland versus Estonia in October 1996 (see 'Up the Existentialists') came close to this. But that was a farce of the amusing kind. There was little funny about events in Santiago in late 1973.

Chile failed to win a game at West Germany '74. Pinochet retained power until 1990, but was arrested in London in 1998 – over a Spanish extradition warrant concerning human-rights violations during his rule – only to be released on 'health grounds' by the then home secretary Jack Straw after a year of house arrest. Russia have never won the World Cup, but at least their 1973 disappearing act was of the right kind.

# THE WHEELS CAME OFF
## GELSENKIRCHEN, 22 JUNE 1974

Benito Mussolini did it for Italy in 1934. Adolf Hitler did it for Germany in 1938. Using the World Cup to promote a nationalistic regime, however dubious, is as old as the hills.

So President Mobutu of Zaïre was quickly on the ball when his newly independent nation miraculously qualified for the tenth World Cup in Germany in 1974. No black African nation had ever reached the finals before, so it was a perfect opportunity for Zaïre's footballers to uphold everything Mobutu's name stood for.

Since he'd changed his forename from Joseph to Sese Seko Nkuku Wa Za, there was quite a lot at stake. It meant 'the all-powerful warrior who, because of his endurance and inflexible will to win, will go from conquest to conquest leaving fire in his wake'. No pressure, then.

Much else had changed since Mobutu's military coup. Citizens were forced to adopt traditional African names and dress. Towns were renamed. 'A sweeping anti-European rebranding', the historians called it. Now, with West Germany '74 beckoning, Mobutu promised lavish incentives to the players in the spirit of pressing the message home.

Each was to receive a car, a holiday and a house. Nor were the gifts dependent on performance. As long as 'The Leopards' maintained their pride and dignity, all would be well. The main thing was to avoid becoming a laughing stock.

But nothing worked out as planned. Years later, the Zaïre defender Ilunga Mwepu reflected bitterly, 'Mobutu was like a father to us before we went. We thought we would all come back millionaires. But we got back home with nothing in our pockets. Now I live like a tramp.'

So where did it all go wrong? The uneasy relationship between Mobutu and the side's Yugoslav coach, Blagoje Vidinic, certainly didn't help. Even so, Zaïre started with a 'respectable' 2–0 defeat against Scotland in Dortmund. As they left the stadium on their luxury BMW coach, lent to them by German sponsors, they were getting a taste for the high life to come.

Then the wheels began to come off. Rumours circulated that wages were being withheld, and the promised incentives withdrawn. Evidently, Mobutu had no taste for defeat of any kind. The players reacted angrily, threatening not to show for the next game against Yugoslavia. Although they relented at the eleventh hour, their hearts weren't in it.

After they fell behind 3–0 in eighteen minutes, midfielder Mulamba Ndaye was irresponsibly sent off. When the score reached 8–0 in the 62nd minute, Vidinic withdrew Muamba Kazadi, the first goalkeeper in World Cup history to be taken off for reasons other than injury. His tiny replacement, Tubilandu, stemmed the flow, conceding only once on 89 minutes, but the game finished Yugoslavia 9 Zaïre 0. It equalled the then record defeat in World Cup finals. The video still circulates under the 'blooper' category.

Vidinic got it in the neck. Mobutu ridiculously accused him of leaking tactical secrets to his Yugoslav countrymen. Now, with only the World Cup holders Brazil to come, the Zaïre president turned the screw. His guards sealed off the team's hotel and delivered a sinister warning: 'Lose 4–0 or worse and you won't be allowed home.'

There were some nervous men at the Park Stadium in Gelsenkirchen on 22 June 1974 – none of them Brazilian. Ilunga Mwepu was particularly affected. Lining up in the wall to face a free kick, he hit on a brainwave. As Brazil pondered a bender, Mwepu rushed from the wall, slammed the ball upfield and spread his arms to the referee in a gesture of childish innocence. 'What did he do that for?' gasped commentator John Motson. A yellow card was swiftly shown. Thirty years later Mwepu's one-man cavalry charge was voted 17th in Channel 4's *100 Greatest World Cup Moments*.

The only consolation for football's most celebrated fall guys was the score. Things had looked ominous at 3–0, but Brazil soft-pedalled. 'The Leopards' held out to clinch their journey home. Even so, their record of no wins, no goals, fourteen against and no points made sorry reading. And one final indignity lay in store.

When the BMW representative called to collect the luxury coach, Zaïre were wallowing in its comfort somewhere on the autobahn, genuinely convinced it was theirs to keep. Like Mobutu's luxury offerings, it was quickly repossessed.

Zaïre's story is the World Cup's ultimate tragicomedy, the more so because millions of chortling television viewers were ignorant of the sinister background. Time has wiped the slate clean to a degree. In September 1997 the deposed President Mobutu died of prostate cancer in exile in Morocco. The same year, Zaïre changed its name back to what it had been between 1964 and 1971: the Democratic Republic of the Congo. But the country has never qualified for the finals again.

Ilunga Mwepu did regain his composure, though. Interviewed by the BBC in 2004, he stood firm: 'I was very proud to represent black central Africa in the World Cup, and still am.' On the subject of the famous cavalry charge, however, he refused to break ranks.

# THE WHISTLE-BLOWER
## BERLIN, 22 JUNE 1974

When World Cup virgins Australia played Chile at the Olympic Stadium, Berlin, in a closing group game, they already knew they were on their way home from West Germany '74. With Chile all but out as well, no contest was less likely to enter the record books. But that reckoned without the intervention of the Welsh referee Clive Thomas.

Thomas was both a stickler for the rules and fond of taking names. That's why they called him 'The Book'. One of his 'best' decisions prior to 1974 was in the game between Coventry City and Sheffield Wednesday in March 1970. Cautioning the Coventry City centre-half Roy Barry was all very well, but wielding the yellow card as he was being stretchered off with a broken leg added insult to injury.

Now Thomas was let loose at a World Cup for the first time. Having handled Poland versus Argentina without provoking a riot, 'The Book' was appointed supervisor/reserve official for the Australia-versus-Chile match. The man in the middle was a nervous-looking debutant, the Iranian Jafar Namdar.

The game was a dire 0–0 draw played in dreadful conditions. The most exciting thing that happened was a brief suspension of play during a torrential downpour. Namdar was quietly assertive. On 37 minutes he showed Australia's Ray Richards a yellow card. And when the midfielder transgressed again, late in the second half, the official fished in his pocket for what everybody knew would have to be an automatic red.

But the occasion got the better of Namdar. Instead he showed Richards a second yellow card and allowed him to play on. That was strictly against the rules. But in the circumstances who cared? The Australian said nothing. Nor did the Chileans complain. The Belgian linesman's lips were also sealed. And the Dutch linesman didn't as much as twitch. Which is more than could be said of a certain Welshman. As Ray Richards became the first man to play 'illegally' in a World Cup game (see 'The Thing From Tring' for the only other), the reserve official who might easily have passed for a traffic warden or a car park attendant was having kittens.

As the game petered tediously towards an inconsequential close, Thomas lasted five minutes before he could contain himself no more. A quiet word to the linesman was all it took for him to 'blow the whistle' from his touchline position. In turn, Namdar was swiftly alerted and Ray Richards walked off for the proverbial 'early bath' in the 83rd minute. Clive 'The Book' Thomas had become the only 'spectator' to send off a player in a World Cup finals game.

Nor was this his only 'jobsworth' moment at the highest level. Four years later, at Argentina '78, he went one better. The first-round game between Brazil and Sweden in Mar del Plata was locked at 1–1 when 'Olive' Thomas (as he was listed in the FIFA programme of officials) awarded a corner to Brazil in the dying moments. It was floated over and firmly headed in by Zico for a last-gasp Brazilian 'winner'. But not in Thomas's book. 'Olive' had blown for full-time as the ball was in the air.

Again, Thomas was within his rights. But his timing was grossly unwise. Confusion reigned as the stubborn Welshman imperiously left the field under a barrage of coins. Brazil still progressed, but the result altered their ongoing fixtures. In the end their bitter rivals Argentina lifted the trophy.

Even FIFA were dismayed by Thomas's egotistical approach. He never refereed another World Cup game. All over the globe there was singing in the valleys.

# THE BUTCHER OF WOLVERHAMPTON
## MUNICH, 7 JULY 1974

World Cup sobriquets can be allotted only once. Billy Wright, England's captain at the finals for 1950, 1954 and 1958, was far too gentle to claim 'The Butcher of Wolverhampton' as his own. That left it vacant for the English referee Jack Taylor. Since he was a butcher and hailed from Wolverhampton, the opportunity was too good to miss. The moniker could be his for life. But first he had to earn it.

Taylor's moment of destiny arrived at the 1974 World Cup final between hosts West Germany and their bitter enemy Holland. Because of deep scars left by World War Two, no fiercer rivalry existed in European football. Not even that between England and Germany. Listen to the Dutch midfielder Willem van Hanegem: 'I didn't give a damn as long as we could humiliate them. They murdered my father, sister and two brothers. I am full of angst. I hate them.' When Jack Taylor was appointed referee for the game, the spotlight beckoned.

Tension reached fever pitch in the build-up. Even jaunty taunts between fans were tinged with hatred: 'The holes in your defence are even bigger than those in your cheese,' sneered the Germans. The press joined in. False allegations about the Dutch captain Johan Cruyff appeared in *Bild* (Germany's answer to the *Sun*) under the screaming headline CRUYFF, CHAMPAGNE AND NAKED GIRLS. A British tabloid fanned the flames with CHEESEHEADS V. KRAUTS.

A crowd of 77,833 packed Munich's Olympic Stadium on Sunday, 7 July. Franz 'The Kaiser' Beckenbauer led out his players. Gerd 'Der Bomber' Müller looked sharp. A gaily clad oompah band played equally gay ditties. A limpid-eyed Cruyff calmly marshalled his troops. The German chancellor, Helmut

Schmidt, and Prince Bernhard of the Netherlands were guests of honour. The tension and excitement were tangible. A record audience of one billion watched on television. How could a Black Country butcher possibly make his mark?

That Jack Taylor was focused, nobody could deny. He delayed the kick-off because he spotted that the stadium staff had forgotten to put out the corner flags. One for the record books even before the whistle. But the problem was, most firsts had already been established. The only one of real significance left was that no referee had ever summoned the courage to award a penalty in a World Cup final.

But Jack Taylor was tough. A man who can eat black pudding and pork scratchings without wincing isn't afraid of making decisions. He awarded a penalty after ninety seconds. Not a single German player had even touched the ball as Cruyff drove into the box and was felled. Beckenbauer hissed to Taylor the worst insult he could think of ('You are an Englishman of course') as Neeskens dispatched the penalty, the quickest goal ever in a World Cup final.

The World Cup aficionado David Miller wrote of that moment, 'Once Taylor had given that penalty, it destructively inflated Holland's real conviction that they could smash their unloved neighbours.' So Taylor had made history *and* turned the game. The Dutch anticipated victory and sat back. Gerd Müller sensed an opportunity for Germany: 'I thought to myself – a referee who gives a penalty so early on could easily give another one.'

Cue theatricals. In the 25th minute Germany's Holzenbein swallow-dived in the penalty area as a defender challenged. Opinion remains divided on the decision, but Taylor pointed to the spot once more. He later gave the odd explanation that it had been for 'intent' rather than 'actual contact'. The big-haired Paul 'Der Afro' Breitner stroked home the equaliser. Forty-four years without a penalty; now, thanks to Taylor, two within half an hour.

Holland were rattled. Two minutes before the break Müller scored what proved to be the German winner. Cruyff left the field at half-time moaning. Taylor sternly brandished a yellow card. Germany lifted the brand-new FIFA World Cup (Brazil won the original Jules Rimet trophy for keeps in 1970) on their home territory. Willem van Hanegem left the field in tears. Another small war was over.

It is both odd and rather disquieting that such an enormous game should be remembered mostly for the referee. But it changed the life of 'The Butcher of Wolverhampton'. Even Taylor, thick-skinned as an ox, noticed it: 'Old ladies who had been coming into my shop for years suddenly started talking to me about sweepers and creating space. That's the power of television.'

In 1999 at a glittering bash in Barcelona, Jack Taylor was admitted to the FIFA International Hall of Fame. Franz Beckenbauer exchanged a cheery word with his favourite Englishman. Johan Cruyff presented the award. As he approached the Dutch legend, Taylor pulled out a yellow card and held it aloft. It brought the house down. Twenty-five years on, 'The Butcher of Wolverhampton' had stolen the show again.

# *AN UNQUALIFIED DISASTER*
## YAOUNDÉ, 31 OCTOBER 1976

Two interconnected milestones were reached in the run-up to the 1978 World Cup in Argentina. For the first time, more than a hundred nations entered the qualifying competition. Despite that, FIFA refused to increase the number of places available at the finals. Of the 103 entrants for 1978, only sixteen would make it to Argentina, exactly the same number FIFA had planned for the 1930 World Cup, when 'qualifiers' had yet to enter football's lexicon.

Little wonder the qualifying tournament for Argentina '78 was one almighty scramble. And scrambles can lead to squabbling and panic. It's a short step from there to milestone number two. The one marked 'Death'.

The World Cup's first match-based fatality occurred in Africa, where increasingly high stakes were in no way matched by increasingly high levels of stadium management skill. Who needed health and safety as long as they had a ball and a referee? Cameroon, as it turned out.

The 'Indomitable Lions' were fiercely ambitious to make Argentina '78 their first finals appearance. But so too were the 'Red Devils' of Congo. So, when the two countries met in a second-round two-leg knockout, something had to give.

The first game finished 2–2 in the Congo capital Brazzaville. The second, played on 31 October 1976 in the Cameroon capital Yaoundé, was abandoned. When Roger Milla put Cameroon ahead after just seven minutes, it looked good for the home side. But Congo turned the game round to go ahead 2–1 in the second half. As the home fans became increasingly restive, Cameroon's potential lifeline came in the 82nd minute, when the Gambian referee, N'Jai Housainou, awarded them a penalty.

Then things really kicked off. The Congolese goalkeeper overreacted to the decision and made for the referee. Had the Cameroon players stayed out of it, order might well have been restored, but instead they piled in. Then as the crowd bayed for blood, further intervention came from an unexpected quarter.

Watching the game on television, Ahmadou Ahidjo felt distinctly uneasy. So he did the obvious thing. Calmly turned off the television? Not on your life. Being the Cameroon president, Ahidjo hastily scrambled a helicopter and sent in his paratroopers. Two people died in the chaos as the referee called the game off.

At the inevitable enquiry, Cameroon claimed 'Congo started it'. Fair enough, but the Cameroon reaction was far too heavy-handed. FIFA docked Roger Milla's goal and awarded the game 2–0 to Congo. All in vain, as it happened. They were comprehensively dismissed in the next round by Ivory Coast.

Such futile loss of life must never be allowed to happen again, cried all right-minded football lovers. But five weeks later it did. On 11 December, Haiti entertained Cuba in Port au Prince. Again it was a second-round knockout that sparked an overreaction. Haiti scored first, but when Cuba equalised someone in the crowd let off a firecracker. Not really a problem, but a section of the crowd panicked, thinking it was gunfire.

The touchpaper thus lit, a bizarre chain of events unfolded. The jostling spectators knocked over a soldier, whose gun went off and killed a small boy and girl. Two people were trampled to death in the chaos and a further man died jumping from a wall trying to escape the crush. The unfortunately implicated soldier made it six dead when he committed suicide. For the record, Haiti won the tie after a play-off, but again in vain. Mexico denied them a trip to Argentina.

There are two postscripts to this double date with death. Sensing the qualifiers had become too highly charged, FIFA increased the number of finalists for Spain '82 to 24. But the 50 per cent rise seemed merely to increase the expectations of the lesser football nations. Same carrot but bigger.

In 1996, twenty years after the deaths in Cameroon, a football match in Africa again proved deadly. But this time the numbers were greater. A stampede in the Zambian capital Lusaka claimed twelve lives. And worse was to come the same year when a staggering 78 were killed in Central America during a game in Guatemala City. Four years after that, three more died in Monrovia, Liberia, and another twelve perished at the clash in Harare between Zimbabwe and South Africa.

The world will watch the 2010 World Cup with baited breath. As will the stadium managers. It will be held on the African continent for the first time.

# *ARCHIE STEALS THE SHOW*

## MENDOZA, 11 JUNE 1978

Scotland supporters looked forward to Argentina '78 with confidence. Team coach Ally MacLeod, blessed with an ego as big as his legendary nose, inspired the Tartan Army to really believe it was their year. And, with England, Wales, Northern Ireland and Eire all failing to qualify, Scotland took centre stage fully intent on grabbing the limelight and delivering the performance of a lifetime.

But the 'theatre' that is football comes in many guises. A brilliant solo dribble may be poetic, but tragedy, comedy and ludicrous farce loiter in the wings. In the event, as music, cinema and even ballet were added to the mix, Scotland's cast of assorted jesters delivered a *tour de force* of them all.

The World Cup's most entertaining campaign began musically. Among scores of lyrics recorded to urge the team on their way, the worst rhyme was delivered by Rod Stewart: 'Ole Ola, we're gonna bring that World Cup back from over tha'. Barely better and again dangerously optimistic was a ditty that Ally MacLeod himself joined in: 'We're representing Britain and we're gaun t'ae do or die/England cannae do it 'cos they couldn'ae qualify'. 'Don't Cry For Us, Argentina' further smacked of confidence. 'Hot Pies For Us, Argentina' smacked of huge-bellied men in kilts having a ball even if it all went wrong. Which it did.

Only sixteen teams competed. Scotland's group of four pitted them against the so-called 'old men and has-beens' of Peru, a useful Holland side without the retired Johann Cruyff, and everybody's rank no-hopers, Iran. With two progressing to the next stage, the bookmakers Ladbrokes made Scotland 8–1 to lift the trophy.

Before the opener against Peru in Córdoba, Ally MacLeod told the Scottish *Daily Record*, 'This is the vital game. We're here to win the World Cup, not friends.' Manchester United's Joe Jordan put them ahead in fourteen minutes, but tactical naïveté tinged with ineptitude saw Scotland lose the game 3–1. MacLeod, having controversially left out Graeme Souness, was cast as villain. Next it was winger Willie Johnston's turn to cut a tragic figure, sent home sniffling after failing a post-match dope test. He blamed Reactivan, taken for 'hay fever'. It was hot. There was grass. Why not? In Scotland, anger raged. Elsewhere we chuckled.

Could it get worse? MacLeod thought not: 'We have to treat the next two matches like Bannockburn. Nothing less than victory over Iran and Holland will do.' After a limp 1–1 draw with Iran, Scotland's fans, some of whom had hitch-hiked from New York, jeered the players from the pitch and hurled their tartan scarves at MacLeod. The *Scottish Daily Express* ran the headline THE END OF THE WORLD. At the post-match press conference in the hotel garden, MacLeod seemed in a resigned mood. 'I've few friends left now,' he told journalists, just as a cute mongrel dog gambolled up to him. 'In fact the only friend I have is this wee brown dog.' He offered his hand for a friendly lick. The dog sank its teeth into his thumb.

Yet amid this poignant farce there remained a dim hope for the game against the Dutch in Mendoza on Sunday, 11 June. A victory by three clear goals would still see Scotland advance at Holland's expense. When they fell behind in the 34th minute, it looked all over. Yet strangely, with the pressure effectively off, MacLeod's men clicked. They stormed into a 3–1 lead in the 68th minute with an individual goal from Nottingham Forest's Archie Gemmill, which is still considered one of the greatest in World Cup history.

Gemmill's mazy dribble and curling finish transported Scotland's supporters to a state of near apoplexy, because they knew just one more strike would see them through. Four minutes later a goal came. At the wrong end. The final score was Scotland 3 Holland 2. Scotland eliminated on goal difference.

The World Cup scriptwriters had killed off the Scots in the first reel yet again. But such was the emotional impact of their strange roller-coaster ride that the scriptwriters back home weren't finished. Countless thousands of words were penned in the name of art as Argentina '78 passed into Scottish folklore.

Two plays opened at the Edinburgh Fringe Festival. First was *The Game* by the aptly named Córdoba Players, which portrayed the agonies suffered by stay-at-home fans. Twenty years later the irreverent *Argentina '78 – The Director's Cut* lampooned the whole campaign. Many of the cruel jokes at the expense of the manager – especially the one about Mickey Mouse wearing an Ally MacLeod watch – didn't bear repeating. But Archie Gemmill's wonder goal certainly did.

It famously appeared at a climactic bedroom-scene moment in the film *Trainspotting*. Later, it formed the centrepiece for a contemporary ballet called *The Nutmeg Suite*. Curious, perhaps, that an entirely meaningless goal should be one of the best remembered in World Cup history, but there's the drama of football. As the Scottish rhymester Alastair Mackie so cleverly captured, Archie's weaving run was a moment of sheer poetry:

> *It's nae o Argentina that I mind*
> *Nor Brazil, passin their triangles neat.*
> *Na, it's o Archie Gemmill's feet streekin*
> *A pattern on the edge o the box.*
> *His skeely needle threaded the ba past*
> *Three men, their legs fooled by the phantom darner.*
> *It was a baldy-headed goblin scored the goal.*
> *His shot, a rainbow, arches ower his name.*

# A GRAIN OF TRUTH?

## ROSARIO, 21 JUNE 1978

It's been said that 'no World Cup is complete without a conspiracy theory'. If that's so, then Argentina '78 was the most complete World Cup of all time. Put simply, Argentina won the tournament, but only after beating Peru to reach the final at the expense of Brazil, who vehemently insisted the Peruvians were 'bought'.

Certainly, conditions were ripe for skulduggery. Two years earlier, the Argentine army had seized power in a coup. Thousands of 'subversive subjects' had since been tortured or killed at the hands of the ruling junta. Even the chief of the World Cup organising committee, General Actis, was hampered in his work. He was shot dead as he travelled to his first press conference.

And money loomed particularly large. The junta's promotional slogan was '25 Million Argentinians Will Play in the World Cup'. It was quickly popularised to '25 Million Argentinians Will Pay for the World Cup'. In *Football Against the Enemy*, Simon Kuper suggests the tournament cost the country $700 million in official staging expenses and $300 million in 'extras', which are 'bribes' to you and me.

The premise of the finger-pointers is clear. For the junta's prestige alone, Argentina *had* to win the World Cup. And everyone knows that 'money talks'. To South Americans, by their own admission, it's a common language.

The hosts began with successive 2–1 victories against Hungary and France. Then they lost 1–0 to Italy. It was just enough for them to finish second in their group and advance to the second round. But neutral observers were already rubbing their chins ruefully. Some of the referees appeared to be abject 'homers'.

124

One commentator described Argentina's win against France as 'a travesty of justice abetted by a monstrous penalty award'. Might there be more to come?

The second round saw Argentina grouped with Poland, Peru and Brazil. FIFA had tampered with the format for this World Cup. It meant the group winner would advance directly to the final. In the event, with Argentina and Brazil neck and neck, all came down to their last games. And FIFA had made an astonishing decision: they staggered the kick-off times.

Brazil played first in the afternoon, capably beating Poland 3–1 in Mendoza. Now everything depended on the outcome of the Argentina-versus-Peru match in Rosario the same evening. And Argentina knew exactly what they had to do to reach the final: not only must they beat Peru, but they had to score a minimum of four and win by at least a three-goal margin.

Despite their talent, that was a very tall order. The black-maned Mario Kempes undoubtedly had match-winning flair, but the fact remained that Argentina had yet to score more than two in a game since the tournament began.

No wonder Brazil questioned the result. Argentina rampaged home 6–0 and went on to beat Holland 3–1 in the final. All Argentina celebrated. The junta had brought together a disparate nation. Brazil's fans were united, too: having seen their team eliminated on goal-difference, all remained convinced the Peru game was an abject fix.

The evidence is intriguing if not compelling. Take Peru's eccentric goalkeeper Ramon Quiroga. Was conceding six goals in 51 minutes really 'just another aberration' from the man nicknamed 'El Loco' ('The Crazy One')? He was certainly keen to make everybody think so. Like the guilty schoolboy who says, 'It wasn't me, sir' even before he's been accused, Quiroga quickly made a completely unbidden statement that 'this was categorically not a fix'. What he omitted to mention was that he was born in Argentina to Argentine parents. He was brought up as 'Peruvian' only when the family emigrated.

Nor was that the end of a strange affair. In 1986, investigative journalist Maria Laura Avignolo made some interesting revelations in the *Sunday Times*. One of the Peruvian players, his tongue loosened by alcohol, had confessed that 'we took money to roll over', but retracted the statement the very next day. More curious still was that, shortly after the 1978 World Cup, Argentina shipped 35,000 tonnes of free grain to Peru as a 'humanitarian gesture'. Arms were thought to have followed, and the Argentine central bank chose that very moment to unfreeze $50 million in credits for Peru's own military junta to draw on. Many Peruvian generals were said to have retired to particularly impressive homes.

'Circumstantial evidence' is what the lawyers call it. Nothing has ever been proven. But nothing will ever change the minds of the accusers, either. Years later, one Brazilian reporter was still chuntering, 'If Brazil had won 50–0 against Poland, Argentina would have won 52–0 against Peru!'

An abiding visual memory of all who witnessed the 1978 World Cup was the glorious snowstorm of blue and white tickertape that greeted the Argentine team at their opening game in Buenos Aires. But how many of us knew then that it was nothing more than cheap toilet paper torn into strips? Could everything about Argentina '78 be a little less savoury than we were led to believe?

# ONE HELLUVA COMMENTARY
## OSLO, 9 SEPTEMBER 1981

There's seldom any dispute among a group of Englishmen about who should win the prize for the greatest piece of football commentary ever delivered in the English language. It's the late great Kenneth Wolstenholme, obviously: 'There are some people on the pitch. They think it's all over. It is now!' Once more in our mind's eye the net billows as Geoff Hurst's rising shot seals World Cup victory for England on 30 July 1966. Good old Geoff. Dear old Ken. Poor old Germans. End of debate.

But add some Norwegians to the mix and they'll give a very different answer. For them, the greatest commentator who ever lived was the late Bjorge Lillelien. And his most memorable moment came in a World Cup qualifying game in Oslo between Norway and England in 1981.

On that famous occasion, Bjorge got more than a little excited. And he gave England's World Cup hopefuls a friendly two-fingered salute in a language they'd readily understand – English. But this is one story that needs putting in context. Without it, you might think Lillelien was some sort of escapee.

Both Norway and England were hoping to qualify for the 1982 World Cup in Spain. But, when they were drawn in the same group, everybody knew it was a case of David versus Goliath. Norway's all-time record against England wasn't good. Although they had met in only four friendly games, England had won them all. Norway had scored two and conceded twenty. It didn't take much analysis to discern a pattern.

The trend continued for the opening qualifying game at Wembley. On 10 September 1980, Ron Greenwood's England swept Norway aside 4–0. Not that it unduly bothered the Norwegian fans. Most of them supported English football more than their own domestic game. Television coverage had made stars of the English players in Norway. It would be a privilege simply to welcome them back to Oslo for the return fixture.

A year later the wait was over. The biggest game in Norway's history was played on 9 September 1981 at the Ullevaal Stadium. A packed house awaited the inevitable. When Bryan Robson put England ahead after fifteen minutes, the familiar script looked set to run. The locals sportingly clapped the goal. And, when Norway amazingly equalised in the 35th minute, most regarded it as a mere consolation. England would obviously prevail. They always did.

Even when the unthinkable happened as Norway went ahead four minutes before half-time, no one seriously thought they'd win. England had 45 minutes to repair the damage – England, the inventors of the game, England the former World Cup winners, England the invincible. Most in the crowd would have happily put money on Norway's losing.

But as the minutes ticked away Norway remained ahead. Then it happened. The referee blew for full-time. It was one of those not-knowing-whether-to-laugh-or-cry moments. The big friendly giant had been slain. Nothing would ever be the same again. That was how all Norwegians felt on that memorable night.

As the crowd, officials and media spilled deliriously onto the pitch to indulge in a strangely surreal celebration, Bjorge Lillelien opened his mouth. What came out was a screaming rant, which lapsed manically into English. It was a perverse way to pay tribute to Norway's finest hour, but it captured the mood of a nation:

'There! He blew the whistle! Norway has beaten England 2–1 at football and we are the best in the world! England, the home of the giants! Lord Nelson! Lord Beaverbrook! Sir Winston Churchill! Sir Anthony Eden! Clement Atlee! Henry Cooper! Lady Diana! Maggie Thatcher! Can you hear me, Maggie Thatcher? I have a message for you in your campaigning. We have beaten England in the World Cup! As they say in the boxing bars around Madison Square Garden in New York, your boys took a hell of a beating! Your boys took a hell of a beating!'

Even allowing for the shameful omission of Ian Botham and Basil Brush, it was pretty stirring stuff. And Kenneth Wolstenholme it certainly wasn't.

Naturally, Norway failed to qualify for Spain '82. They finished bottom of the group while England crept through. But it mattered not. Whatever the Norwegian is for 'It was our Cup final', they were all saying it that night. And still do, given half a chance.

## *KISSED GOODBYE*

### ELCHE, 15 JUNE 1982

The last time El Salvador had qualified for a World Cup, they suffered a bit of a spat with their Honduran neighbours en route (see 'Now It's War'). Nor was their debut appearance at the tournament itself any less fraught. They lost all their three games at Mexico '70, scoring none and conceding nine.

Now they had battled through to Spain '82 for a second try. And this time they intended to show the football world they were more than just trivia fodder. The word was spread that they meant to enter the record books for the right reasons.

I'm not sure if there's a Spanish translation of the phrase 'fine words butter no parsnips', but there ought to be. In El Salvador's opening fixture against Hungary, the World Cup floodgates opened as never before or since.

Hungary were already renowned as World Cup high scorers. At Switzerland '54 the incomparable Puskas and his 'Magnificent Magyars' saw off West Germany 8–3 and South Korea 9–0. So why not go one better? On 15 June 1982 at the Nuevo Estadio in Elche, near Alicante, El Salvador were taken apart 10–1.

They remain the only team to have conceded double figures in a World Cup finals match. And Hungary, leading by a mere 3–0 at half-time, became the only side to score seven in a single half.

This is one of those occasions where records beget records, for three of those second half goals were scored by Laszlo Kiss, who hadn't even started the game. The 26-year-old from the Budapest club Vasas came on as a 55th-minute substitute when the score was 5–1.

In the 69th minute he planted a low shot past the El Salvador keeper Luis Mora. Four minutes later he pulled off a neat lob from the left. And he completed his unprecedented hat trick in the 76th minute with another low drive. That was three goals in seven minutes.

Kiss is the scorer of the fastest World Cup hat trick ever and the only substitute to have performed the feat. When it comes to bestowing the 'Supersub' tag, the Hungarian must rival Roger Milla (see 'Roger and Out') for the all-time title.

As El Salvador left the field, it was hardly a morale booster that Kiss wore the fateful Number 10 on his back. So four days later it was almost a triumph to lose 1–0 to Belgium. And El Salvador gave a huge sigh of relief when they finished their fixtures in Alicante on 23 June. They lost only 2–0 to an Argentina side that included three potential destroyers – Kempes, Ardiles and Diego Maradona.

The Salvadorans had played three, won none, scored one and conceded thirteen. Despite the fact that their record was even worse than their performance at Mexico '70, ardent fans pointed to the solitary goal by Ramirez Zapata as a landmark in their history.

In Spanish the name El Salvador means 'The Saviour', but the smallest of the Central American states is still looking for one. When the team kissed goodbye to Spain '82, it was a farewell that has so far remained final and certainly not fond.

# *A SHEIKY DECISION*

## VALLADOLID, 21 JUNE 1982

FIFA had an attack of generosity in allotting the places for Spain '82. For the first time they allowed 24 teams to compete. That made for an almighty scramble in the qualifying tournament as the smaller nations saw their chance. A total of 107 countries had a go, between them playing 306 matches and scoring 797 goals.

Kuwait were the only team from Asia to win through. Putting one over Iraq and Saudi Arabia was seen as a major coup in the Middle East power struggle. Kuwait's mega-wealthy Arab backers were so pleased that they showered the players with lavish gifts – a Cadillac car, a luxury villa, a plot of land, a gold watch and a speedboat for each of the 24-man squad. A mere wave of a Sheik's hand could work miracles in Kuwait.

Once in Spain, they started well. A confident performance against Czechoslovakia earned them a 1–1 draw. But next came France, full of invention and Gallic flair. When goals from Bernard Genghini, Michel Platini and Didier Six put 'Les Bleus' 3–0 up by the 46th minute, Kuwait looked beaten. But a goal from Al-Bouloushi with fifteen minutes remaining gave them a glimmer of hope.

It soon faded, however. Few things in football are harder to bear than a hope cruelly dashed. Kuwait's humbling encounter with World Cup reality led to the most extraordinary transgression of the rules ever to occur at a World Cup. No sooner had the Kuwaiti celebrations died down than Alain Giresse scored what appeared to be France's fourth goal. Drifting in on the blind side, he slammed the ball past the despairing Kuwaiti keeper. 'No doubt about that one,' the commentator told British TV viewers as the referee signalled the goal.

But he had spoken too soon. The Kuwaitis had hesitated as Giresse received the through ball. Claiming to have heard a whistle from the crowd, they surrounded the Russian referee, pleading for a reprieve. It should have been futile. 'Play to the whistle' is an old football maxim. But it must be the referee's whistle.

There was only one thing for it. High in the stands at the Zorrilla Stadium sat the resplendently robed Sheik Fahad Al-Ahmad Al-Jaber Al-Sabah. With a name that long he had to be important. He was Prince Fahad, president of the Kuwaiti FA and brother of the ruling emir. The princely hand was duly shaken and the entire Kuwait team instantly stirred. They all left the field.

The delay lasted nearly ten minutes. Kuwait refused to play on. There was jostling and much hand-waving. The brooding Prince Fahad, now on the pitch, cut an imposing and sinister figure. The referee Miroslav Stupar looked scared stiff. The French manager Michel Hidalgo was hit in the face by a flailing camera. Spanish soldiers encircling the mêlée added to the sense of drama.

Exactly what negotiations took place will never be known. The Kuwaitis did resume the game, but apparently on one condition. The French looked on stunned as Miroslav Stupar disallowed the goal and restarted play with a bounce-up. The sheik returned to his seat looking royally self-satisfied.

Luckily for the weak-kneed referee, Kuwait failed to rally. Bossis completed the scoring for France with a minute to go. Four days later England finished off Kuwait with a solitary goal from Trevor Francis in Bilbao. The extraordinary entourage were homeward bound from their one and only finals.

Fahad was fined £8,000 by FIFA, hardly a princely sum to a multimillionaire. Stupar never refereed another finals game. France remain the only team to have had a goal disallowed by a member of the crowd.

# THE SHAME IN SPAIN
## GIJÓN, 25 JUNE 1982

Spain '82 was an incident-packed World Cup – Bryan Robson scoring for England after just 27 seconds against France; Norman 'Babyface' Whiteside playing for Northern Ireland aged 17 years and 41 days; England being eliminated without losing a game; Scotland going out on goal difference for the third World Cup running; the diabolical defending from Alan Hansen that led to the killer goal in their game against USSR.

Not one of them made the final cut for *The World Cup's Strangest Moments*. But an exceptionally dull game between West Germany and their neighbours Austria did. Here's why.

Group 2 of the first round comprised Algeria, Chile, West Germany and Austria. It started with an unforeseen shock as Algeria beat West Germany 2–1. The Germans recovered to beat Chile 4–1, while Austria took care of both Chile and Algeria. But then the Algerian underdogs struck again, beating Chile in Oviedo on 24 June by three goals to two. That result really put the cat among the pigeons.

It left Austria top of the group and Algeria second. With only two teams to progress to the next stage, Germany languished in third. But there was still one game to come. A truly crass decision by FIFA had scheduled the last remaining Group fixture for the next day. It was West Germany against Austria.

Football managers have many skills. Jupp Derwall of Germany and Georg Schmidt of Austria were no slouches at maths and logic. With one night to mull it over, they knew the score. Some would say literally.

A draw or a win for Austria would eliminate Germany and see Austria and Algeria through. A win for Germany by three goals or more would knock out Austria and see Germany advance with

Algeria. But, and here is the key, a win for Germany by a mere one- or two-goal margin would see 'both' Germany and Austria advance at Algeria's expense.

It may smack of 'Mary had three apples and Johnny had two, so how old is Henry's sister Linda on her next birthday?', but the conundrum didn't fool Jupp and Georg. German lager and Austrian *apfelstrudel* went very well together that night.

On 25 June, 41,000 honest punters paid good money to enter Sporting Gijón's Estadio El Molinón ('The Windmill'). But what they saw wasn't sporting. And it took the wind right out of Algeria's sails. West Germany beat Austria 1–0.

The game started conventionally enough. Germany attacked vigorously because they knew they were out unless they scored. After ten minutes, Horst 'The Giraffe' Hrubesch nodded in a cross from Pierre Littbarski. And that was it. Both teams effectively stopped playing. One British football magazine later used the irresistible headline WHAT A LOAD OF HRUBESCH.

Austria were afraid to push forward in case they conceded twice more. Germany daren't attack lest they should let in an equaliser. It came to be known as 'The Game of Shame', as most of the remaining eighty minutes were played in the middle third of the field. The ball was passed sideways, backwards and sideways again, listlessly or at walking pace. Neither side made genuine attempts to score.

The spectators jeered and hooted throughout, but the Scottish referee Bob Valentine could do little more than join in the stroll. The many Algerians in the crowd waved banknotes in the air and wailed *baksheesh*. They knew their fate long before the final whistle.

After they'd gone out on goal difference, there was a massive Algerian protest. But there was nothing FIFA could do except change the format for future World Cups. All 'related' games are now played simultaneously.

The conspiracy theorists shouted 'fix', but no collusion could be proved. In a sense it was neither. Both teams just settled for what they had, joining the 'self-preservation society' at the expense of the fans. Could England and Scotland have abandoned the 'Corinthian spirit' in the same way? Probably not.

The German FA president, Hermann Neuberger, spoke to the press: 'There is no FIFA rule saying teams cannot play as they wish.' Austria failed to come through the second round. West Germany advanced to the final but lost 3–1 to Italy. The German magazine *Fussball* ran a self-pitying headline: A WORLD CUP WITHOUT A HAPPY END. The rest of the football world found it all very satisfactory.

# 'JACK THE RIPPER'

## SEVILLE, 8 JULY 1982

By the end of the 2006 World Cup, 708 finals matches had been
played and around 13,000 transgressions of the rules perpetrated
since the competition began. So it's quite something to be
remembered for what is routinely described as the tournament's
'worst ever foul'. Take a bow, Harald 'Toni' Schumacher,
Germany's goalkeeper in the 1982 semifinal against France.

Enormous anticipation surrounded the game. It was billed as
'Artistes' versus 'Automatons'. The French played football as
their names sounded. Was there ever a more finesse-filled
midfield than Alain Giresse, Michel Platini and Jean Tigana,
alias the 'Three Musketeers'? And how could Didier Six,
Dominique Rocheteau and Marius Trésor exude anything but
Mediterranean flair and Gallic charm in their dashing shirts of
azure blue? All for one and one for all.

Ranged against them were the sterile white-shirts: Uli Stielike,
Felix Magath, Manfred Kaltz, Wolfgang Dremmler. Teutonic
efficiency personified. With the hosts Spain and favourites Brazil
already eliminated, popular opinion swung firmly in favour of
France. Not least in Seville, a sultry city where dark-eyed gypsy
girls still danced the *sevillana* with all the passion and grace of
old Andalusia. France had to win there. It was right.

A crowd of 71,000 in the Estadio Sanchez Pisjuan witnessed a
classic. After ninety minutes the sides were locked at 1–1. France
cruised into a 3–1 lead in extra time, only for the Germans to
claw level twelve minutes from time. The conflict between
'style' and 'steel' would be resolved by the World Cup's first
penalty shoot-out.

But it's not for that dramatic finale that the game is best
remembered. In the 65th minute, the French substitute, Patrick

Battiston, had raced clear onto Michel Platini's exquisite lobbed through ball. As the German keeper instinctively advanced and the ball sat up, all it needed was a delicate dink over his head.

But the manner of Schumacher's advance, at once furious, reckless, menacing and utterly unstoppable, caused Battiston to take his eye of the ball and prod it tamely wide. Schumacher took his eye off the ball too. Anticipating the lob, he leaped and clawed the air like a wild man. He was a juggernaut out of control.

The 'unavoidable' collision occurred just inside the box. Battiston lost two teeth and suffered fractured vertebrae. An incredible photograph taken a split second after impact shows him perfectly horizontal in midair like some levitating fakir. He was stretchered off unconscious and given oxygen in the dressing room. Some spectators genuinely believed he was dead. As it was, he spent several weeks in hospital.

This was football's equivalent of drink-driving. Given Schumacher's speed and trajectory, the clash *was* unavoidable. But he was totally responsible for it. Then came the shock. Faced with no option but to show a red card, the Dutch referee Charles Corver did nothing but give Germany a goal kick. Unbelievably spared by one of the worst decisions of all time, the patently culpable keeper retreated to the edge of his box and callously indulged in some stretching exercises.

Schumacher had got away scot-free with what the press dubbed 'the foul of the century'. He was whistled, hissed and booed for the rest of the game and later labelled 'The Beast of Seville' and football's 'Jack the Ripper'. Even his mother told him 'it was dreadful, Harald', and *The Times* stiffly condemned 'that grotesque poodle-permed innocence feigned by the doyen of a long line of slightly deranged German goalkeepers'.

Naturally, Schumacher denied intent, but this was a man whose ritual pre-match mantra was 'You are a tiger – the ball is your prey.' Battiston was the nearest option on the day. It was almost inevitable that the man who should have played no further part in the game proved to be the hero in the penalty shoot-out. Germany went through 5–4 as 'The Beast' saved twice.

All Seville cried with France. Schumacher was voted the most unpopular man in history by a French newspaper poll. Adolf Hitler came second. No wonder the football world united in rejoicing when Italy beat Germany in the final three days later (see 'Vintage Rossi').

Some would take retributive satisfaction from the curious ongoing postscript to this gruesome tale. Four years later, Germany lost to Argentina in the 1986 final and Schumacher was blamed for two of the goals in their 3–2 defeat. He never did win a World Cup medal.

Then in 1987 his book *Anpfiff* ('Blowing the Whistle') made such sensational claims about drug-taking and the popularity of call girls among *Bundesliga* players that Schumacher was stripped of the captaincy of his club and dropped for good from the German side. The final ignominy came on 15 December 1999, when he was sacked as boss of Fortuna Cologne during the half-time break of their match against Waldhof Mannheim. Maybe there is justice after all.

# VINTAGE ROSSI

## MADRID, 11 JULY 1982

Even the most optimistic fans accept that players need to be meticulously prepared to perform in a World Cup. That's why all devotees of the *azzurri* (the Italian national team, 'The Blues') knew for sure that Paolo Rossi would be missing from the Italian squad that travelled to Spain '82.

The tournament was due to start in Barcelona on 13 June. As things stood on 28 April, Paolo 'Pablito' Rossi had not played competitive football for two years. Both his morale and standing in the game were at rock bottom, for Italy's former star striker had been a very naughty boy.

In 1980, while on loan to Perugia from Lanerossi Vicenza, Rossi had been accused of accepting money to 'influence the outcome' of Perugia's game against Avellino. It was an odd affair. The result was 2–2 and Rossi scored both Perugia goals. Presumably he'd have routinely completed a hat trick if the 'fixing' syndicate had called for a Perugia win.

Notwithstanding the doubts over the truth of the allegations, an investigation found him guilty. He received a three-year ban, later commuted to two. With his reputation irreversibly tarnished, Juventus bought the shamed striker on the cheap. No one expected much when he was freed to play again on 29 April 1982.

But, having appeared in the final three games of a championship-winning season for Juventus, the 27-year-old Rossi found himself suddenly thrust back into the spotlight. Italy's pipe-chomping manager, Enzo Bearzot, shocked the football world by selecting 'Pablito' for the World Cup squad: 'Paolo takes opportunities. I need an opportunist,' said the careworn old-stager.

Very few people agreed with the selection. The former Scotland striker Denis Law, who had played in Italy for Torino, summed up the mood: 'You can't be out of the game for two years and come back in a tournament like the World Cup.'

The first-round games appeared to prove Law a shrewd judge. Italy struggled to feeble draws against Poland, Peru and Cameroon. In the Peru game, Rossi was substituted at half-time. Italy scored only two goals in the opening phase, neither from Bearzot's master 'opportunist'.

They scraped through to the next round (which was another group scenario) only by virtue of scoring one more goal than Cameroon. But that condemned the dispirited Italians to a triangular showdown against the holders Argentina and the favourites Brazil. The Italian fans and press were up in arms. They called for the manager's head and for Rossi to be dropped. Some even said his selection was morally wrong. Bearzot responded by chewing even harder on his pipe and banning the players from talking to journalists. Italy were a squad in crisis.

What happened next has entered World Cup folklore. On 29 June Italy beat Argentina 2–1 in the first game. Rossi again failed to score but showed signs of his old self. On 2 July Brazil beat Argentina 3–1. That made the decider Italy against Brazil. On 5 July, in what some regard as the greatest World Cup game of all time, Italy beat the favourites 3–2. The game became known as 'Rossi's Match' as the comeback striker scored a hat trick.

In the semifinal against Poland, Italy won 2–0. Both goals again came from the 'opportunist'. Bearzot's cadaverous expression changed not one bit. The final was against Germany at Real Madrid's Santiago Bernabéu Stadium on 11 July. It proved almost a formality. Italy's first goal was their sixth in a row scored by Rossi. They won the game 3–1 to lift their second World Cup.

All the Italian fans and pressmen agreed that Rossi's inspirational brilliance had transformed the tournament. 'Good old Bearzot,' they chorused. 'He had us fooled all along. How could we have doubted him? What a wily old fox he is.'

Paolo Rossi was awarded the 'Golden Boot' as the tournament's leading scorer. He was named 'World Footballer of the Year' by *World Soccer* magazine. Readers of *France Football* voted him 'European Footballer of the Year'. Wine growers from his native Tuscany presented him with a thousand litres of their finest produce. No 'Hall of Fame' is complete without him.

As swings of fortune go, none has matched the 'shame to fame' leap of the 'Prodigal Son' of Italian football. One newspaper headline summed it up nicely: CHEERS, PAOLO – ITALY RAISES A GLASS TO VINTAGE ROSSI. The masterful Enzo Bearzot took a satisfied puff of his pipe. Denis Law was unavailable for comment.

# *ANYTHING YOU CAN DO . . .*

## RIO DE JANEIRO, 20 DECEMBER 1983

When England's Football Association suffered an unfortunate mishap involving the World Cup trophy in 1966, their Brazilian counterparts were not impressed. Having triumphed at Chile '62, Brazil were the holders of the Coupe Jules Rimet. So, when 'their' trophy was stolen in London while in the custody of the FA (see 'Cheers and Pickles'), Brazilian officials took it personally.

Abrain Tebel of the Brazilian Sports Confederation told *The Times* exactly what he thought of England's abject carelessness: 'This shameful theft would never have happened in Brazil. Even Brazilian thieves love football and would never have committed such a sacrilegious crime.'

Brazil had a chance to put that bold assertion to the test four years later. Pickles the dog had famously recovered the cup in 1966, and at Mexico '70 a magnificent Brazil side won it for the third time after beating Italy 4–1 in a truly memorable final. According to an age-old challenge laid down by FIFA, that entitled Brazil to keep the coveted trophy for ever.

While FIFA commissioned the completely new and radically different trophy that is still played for today, Brazil jealously guarded the grand old original. Their priceless gem was given permanent residence at the Brazilian Soccer Federation in Rio de Janeiro. Having secured the most romantic treasure in world sport, they would allow nobody to take it away from its rightful home.

Nobody except a team of Brazilian crooks, that is. In the early hours of 20 December 1983, hooded men broke into the premises, tied up a nightwatchman, and made off with the Jules Rimet trophy. They obviously hadn't listened to Abrain Tebel back in 1966.

Despite appeals from the great Pelé to return it 'for the sake of the soul of Brazilian football', the gang were in no mood to compromise. And this time there was no Pickles to save the day.

By the time three Brazilians and an Argentine were apprehended and tried, police were convinced the cup had been melted down. Meanwhile, conspiracy theorists suggested it had been stolen to order for a fanatical collector. That sounds feasible. Either way, the original Jules Rimet trophy has never been seen again. All Brazil are left with now is the replica they had made by a German goldsmith to cover their acute embarrassment.

England's Football Association were far too polite to gloat, but Brazil's own 'abject carelessness' prompted FIFA to tighten security for good. Even the three-times World Cup winners (Germany and Italy have both achieved the feat since Brazil) are no longer allowed to keep the trophy for good. And each tournament's victor is obliged to hand it back to FIFA in return for a replica.

The strangely insecure life of football's premier prize has earned it a newsworthy status in itself. Many thousands of fans have filed past display cabinets throughout the world just for a glimpse of 'the real thing', sometimes blissfully unaware that FIFA are wont to substitute a copy at their whim.

The current trophy is certainly striking. Designed by the Italian sculptor Silvio Gazzaniga and first won by West Germany in 1974, it was chosen by FIFA ahead of 52 other submissions. It stands 36 centimetres high, weighs nearly 5 kilograms, is made of 18-carat gold, and depicts two fluidly stylised players cradling the Earth itself on high.

While the sculptor explained it was 'an organic depiction of symbolic exertion coupled with the harmony and simplicity of world peace', others weren't so sure.

On television's *Fantasy Football*, Frank Skinner and David Baddiel irreverently delivered a 'how to make your own World Cup' masterclass: 'Roll up your sleeve, clasp a grapefruit firmly in one hand, plunge your arm up to the elbow in a bucket of custard, remove arm and raise vertically.' Trust me, it works.

An even odder story emerged in February 1999, when scientists proudly announced they had constructed a replica World Cup consisting of just a single molecule. It measured three nanometres, less than a ten-millionth of the real thing. Strangely, they never explained why.

When the present cup is retired after the 2038 tournament (there will be no room for any more winners' plaques) maybe FIFA should use the miniature as the third trophy. Then no one would know whether it had been stolen or not.

# TIME WARP

## LEEDS, 28 JULY 1985

But for a carelessly discarded cigarette, the most surreal game in World Cup history wouldn't have happened. Neither the time nor the place was the same. Most of the waistlines were thicker, the jowls heavier and the hair thinner. But England wore red shirts and Germany wore white shirts, just as they had on 30 July 1966. And beneath the wrinkles the faces were unmistakeable.

It was the only World Cup final 'replay' in the tournament's history. Nineteen years late, it's true. Nor did the result matter. But that wasn't the point. This one was for an even better cause than national pride.

On 11 May 1985 British football suffered one of its worst disasters. A crowd of 11,076 went to Bradford City's home game against Lincoln City to celebrate the club's success in winning the Third Division championship. But 56 of them, many elderly or very young, never made it home from Valley Parade.

Shortly before half-time a small fire began in rubbish below the historic Main Stand. It seemed innocuous at first, but wind fanned the flames and the fire spread. Within minutes the entire structure was ablaze. The agile jumped over seats to clamber onto the pitch, but the least able stood little chance. The club's oldest supporter, 86-year-old Sam Firth, was one of the 56 fatalities. Several hundred more spectators survived but were badly burned or injured. Television cameras captured the entire tragedy.

The 'Bradford City Disaster Fund' was speedily launched. Football, for all its faults, always honours its own. While national and local appeal funds began to mount, Leeds United came to Bradford's aid by offering them the use of Elland Road while Valley Parade was closed. The Bantams played three 'home' games at their illustrious rivals' ground, but an odder spectacle still was the World Cup rematch on 28 July.

The media attention was eerily scant. Many football journalists were enjoying their summer holidays. And anything that smacked too much of circus didn't sit well with the poignancy of the appeal. But the fans who turned up witnessed a curious slice of history. In 1966 England beat West Germany 4–2. This time the result was half as good again, as England triumphed 6–4.

Everybody thanked the Germans for their generous participation. There were no old scores to settle any more. But just in case Franz Beckenbauer and his men thought it really was 'all over', they were handed a gentle reminder of 1966 by a rather florid-looking 46-year-old who showed all the signs of having enjoyed a very full life on the corporate functions circuit.

The most famous cheeks in football were puffed out one more time as Geoff Hurst helped himself to another three goals. Sir Geoff is the only man to score a hat trick in a World Cup final. When asked about the repeat performance he had a ready answer: 'Showing the Germans the action replay was all in a good cause.' Just as in 1966, he was bang on target. The time-warp game raised £46,000 for the Bradford City Disaster Fund.

# UNCLAIMED BAGGAGE

## CARDIFF, 10 SEPTEMBER 1985

For sheer tension and high drama, no World Cup qualifying game has been more sensational than Wales against Scotland at Ninian Park, Cardiff, on 10 September 1985.

It was the last group qualifier for both sides. Wales needed victory to progress to a play-off against Australia. Scotland required only a draw to achieve the same end. A place at Mexico '86 was the ultimate prize.

Thousands of Scots travelled to Cardiff with high hopes. Their legendary manager Jock Stein (25 trophies for Celtic alone) had already led them to Spain '82, and much was expected again of the one they called the 'Big Man'. Quietly spoken but bluff. Broad-shouldered with a stomach to match. A determined face under wavy Brylcreemed hair. And a heart that beat for Scotland like no other. Surely the 'Big Man' would see them through.

The tension in the run-up to the game was palpable. Even Stein, normally so calmly authoritative, seemed unusually agitated prior to kick-off. A television interview had to be stopped and started several times because his attention kept slipping. And, on a mild September day, he was lathered in sweat.

Wales tore into the Scottish side from the start. After thirteen minutes, Manchester United's Mark 'Sparky' Hughes bustled through to shoot them ahead. The Welsh fans roared. Scottish shoulders drooped. Stein urged his men forward from the dugout. They responded with frantic urgency. But the vital goal eluded them.

As half-time approached, Stein planned his talk. It would be calm, clear, logical and convincing. But that was upset by a bizarre confession. Midway through the first half, Scotland's goalkeeper Jim Leighton had looked unsure of himself. Crosses were fumbled, and he made heavy weather of innocuous shots. Stein suspected concussion, but only in the dressing room did Leighton admit he'd lost a contact lens in the mud. Seven years he'd played for Scotland, and not a soul knew he wore them.

Stein scrambled to get substitute keeper Alan Rough on for the second half. It was another pressure, a distraction he could do without. Again Scotland pressed as their fans bayed for a single strike. Even the England mascot Ken Baily (see 'Beyond Our Ken') was there to lend support. Still nothing came.

The 'Big Man' rocked back and forth uneasily. Scotland looked beat. Already, with twenty minutes remaining, photographers clustered round the dugout to record the downfall. Stein turned to physio Hugh Allan to signal a last-throw substitution. Off went Gordon Strachan. On came Davie Cooper.

On eighty minutes, a shot from David Speedie struck the hand of David Phillips. Penalty to Scotland. Substitute Cooper (fated to die of a brain haemorrhage ten years later) seemed to sense a providential moment. Amid unbearable tension, he took the ball and stroked it past Neville Southall. Scotland were all but Mexico-bound if they could only hang on.

The pandemonium around the Scottish dugout reached hysteria. Now the snappers wanted the triumphal shot. With barely a minute left, referee Keiser issued a piercing blast for a free-kick. Stein mistook it for the final whistle. Suddenly unburdened of huge pent-up tensions, he clambered to his feet, only to fall back. Three words told the physio all he needed to know: 'I'm away, Hugh.'

Seconds later, the final whistle sounded. But, as Scotland's players and fans reeled in delight, Stein was already in the dressing room laid flat on the treatment table. At 9.50 p.m. the 62-year-old was pronounced dead from a massive heart attack. His recorded last words ('Doc, I'm feeling much better now') were typically upbeat.

The entourage who returned to Edinburgh airport on that eerie night were in shocked and sombre mood. Once the luggage had been claimed, one small holdall remained on the conveyor. Inside was a book, a bottle of white wine, jars of medication and a letter that said, 'These items belong to J Stein Esq.' Only then did it really sink in that the 'Big Man' was dead.

Ten thousand people lined the streets of Glasgow for the funeral. Scotland beat Australia in the play-off and Aberdeen's Alex Ferguson took charge of the side at Mexico '86, where they finished bottom of their group and failed to win a game. Who knows what might have happened if the 'Big Man' had only survived?

# THE FLYING DANE
## DUBLIN AND MUNICH, 13 NOVEMBER 1985

In the film *Bend It Like Beckham*, the heroine Jesminder 'Jess' Bhamra makes a frantic dash from a family wedding to play in a cup final for the Hounslow Harriers ladies' side. Arriving late, she whips off her sari just in time to score the winner from a free kick that 'Goldenballs' himself would have been proud of.

Similar things happened almost routinely to the Melchester Rovers' striker Roy Race. In 1977 his inconsiderate wife Penny gave birth during the Championship decider against Tynecaster. Racey nodded a goal in the ninetieth minute, dashed to hospital still in his kit, and arrived to discover he was a proud father of twins.

That's *Roy of the Rovers* and girlie movies for you. Great fun, shame about the ludicrous plots. Nothing even remotely like it could happen in real life, especially in the World Cup. Unless Søren Lerby were involved.

In 1985, the Danish international was faced with a classic club-versus-country dilemma. On 13 November, Denmark faced Ireland in Dublin in their final World Cup qualifier, a game the Danes had to win to be sure of topping the group and sending the side off to Mexico '86 in good spirits. Lerby's stylish midfield presence was an absolute must.

That made life difficult for his club, Bayern Munich, who had a third-round cup-tie at home to Bochum later the same day. And Bayern paid Lerby's wages. Again, his presence was a requirement rather than a preference. Being a proud Viking, Lerby naturally played against Ireland in Dublin. But only for 58 minutes. Having helped Denmark to establish a 3–1 lead, he was substituted, leaving the Lansdowne Road pitch in what seemed to be a hurry. The Danes went on to win 4–1, but Lerby didn't join in the 'We're off to Mexico' celebrations – because he was already on his way to Munich in a private jet laid on by Bayern's board. The 'Flying Dane' arrived at the Olympiastadion just in time to come on as a half-time substitute in a 1–1 draw. After this unique double-header, his post-match analysis was to the point: 'My legs feel pretty tired. The pitch in Dublin was really heavy.'

Bayern Munich won the replay and went on to lift the German cup. Lerby went on to captain Denmark at Mexico '86, where they beat Scotland, Uruguay and West Germany to finish top of their first-round group with a 100 per cent record. Had this been a fictional tale 'The Vikings' would have won the World Cup in rampaging style, but neither Roy Race nor Jess Bhamra was available to help out. Denmark were hammered 5–1 by Spain in the knockout stage.

Søren Lerby never got the chance to play in the finals for Denmark again, but he remains the only footballer to play in a World Cup match and a club match in two different countries on the same day.

# *MAKING WAVES*

## MEXICO CITY, 3 JUNE 1986

On the face of it, the facts are straightforward. But the fevered debate that ensued is strange if not downright odd. On 3 June 1986, the World Cup hosts Mexico beat Belgium 2–1 in their opening group game in the magnificent Azteca Stadium. Several times during the game, the crowd performed a coordinated routine of progressive standing up and sitting down known to the locals as 'La Ola'. In English it was quickly dubbed the 'Mexican Wave', a term now firmly established in the *Oxford English Dictionary*.

Forgive me if you are an enthusiastic 'waver', but I just don't get it. Waves start because people are bored. Either because the match is excruciatingly dull or the initiators don't appreciate the finer points of what's going on. Youngsters at a schoolboy international game might be forgiven, but surely not real grown-up football fans.

But it appears I may be a lone dissenter. Some people took the wave so seriously that a fierce row developed in the United States over who was the inventor of the phenomenon. The 'Mexican Wave' may have been *named* at the 1986 World Cup, but it certainly wasn't 'invented' there. That dubious honour has been vociferously claimed by the American cheerleader 'Krazy George' Henderson.

Krazy claims he first experimented with 'the crowd-exciter known simply as the wave' at ice-hockey games in the 1970s. Much later he 'got a real good one going for the first time' at the televised baseball play-off between Oakland Athletics and New York Yankees at the Oakland Coliseum on 15 October 1981. What's more, he has the video to prove it.

But that didn't stop George's rival, Robb 'Husky Leader' Weller, trying to queer his pitch. In 2002, the one-time megastar

153

presenter of US television's *Entertainment Tonight* claimed he initiated the first 'proper' wave on 31 October 1981 at a football (US-style) game between Washington Huskies and Stanford. Weller was dismissive of George's claim to have beaten him by sixteen days: 'His wave was way too stiff, not at all fluid.'

With the battle lines thus drawn, the debate widened. The *Guardian* fanned the flames by running a readers' forum. The overwhelming consensus was that waves had broken much earlier. Many correspondents recalled seeing them on the first occasion Mexico hosted the World Cup in 1970.

Then an Olympic Games buff entered the fray: 'The wave *was* born in Mexico at the Azteca Stadium, but not in 1970. I distinctly remember seeing one at the 1968 Mexico Olympics.' Krazy George twitched uncontrollably. Husky Leader Weller slunk away with his tail between his legs.

Perhaps the best comment on this increasingly 'anorakean' debate was made in the 2001 movie *A Knight's Tale*, which included a great scene of a medieval crowd performing the wave at a jousting match. Now there's a director with a sense of humour. One not shared, though, by the po-faced team of biological physicists at Budapest University. Their paper entitled 'A Quantitative Analysis of the Propagating Human Wave' was published on 12 September 2002 in the scientific journal *Nature*. Presenting a plethora of complex mathematical equations, they claimed their conclusions represented a major breakthrough in football science.

Three-quarters of waves apparently travel clockwise. In my experience it's the other way round. They typically take 25 people (known as 'critical initiators') to start them. Each wave travels at around 40 feet (20 seats) per second and is generally 15 to 20 seats wide at any given point.

Waves as 'art forms' can include 'dual waves', 'silent waves' and the rarely seen 'simultaneous wave'. That's the one that goes in opposite directions at the same time. Participants in the wave can be 'inactive' (sitting), 'active' (moving upward), or 'refracting' (moving back down), but all waves begin with an 'initial perturbation' which 'propagates a single planar reaction'. They are most likely to happen during lulls in the tempo of play.

So now you know. The only flaw in this stunning piece of 'original' academic research (which incorporates realistic computer simulations) seems to be that it doesn't allow for boring old geezers like me who actually want to watch the football and are apt to fret endlessly if they don't see every last second of the action. Silly games at a football match? They'll bring back community singing next.

On balance I think the Americans must be to blame somewhere along the line. Which leaves me with only one thing to say: 'Siddown!'

# THE HAND OF GOD

## MEXICO CITY, 22 JUNE 1986

'Cheats never prosper' was once thought to be a plausible English motto. But, when England faced Argentina in the 1986 World Cup quarter-final, the sentiment was single-handedly torn asunder by the 'greatest player in the world'. In front of 114,000 witnesses at the Azteca Stadium in Mexico City, England were brazenly duped by the Argentine captain Diego Armando Maradona. A week later he lifted the World Cup trophy without a shred of guilt.

Rivalry between the countries had been much hyped ahead of the game. Four years earlier English forces had overcome the Argentines to emerge triumphant from the Falklands War. This was the first football encounter since that bitter conflict. Even the controversy of England's victory in the 1966 quarter-finals (see 'Animals!') was gleefully rekindled by the press. Argentina desperately wanted revenge.

They got it six minutes into the second half. With the game goalless, a dreadful sliced clearance by England's Steve Hodge ballooned back towards his own goalkeeper. It was a routine matter for Peter Shilton to advance and punch the ball to safety. He hardly needed to jump, since the five-foot-six Maradona was the only challenger. Shilton knew instinctively that his fully extended arm would beat Maradona's head to the ball no matter how prodigious the Argentine's leap.

But the ball ended in Shilton's net. Maradona had found crucial extra inches by slapping the ball over the England keeper with his raised left fist. The action replay was clear. The act was deft and cunning but overwhelmingly illegal. Shilton fully expected the 'goal' to be disallowed and Maradona to be booked.

But astonishingly the goal was given. As he wheeled away to celebrate, the Argentine sneaked a crafty look at the referee.

156

Shilton protested wildly. But the Tunisian official Ali Ben Nasser had been fooled by the sleight of hand. So too had his linesmen and many spectators. But England and a television audience of millions knew they had been cheated.

Salt was rubbed into the wounds four minutes later. Maradona prodded home his second after a surging run that left five England players trailing in his wake. The strike was later voted 'Goal of the Century'. The brilliance of the solo effort was undeniable, but the earlier goal had undoubtedly disturbed England's focus. Without the first, the second might not have happened. Although Gary Lineker pulled a goal back in the 81st minute, England lost the game 2–1. Then the inquest began.

Maradona's post-match interview defined the most infamous goal in World Cup history: 'It was a little bit by the "Hand of God", another bit by the head of Maradona.' The reaction of the English press was unforgiving. The *Sun* snarled, DIEGO THE CHEAT, and the *Mirror* wailed, BANDIT DIEGO HANDS GLORY TO ARGENTINA. An apt alternative was HAND OF THE DEVIL.

Far from being chastened, Maradona brazened it out. Nor did his World Cup handiwork finish at 1986. At Italia '90 the USSR were eliminated with the help of another sly handball by the Argentine captain. This time he used his right hand to palm away a goal-bound header by Oleg Kuznetsov, but the Swedish referee played on. One newspaper dubbed it THE HAND OF GOD II. Much more imaginative was THE HAND OF A CLOD.

Again, it helped Argentina reach the final, but this time they were beaten 1–0 by Germany. Maradona blubbed inconsolably at the medals ceremony and proved himself a real wet fish by refusing to shake hands with the president of FIFA. The most contrived tagline for that one was THE HAND OF COD.

No one exacted revenge on Maradona for his misdeeds. There was no need to. He pressed the self-destruct button unaided. Two games into USA '94 he was sent home after testing positive for no fewer than five illegal substances. The *Sun* marked his World Cup farewell with another choice headline: DIRTY DIEGO GONE FOR GOOD.

He later declared himself a drug addict, admitting to having used cocaine since 1982. A shooting incident, seedy liaisons with call girls, gangland disputes and scuffles with journalists all followed. After he ended his professional career in 1997, his weight ballooned alarmingly. When he was hospitalised with heart trouble in 2004, the less charitable were heard to mutter, 'What comes around goes around.'

One final indignity befell the bloated former star in March 2005. With his weight topping 19 stone he underwent a stomach-stapling operation in Colombia. One magazine headlined the story MAN OF PODGE. England fans of the 'cheats never prosper' persuasion came up with their own explanation for the 44-year-old Maradona's sorry demise. Most put it down to 'the hand of God'.

But what they didn't know was that Maradona was by no means finished. In November 2008 after a period of rehabilitation he was appointed manager of Argentina. And amidst much further controversy he narrowly steered them to qualification for South Africa 2010. Who knows what further twists in the saga may yet unravel? But expect the unexpected – the wise old saying that 'God moves in a mysterious way' might also have been created for Diego Armando Maradona.

# ON YOUR BIKE, MATE

## MEXICO CITY, 29 JUNE 1986

On 29 June 1986, Argentina beat West Germany 3–2 at the Azteca Stadium in Mexico City to lift the World Cup for the second time. The game had individual skills, excitement, drama and a cliffhanger finish. It was far from unlucky: those who had tickets for the thirteenth World Cup final were privileged to witness a classic.

Argentina were two up by the 56th minute, but West Germany staged a typical comeback to level through Rummenigge and Völler with just eight minutes remaining. Extra time looked a certainty, but with only five minutes left Jorge Burruchaga won it for Argentina. Their captain Diego Maradona hoisted the trophy skywards with the very guilty hand that had earlier sent England reeling out of the tournament (see 'The Hand of God'). Not one of the 114,580 spectators would ever forget the Mexico '86 final.

Nor would one man who wasn't part of the crowd – because he should have been. Everything that is right and just in the world of football supportership says the attendance figure ought to have been 114,581. But the missing man knew there was nothing fair about being a fan. He had the sore buttocks to prove it.

Many fans have endured untold hardships and arduous journeys to follow their national side, but none more so than 52-year-old Pedro Garita. Months before the tournament began he felt it in his waters that Argentina would triumph, and he longed to be in Mexico to see it. But Pedro couldn't afford the air fare or a corporate ticket package, so he resolved to do it the hard way.

At the beginning of May, he started out from his home in Buenos Aires and pointed himself north. Apart from the odd puncture, the bike stood up well. Which was more than Pedro did when he arrived in Mexico City. He had cycled all the way, covering more than seventy miles a day. Buenos Aires to Mexico City is 4,360 miles as the crow flies. As the Argentinian pedals, who knows?

But Pedro knew it would be worth it when he had that final ticket in his hand. And the grim-faced ticket office assistant knew that Pedro was a simple soul who had set off on his pilgrimage without doing his consumer research. He couldn't afford a ticket, even if there had been any left.

All that faced the disconsolate fan now was the journey home by the means that he'd arrived. But even that wasn't possible. He wandered forlornly away from the ticket window to discover that someone had stolen his bike.

And that's where my journey ends but Pedro's must somehow have started again. Try as I may, I have been unable to discover the fate of Argentina's most determined but unfortunate supporter. Did he make it out of Mexico? Could he have got stuck en route in Colombia, Brazil or Bolivia?

The intrepid cyclist will be long in the tooth by now, if he's still with us. Should anyone know what happened to the loyal but hapless Pedro Garita, please write to me care of the publisher. I've barely been able to finish the book for worrying about him.

# IN THE LINE OF DUTY
## LAGOS, 12 AUGUST 1989

Basic statistics may never truly lie, but they can certainly belie the truth. On 12 August 1989 Nigeria entertained Angola in the Surulere Stadium in Lagos. It was Nigeria's penultimate game in the qualifying tournament for the 1990 World Cup. They beat the 'Palancas Negras' (Black Panthers) 1–0 to go top of the group. Their chances of going to Italia '90 looked good.

One particular player figured twice in the record books. In the fifth minute Nigeria's dreadlocked midfielder Sam Okwaraji received a yellow card, the first of his international career. In the 77th minute he was substituted.

Okwaraji had astonishing vision, blistering pace and all-out commitment. Those not at the game would be forgiven for assuming that the 'Green Eagles' (they weren't yet 'Super' – see 'Black Magic') were saving their star man for their final key game against Cameroon. Okwaraji's very presence had always given Nigeria a lift, for he was that rare creature, a footballer with true brains. Samuel Sochukwuma Okwaraji spoke English, Italian, Spanish, German, Yugoslavian and his native Ibo fluently. He had first and second degrees in law and was about to complete his PhD.

But through it all he had remained remarkably focused: 'I intend to represent my country in the World Cup in Italy in 1990. First and foremost I am a Nigerian. I will die fighting for the dignity of my country.' High-ups in the Nigerian FA spoke glowingly of his 'honesty, dedication and accountability'. The FA chairman, Group Captain John Obakpolor, paid him a fine tribute: 'He is just the role model Nigerian football needs.' Popularity in both the 'dressing' and 'board' rooms is something few players achieve. Okwaraji was special.

161

Now for the subtext to the same fixture. Saturday, 12 August 1989, was a blisteringly hot and oppressively dry day in Lagos. Nearly 80,000 were crammed into the '60,000 capacity' National Stadium fully four hours before kick-off. Millions watched on live television. Nigeria led 1–0 in the 76th minute when a bad tackle sparked fury in the crowd. The referee dismissed the Angolan perpetrator, but even as he did so there was an 'unfamiliar' movement elsewhere on the field. Okwaraji slumped to the ground with no one near him. Just as the statistics said, he was substituted. He was pronounced dead on his arrival at hospital. Cardiac arrest had claimed the 25-year-old star.

As if that weren't bad enough, twelve spectators died of heat exhaustion during the game, unable to extricate themselves from the packed terraces. Despite Nigeria's 1–0 win, a day that had started with so much hope had turned into a nightmare. Utterly dispirited and without their inspirational figure, they lost the group decider against Cameroon, who snatched their place at Italia '90 at Nigeria's expense. The 'Indomitable Lions' sensationally advanced to the quarter-finals before England narrowly edged them out by three goals to two.

The world watched enthralled. West Germany lifted the trophy. Nigeria against Angola was already a mere statistic. The fans at large were totally unaware of Samuel Okwaraji's tragic and untimely demise. He is one of just a handful of players to die 'with their boots on', and the only one to perish while on World Cup duty.

# *DOUBLE EXPOSURE*

## RIO DE JANEIRO, 3 SEPTEMBER 1989

With only three teams in their qualifying group, Chile had a plausible chance of reaching Italia '90 at the expense of Venezuela and mighty Brazil. Already Chile had drawn with the 'Samba Boys' in Santiago. Now just one fixture remained: the group decider on Brazil's own territory in Rio de Janeiro. Brazil needed only a draw. Chile required a win by two clear goals.

In front of a typically colourful following in a throbbing Maracana Stadium, it was no surprise that Brazil dominated. But, with the score 0–0 at half-time, Chile were well in with a shout. So the home relief was palpable when Careca put Brazil 1–0 ahead in the fiftieth minute. Now Chile needed to score three times.

Brazil's fans began to celebrate, none more demonstratively than a 24-year-old secretary, Rosemary de Mello, who in the 69th minute joyously hurled a smoking green flare onto the field. Quite normal in South America. 'Signal flares' are generally regarded as harmless. But apparently not this one. When it landed by the Chilean goalkeeper and captain Roberto Rojas, he dramatically fell to the ground clutching his face.

All hell broke out. Chilean players and officials surrounded the stricken keeper and hastily bore him off the field with blood pouring down his face. Such was the crisis that they didn't even wait for an official stretcher. Things looked truly grim for Brazil as the rest of the Chilean team followed Rojas to the dressing room. The punishment for serious crowd disorder could be an automatic forfeit of the game.

The Brazilian players stood around talking. The match officials waited. When spectators in the 130,000 crowd became restive, troops were sent to the Chilean dressing room to investigate. FIFA delegates quickly followed as Chile announced their withdrawal from the match. They were too traumatised to continue. Their goalkeeper certainly couldn't carry on. Indeed the Chilean camp made it clear that they considered lives to be in genuine danger.

Thousands of spectators hung on, many for as long as two hours, to see if the game would resume. But news eventually filtered through that it was abandoned. The Chilean team doctor reported that Rojas had required five stitches in a facial cut. But some of the Brazilians were suspicious. They suggested the flare had landed well away from Rojas, and that the blood miraculously appeared only after the arrival of the Chilean trainer. A full FIFA investigation followed.

FIFA's general secretary later described the Rojas affair as 'the biggest attempt at swindle in the history of our organisation'. Television pictures backed the Brazilian version. Rojas had surreptitiously slashed himself with a surgical scalpel, and the team doctor had issued a false medical certificate. The equipment assistant had quickly disposed of the keeper's jersey and gloves to evade the forensic search for evidence of a direct hit by the flare. He knew there wouldn't be any.

Brazil were fined $31,000 for the crowd disorder but awarded the game 2–0. Chile's audacious 'Oscar performance' was not a winning one. They forfeited their Italia '90 chance, suffered a $100,000 fine, and were banned from USA '94 as well. Rojas was barred from international competition for life.

But he wasn't the only one exposed. The curious workings of the media made Rosemary de Mello a celebrity. Brazil's unwitting match clincher worked as a PR agent for the team at Italia '90 and appeared nude in *Playboy*. Most Brazilian men expressed themselves quite happy with the outcome of the most shameful flare-up in football's history.

# THAT'S IRISH!

## CAGLIARI, 11 JUNE 1990

'That's Irish' will never top the league of politically correct phrases. At best it suggests that something doesn't quite add up. At worst it implies crass stupidity. So, when the Republic of Ireland qualified for the World Cup for the first time, everybody expected the unexpected.

Even before they clinched a coveted place at Italia '90, events took an unusual turn. In February 1986 the Football Association of Ireland (FAI) provoked a huge controversy when the Englishman Jack Charlton was appointed manager of the Republic side – no matter that 'Big Jack' had won a World Cup medal with England in 1966. As the first man born outside Ireland to manage the team, he was on trial right from the start. Most sane Irishmen expected the Republic's long run of inglorious failure to continue unabated.

But Charlton began to make things happen. Soon after he took over, the Republic won their first ever trophy. A triangular tournament in Reykjavík against Czechoslovakia and Iceland wasn't exactly the World Cup, but it was a start. 'Icelandic Cup Winners' had a nice Irish ring to it.

It gave the side confidence at any rate. And when they qualified for the 1988 European Championships, the long-suffering Irish fans began to entertain very strange thoughts indeed. They didn't just hope their country would qualify for the 1990 World Cup. They believed it.

So did Jack Charlton. What he didn't seem to believe was that he needed home-bred Irishmen to do it. Stretching the eligibility rules to their limits, Charlton scoured the English league for recruits. Anyone with an Irish grandmother would do. Maybe even a great-grandmother. Soon the critics were joking that FAI stood for 'find another Irishman'.

When the side failed to win any of their first three qualifying games, the knives were out for Charlton. But then the joke began to wear thin. After turning the corner with a victory against Spain, the Republic won their last four games to qualify for their first World Cup at a canter. Needless to say, 'Big Jack' was hailed as 'a true Irish hero' and hastily rechristened Jackie O'Charlton.

Even then the realists were convinced the Republic would flop. Their World Cup debut game was against England in Sardinia. Surely that was a step too far. Some conspiracy theorists even questioned how 'an Englishman' could possibly give his all against his own countrymen. But 11 June 1990 proved a memorable day for Irish football. England were comfortably held to a 1–1 draw in Cagliari. Ireland's goal was scored by Everton's Kevin Sheedy, who was born in the Welsh town of Builth Wells.

Charlton was dubbed the 'new messiah' as the roadshow next moved on to Palermo for the Republic's game against Egypt. After it finished 0–0, Jack demonstrated how quickly he had assimilated Irishness into his mental approach. The first question at the press conference seemed simple enough – 'Jack, which of the Egyptians impressed you?' – but the answer was less than incisive: 'I couldn't tell you. I don't know their names. There was the boy with the beard, the dark lad in midfield, the keeper, the little dark lad who played centre-midfield, the very coloured boy, and the boy who played up front.'

The world watched agog. Charlton caused further amusement when he accused the Egyptians of 'killing the game'. That seemed a bit rich. Ireland were hardly renowned for their attacking flair. No wonder an Egyptian official retaliated in kind: 'They say football is the beautiful game. Any match would have to be more beautiful than playing against the Irish.'

The jibes didn't worry Ireland, even though their final group game was against Holland. The Dutch line-up included some really big names: Ruud Gullit, Marco van Basten, Ronald Koeman, Frank Rijkaard. But the Republic had weapons just as effective: spirit, belief, determination – and the magic Charlton touch. Gullit gave Holland the lead after ten minutes, but Ireland snatched the 1–1 draw late in the game. The wags were quick to note that the result preserved Ireland's all-time unbeaten record in the finals. They qualified for the second round. But bizarrely they had yet to win a game.

Next stop was Genoa for a knockout tie against Romania. It finished 0–0 after ninety minutes and extra time, but the Irish went through 5–4 on penalties. That secured them a dream quarter-final against Italy. The heroic scorer of the last decisive spot kick was Arsenal's David O'Leary, who was born in London.

The Irish agenda got no less strange as it progressed. They had reached the quarter-final without winning a game in regulation time. They were the first team ever to achieve that singular feat. And now they were summoned to an audience with Pope John Paul II at the Vatican. Charlton was formally introduced to the pontiff – 'I know who you are,' said John Paul, veering towards hero worship. Back in Ireland, they were already talking of 'Saint Jack'.

But dreams have to end somewhere. Ireland's ended in Rome on 30 June as the hosts beat them 1–0 with a goal from Salvatore 'Totó' Schillaci, who went on to finish as the tournament's top scorer. That was quite a turn-up, since Schillaci's selection had come right out of the blue. Nor did the Irish record make any more sense. They had played five and not won a single game in normal time. They had scored only two goals and conceded three. At no time was their football stunning, but some of their tackling certainly was. Their captain, Millwall's Mick McCarthy, won the unofficial 'dirtiest player of the tournament' award for his 23 fouls in five games. He was born in Barnsley.

Not one of the Republic of Ireland's 22-man squad for Italia '90 played his regular football in the Emerald Isle. Yet 500,000 Irish fans lined the streets from Dublin airport to the city centre when the heroes returned 'home'. After further adventures of a peculiarly Irish kind at USA '94 (including a £10,000 fine for letting his players drink water on the pitch), Jack Charlton stepped down in 1996 and was succeeded by Mick McCarthy.

The Englishman whom nobody had wanted is now Ireland's most celebrated honorary citizen. A bronze statue of 'Big Jack' adorns the arrivals lounge at Cork Airport. Understandably, the figure is not dressed in an England '66 kit. But nor does it wear an Irish shirt. The great outdoorsman is clad in full fishing garb, dangling a rod over an ornamental fountain and clutching a nice big salmon in his hand. Everything about the Republic's World Cup adventure is truly Irish.

# TEARS ALL ROUND

## TURIN, 4 JULY 1990

In 1990 Italy became the first European country to host the World Cup more than once. Some would say it was once too many. In his *Complete Book of the World Cup*, Cris Freddi describes Italia '90 as 'the worst tournament ever'. Many England fans agree, for this was the one that 'all ended in tears'. And for once that was no mere metaphor.

English expectations were quietly optimistic. Bobby Robson's side had romped through the World Cup qualifiers without conceding a goal. But they began Italia '90 only moderately. A win against Egypt and draws against the Republic of Ireland and Holland were just enough to see England top their group.

In the second round they beat Belgium 1–0 with a dramatic goal by David Platt in the last minute of extra time. The supplier was Tottenham Hotspur's brilliant but temperamental (unstable?) midfielder Paul Gascoigne. Bobby Robson labelled him 'daft as a brush', but 'Gazza' had the flair to work miracles.

Now the English nation dared to dream. Even the *Sun*, fiercely critical early in the tournament, yelled, WE CAN DO IT. In the quarter-final England beat Cameroon 3–2 after extra time, despite trailing 2–1 with just seven minutes of normal time remaining. Robson's men had the gods on their side.

That set up a semifinal with the old enemy West Germany on 4 July 1990. England became gripped with football fever. There were only 62,628 inside the Stadio delle Alpi in Turin, but a staggering (reported) 30 million watched the game on television in the UK. None of them would ever forget it. And the drama turned football into a consumer commodity on an entirely new scale.

The game stood 1–1 at ninety minutes. What happened in extra time remains etched into the English consciousness fifteen years later. The World Cup had witnessed many strange sights in its history. But a player bursting into floods of tears during the game was a new one. Paul Gascoigne had already been booked against Belgium. Another yellow card would see him suspended for the final should England reach it. It came nine minutes into extra time after a needless late challenge on Berthold. As the Brazilian referee José Wright did his duty, the implications hit Gazza full in the face. The English fans chanted his name in sympathy. The lip twitched. Then the tears flowed. And at the final whistle they positively gushed. Gascoigne mopped them up with his England shirt.

No footballer had ever cried more publicly and more spectacularly during a game. Yet, far from being ridiculed, 23-year-old Gascoigne became a national hero. Advertising deals poured in. He made several records. His *Spitting Image* puppet spurted tears of fountainous proportions. Signed limited-edition prints of the iconic moment are still being sold. 'Gazzamania' was born.

Football sociologists insist that the tears of despair changed English football. The game became 'sensitive' at a stroke. Liking it no longer implied feeble-mindedness. Football became a chic consumer commodity that few intelligent men and women were prepared to denounce. A crying shame, some would say. Like 'New Labour' usurping 'Labour'. And all because of the tears of a clown.

The small matter of 'penalties' also contributed, for Gascoigne's were not the only waterworks that day. The game finished 1–1 and went to a penalty shoot-out. At 3–3 England's normally reliable Stuart Pearce had his fierce down-the-middle shot saved by the German keeper's legs. Then Olaf Thon put Germany ahead. All rested on Chris Waddle (hunched shoulders, loping run), who blazed over the bar with the final spot kick of the agonising drama. Germany had won the shoot-out 4–3.

Pearce manfully heaped the blame on himself. As England's iron man left the field blubbing, ITV's Brian Moore delivered one of the crassest pieces of commentary on record: 'Oh, he's in tears, Stuart Pearce. And I thought he was a really hard man.'

Lots of hard men cried that day. Even Argentina's defeat in the subsequent final was scant comfort. It was Germany who beat them. The bitter tears of Diego Maradona provided a momentary uplift (lachrymal outbursts were becoming commonplace), but Jürgen Klinsmann's clinical analysis soon dampened the mood again: 'The reason we Germans are so good at penalties is that we have lost two world wars and each time had to rebuild our country.'

Only when England beat Germany en route to another World Cup final victory will the tears be truly wiped away. Meanwhile it was left to Gary Lineker to restore a wry smile to English faces: 'International football is a simple game. Twenty-two men play for a hundred and twenty minutes and then the Germans win on penalties.'

# AN AERIAL NIGHTMARE
## LIBREVILLE, 28 APRIL 1993

'An aerial nightmare' is the sort of vaguely amusing phrase that television pundits like to use to describe defenders whose heading isn't all it might be. But woe betide any smirking expert who ever applies it to Zambia. Their aerial nightmare was all too real.

When the qualifying competition for the 1994 World Cup in the United States got under way, Zambian hopes were high. The closest 'The Mighty Zambia' had ever been to a finals place was fully twenty years earlier, when they reached the last round of qualifiers for West Germany '74. But now they had a band of promising young players dubbed the 'Dream Team', who were hotly tipped to go all the way.

The campaign started well with a 4–0 win over Namibia in October 1992. The squad were still on track six months later as they prepared to fly to Senegal for a key second-round qualifier in Dakar. What happened next stunned a nation. On 28 April 1993 they left Zambia aboard a Buffalo military aircraft, which touched down in Gabon for a 'technical stop'. Shortly after it took off again, the plane exploded in midair, plunging into the Atlantic Ocean off Libreville.

All thirty passengers on board were killed. Eighteen of the 'Dream Team' squad perished at a stroke. They were later buried at Zambia's National Stadium in Lusaka in a designated memorial ground dubbed 'Heroes' Acre'. And to think that some of the 'big' nations go into hysterics when their fourth-choice goalkeeper tweaks a hamstring. Zambia's 'injury list' is the worst in World Cup history.

Yet the strange thing is, their qualification campaign continued apace. Miraculously, their star player Kalusha Bwalya avoided the disaster because he planned to fly to Senegal direct from his Dutch club, PSV Eindhoven. He never did meet up with his teammates in Dakar, but he vowed to honour their memory by leading a new squad into the remaining games.

Unexpected help came from the English Football Association, who assisted the former Sunderland striker Ian Porterfield (scorer of a famous winning goal against Leeds United in the 1973 FA Cup final) to take over as coach in the biggest rebuilding job of all time.

In these unlikely circumstances, and on a huge wave of national sentiment, Zambia first beat their main rivals Morocco, and then drew the rearranged away fixture with Senegal. They followed that by beating Senegal 4–0 in Lusaka. Some supporters claimed they knew why: 'We felt the spirits of the dead players rising from their nearby graves to will the side to victory.'

All came down to the last group game against Morocco in Casablanca on 10 October 1993. A draw would be sufficient to see Zambia qualify for USA '94. If this were a fairy story, they'd have done it. Alas, it isn't. Morocco scored the only goal of the game in the second half. The 'Mighty Zambia' revival dream was over.

That signalled the start of another bizarre chain of events as Zambia's fans and relatives of the crash victims sought to apportion 'blame' for the 'Gabon Air Disaster'. Twelve years later, as Zambia tried to qualify for Germany '06, they were none the wiser. The 'official report' took ten years to appear, and when it did it seemed to fudge the issue. A 'technical fault' and a 'tired pilot' were blamed. It concluded that 'the left engine malfunctioned' and 'the right engine was switched off by mistake'.

Many remain unconvinced. The conspiracy theorists talk of a bomb, 'cover-ups' and deliberate sabotage. The likelihood is that no one will ever know what really happened aboard the Dream Team's fateful flight. What is less disputed is that no team deserves to qualify for their first World Cup finals more than 'The Mighty Zambia'.

# BLACK MAGIC

## ABIDJAN, 2 MAY 1993

Paul Ince never put his shirt on until he'd left the dressing room. Gary Neville didn't sing the national anthem. The legendary Argentine manager Carlos Bilardo always liked to wear the same tie even in sweltering heat. Catholics cross themselves as they take to the field. British squads rarely include a Number 13. And in February 1999 Steve McManaman told *The Times*, 'I always keep a false moustache in the car as a lucky charm.'

McManaman's impish 'porkie' apart, superstition and football go back a long way. So why has it become fashionable to make fun of the 'peculiar' beliefs held throughout Africa? Who's to say they're any odder than those adhered to elsewhere? On that continent they like their *muti* men, *sangomas* and *marabouts*. 'Witch doctors' to you and me. And their medicine is 'black magic'.

So strong is the belief in divining, healing and psychic skills in Africa, that magic and football regularly make the news together. In August 2000 the magazine *African Soccer* ran a ten-page special investigating witchcraft within the game. Animal sacrifice, self-mutilation, spells, noxious unctions and odious potions were all on the agenda. The start of one international game was delayed for an hour while the teams argued about who would be first to set foot on the pitch.

But does it work? Or is it mere mumbo-jumbo after all? On 2 May 1993 'The Elephants' of the Ivory Coast played host to the 'Super Eagles' of Nigeria in a World Cup qualifier in Abidjan. The nicknames said it all. This was Plodders versus High Fliers. It called for desperate measures on the part of the Ivory Coast.

Cue the entry of a suitably 'desperate' witch doctor. Shortly before kick-off, clad only in a loincloth and balancing a pot on his

174

head, the *muti* man encroached onto the pitch and ceremoniously relieved himself on the playing surface. Ivory Coast won the game 2–1. Devotees of the dark arts chorused QED.

The African Football Confederation condemned the incident: 'We need to shake off this Third World image,' said a spokesman. 'We are no more willing to see witch doctors on the pitch than cannibals at the refreshment stalls.'

But supporters of 'The Elephants' weren't complaining. Many are the times when a big side has extracted the urine from a minnow. Ivory Coast returned it to Nigeria with interest.

# PLEASE, SIR
## IRBID, 22 MAY 1993

In May 1993 five teams gathered in Irbid, Jordan, for the first round of the Asian Group qualifiers for the 1994 World Cup. No one expected any new records to be established by Iraq, China, Yemen, Jordan or Pakistan. But that was because nobody believed that dreams really can come true.

First the tired old cliché: 'It is every schoolboy's dream to play for his country in a World Cup match.' Now the reality. On 22 May China faced Pakistan in the Al Hassan Stadium in Irbid. It was the first qualifying game for both teams. Far away in the classrooms of the Lahore Pakistani Railways High School, the boys were taking more than a usual interest in the fixture – not least because one of their pupils had asked for time off to travel to the game.

As selection problems go, the one facing the Pakistan coach was particularly unusual. Unless the school's headmaster gave permission to Farooq Aziz to bunk off, then Pakistan would be short of a forward. Fortunately, the head saw the selection of his charge as an honour. Thus it was that Farooq Aziz became the youngest World Cup debutant at the age of 15 years, 4 months and 28 days.

While the rest of his classmates grappled with the laws of physics, Aziz was figuring out how to unlock China's defence. But, alas, he had literally left his class behind in Lahore. All he got was a Chinese burn and a rather nasty deadleg as Pakistan were trounced 5–0.

The canny Scottish pundit Alan Hansen was once proved very publicly wrong by Manchester United when he pronounced 'you win nothing with kids'. But on this occasion the adage proved all too true. Pakistan's bold youth policy failed to pay off. Their group record was 'Played 8, Won 0, Drawn 0, Lost 8, For 2, Against 23'. Aziz made little impact. For once the age-old accusation of 'far too many schoolboy errors' was absolutely justified.

# HE WASN'T WORTH IT

## PARIS, 17 NOVEMBER 1993

France was blessed by a squad of exquisite vintage in 1993. It was so full of talent that qualification for USA '94 was regarded almost as a formality. They had Marcel Desailly, Emmanuel Petit, Laurent Blanc, Didier Deschamps, Jean-Pierre Papin and Eric 'The King' Cantona. And the most typically Gallic of the lot was David Ginola, the pouting god with the flowing locks who would come to be known for the most mimicked catchphrase in football: 'Because I'm worth it.'

Things started badly though. France kicked off their qualifying campaign by losing in Bulgaria. They later managed only a draw in Sweden. But by mid-October 1993 they were back on track. With two games remaining, both at home, they needed only one point to clinch a berth at the 1994 finals. And blessedly the first game was against bottom-of-the-group Israel, yet to register a win.

But 13 October 1993 proved to be a great day for Israeli football. At 2–1 down with seven minutes to go, the underdogs felt they had done well against their illustrious opponents. But more was to come. Two goals in the final minutes gave Israel a victory which stunned France and the football world at large. It was just as well the French had a second chance.

All came down to the very last game of the group on 17 November 1993. Bulgaria were the opponents. Parc des Princes was the venue. France required only a draw. As the clock showed ninety minutes they had it. The score was 1–1. What was more, they had the ball. Barely twenty seconds remained when they were awarded a free kick close to the corner flag deep into Bulgaria's territory.

Sound tactical logic and good old common sense called for a round of keep-ball to eat up the seconds. But unsound Gallic flamboyance and an inflated ego got in the way. When the ball was played to David Ginola, on as a substitute, he inexplicably slung in a deep cross that went way beyond the unprepared French forwards. The Bulgarians latched onto it and swiftly moved the ball forward to Emil Kostadinov, who buried the winner with ten seconds to go.

So Bulgaria went to USA '94 and France rued a self-inflicted missed qualification, which many observers regard as the most disastrous on record. For once, not even a Gallic shrug could dispel the gloom of the French supporters. Their team had shot themselves in the foot, and it hurt.

As for the man who pulled the trigger, the simpering pout and twinkling eyes gave way to a sheepish grimace: 'Zis fing is truly terrible,' he said. 'I 'ave no words to describe zis moment.' The most appropriate words might have been 'It is the end of my international career.' Ginola never played in another World Cup game.

Football fans outside France looked on with undisguised amusement. Those with cantilever beer guts, premature baldness and rampant acne seemed particularly pleased by Ginola's downfall. And once his lucrative advertising deal with L'Oréal was hatched, the 'overpaid loser' jibes redoubled. The popular vote was unanimous – when it came to the crunch, David really 'wasn't worf it'.

# BEYOND OUR KEN
## BOURNEMOUTH, 10 DECEMBER 1993

On Friday, 10 December 1993, the World Cup changed for ever – not in the seething cauldron of the Maracana Stadium, nor even the luxury office of an addle-headed FIFA executive intent on splitting the game into quarters. This particular pivotal moment occurred at the Bramley House Nursing Home in the south coast resort of Bournemouth. In those genteel surroundings, England's long-serving honorary mascot and standard bearer, Ken Baily, lost his short and dignified fight against liver cancer, aged 82.

Never before had a mascot obituary made the national press. But never before had Kenneth Henry Highett Baily (1911–93) passed away. No more would his cheery smile and trademark sparkling gnashers grace the World Cup stage he had made his own. Never again would he enter some far-flung arena, England shield and Union Flag held proudly aloft. And gone for ever were those incongruous moments when he was pelted with ribald abuse and sundry exotic fruit by England's travelling army.

Ken's 'old school' approach wasn't to everybody's taste. He was a civil servant and middle-class Tory councillor to boot. He was a confirmed bachelor who neither smoked nor drank and openly declared a marked indifference to the opposite sex: 'The ladies are all very nice, but I'm in love with the flag, you see. My only vices are coffee cream chocolates and trifle.' And Ken was a royalist so patriotic he always rose for the national anthem, even when alone. Hardly one of the lads.

But you must be the judge: 'model mascot' or 'eccentric loony'? Certainly, Ken was unforgettable. It's difficult to ignore someone sporting a Union Flag waistcoat, scarlet tails, white gloves and top hat, especially when they're leading a panting bulldog named Winston into the Jalisco Stadium in Guadalajara in a hundred-degree Mexican heat. Forget 'mad dogs and Englishmen'. Noël Coward should have written a verse especially for Ken.

To his admirers he was 'nutty but nice' – simply 'our Ken', English to the core and always there when we needed him. There for England's 1966 World Cup triumph, there for remote qualifiers, there for the toss, there for training, there to greet the team bus. No England player risked hanky-panky with Ken around. Chances were he'd emerge from under the bed and deliver his time-honoured two-fingered salute. The Churchillian 'victory' one, naturally. No wonder England fans hailed his appearance with a lusty 'He's here, he's there, he's every-fucking-where.' He was.

But there was more to this pantomimic figure than met the eye. Afflicted by a cleft palate from birth, young Kenneth found communication difficult. So he took to solo running. No one told him to stop, and he kept a record of every step. By his eightieth birthday he'd clocked up 190,805 miles and was in *The Guinness Book of Records*.

Carrying the torch for the 1948 London Olympic Games was another claim to fame, but his greatest athletic feat was 'running' across the Atlantic in 1939 to try to prevent a war. With three colleagues, he completed a nonstop relay around the decks of the liner *Europa*, covering 997 miles from Southampton to New York carrying a petition in his relay baton urging President Roosevelt to nip the European conflict in the bud. Oddly, the most powerful man in the world declined to grant Bournemouth's best-known resident an audience, so World War Two kicked off without Ken's permission. 'It was worth a try,' he said, 'but America are too isolationist, I'm afraid.'

Undeterred, Ken kept on running. Five miles every day of his adult life. He also ice-skated four hours a week and took daily swims in the Bournemouth briny, even on Christmas Day and at the stroke of midnight on New Year's Eve. Bike riding, often in full mascot garb, was a passion. He played a useful game of football and hockey, loved rugby, excelled at squash, and hit a passable golf ball. He didn't, as far as I'm aware, 'play a mean harmonica', doubtless only because he was too busy writing his gossip column for the *Bournemouth Times* under the pseudonym 'Genevieve'. He never missed a deadline in 45 years.

In his 'spare time' Ken was Bournemouth Football Club's official mascot. He first donned his famous outfit for a cup tie in the 1950s. 'He wore a white pith helmet instead of the topper,' recalls one misty-eyed Cherries fan. 'The only trouble was that most of the kids were scared of him. I think it was the grin.'

It may come as a surprise that Ken lived with his mother in the same flat in Bournemouth's Parsonage Road for fully 56 years. The nearest he came to wooing the ladies was on his regular tours of Bournemouth's nightclubs in his eighties. He handed out red roses to the town's female language students. But only when he wasn't winning countless fancy-dress contests dressed as Winston Churchill or Haile Selassie.

Supporting England, courtesy of a legacy from a kindly aunt, seemed like a good idea to fill those awkward gaps in Ken's diary. In 1966 he even stole the show from the official mascot World Cup Willie. When Subbuteo made a figure of him in 1969, he knew he'd arrived. He was appointed official England mascot in 1970. Forty countries and nearly 200,000 miles later, he was still flying the flag.

It would be remiss of me not to mention that he also followed the British Olympic team, turned up at Wimbledon for the tennis, and cheered on Bournemouth in away legs of *It's a Knockout*. He was also an avid Rugby fan. Regrettably, it was Ken's flag that covered up the pendulous assets of streaker Erika Rowe at Twickenham in January 1982. Never trust a confirmed bachelor.

The jury may now retire. But don't let that lingering vision of Rowe swing your vote in either direction. Nor the hearty greeting from Prince Charles when first introduced to Ken: 'Where did you escape from?'

Loony or national treasure? Whichever side you come down on, Kenneth Baily's passing marked the end of an era. The fatalists say England will never win the World Cup again until a suitable successor is found. Who knows whether mascots really can win matches? Sadly, England's future is well beyond our Ken.

# *DID WE NOT LIKE THAT*

## LIVING ROOMS OF ENGLAND, 24 JANUARY 1994

Failing to qualify for a World Cup is a fraught experience for any manager, but none suffered more than the England boss Graham Taylor, who strangely agreed to have his every agony filmed for posterity.

Thanks to the Channel 4 documentary *An Impossible Job*, screened on 24 January 1994, Taylor was stripped bare of what little dignity and credibility he had left following England's failure to qualify for USA '94. The most public humiliation in World Cup history also spawned a nifty catchphrase.

When Taylor was appointed England manager on 23 July 1990 the future looked bright. He had brought success to both Watford and Aston Villa and was a lively character. But things started to go wrong during the 1992 European Championships in Sweden. When England lost 2–1 to the hosts in Stockholm to finish bottom of their group, the *Sun* newspaper superimposed Taylor's face on a turnip along with the infamous headline, SWEDES 2 TURNIPS 1. The England supremo was thenceforth known as 'Turnip Head', hardly ideal for a man about to mastermind a crucial World Cup campaign.

Ahead of the World Cup qualifiers, which began on 14 October 1992, Taylor changed his telephone number. Another sign that his confidence was low. The other teams in England's group were Holland, Poland, Norway and San Marino. Taylor tried to laugh off the criticism by joining in the joke: 'I'm beginning to wonder what the bloody national vegetable of Norway is.'

But the tabloids had alternative puns up their sleeves. When England lost to Norway 2–0 in Oslo on 2 June 1993, many critics labelled it their worst performance in living memory. OSLO-RANS was almost a kind headline, but the *Star* outdid the *Sun* for bad taste, planting the hapless 'Turnip Head' atop a pile of steaming horse dung under the stinker of a headline NORSE MANURE.

Nor did Taylor's 'refreshing honesty' help his cause. He described his side for the Norway fixture as 'a pig's arse of a team'. And during the game he muttered, 'Do I not like that' when faced with yet another moment of adversity. Once the documentary aired, football fans quickly adopted the ludicrous new catchphrase.

England's crucial penultimate game against Holland in Rotterdam on 13 October 1993 also took up much of the screen time. England succumbed 2–0 amid major controversy. They might have been awarded a penalty. Holland's Ronald Koeman might have been sent off for a blatant 'professional foul'. Graham Taylor might have taken England to USA '94.

In the event it was Koeman, lucky to be on the pitch, who cruelly opened the scoring from a bitterly disputed twice-taken free kick. The gods were not with Taylor, and when Bergkamp clinched it for Holland the England manager bawled his disapproval of the German referee at the nearest official: 'I hope you're happy. Your mate's just got me the sack.' At last he had got something right, although even then he ended up resigning rather than being given his cards.

Despite winning their last game 7–1 against lowly San Marino, England failed to qualify for the 1994 World Cup. Taylor threw in the towel six days later on 23 November 1993. Terry Venables assumed the hot seat.

England's deposed coach probably didn't watch his 'trial by television' two months later, but countless England fans certainly did. The documentary stripped football of much of its mystique. Far from depicting management as a delicate science ruled by intelligent and considered decisions, the fly-on-the-wall cameras revealed its more earthy side. Taylor's favourite response in moments of crisis was to scream the F-word. His tally for the night was 38.

England fans condemned to watch USA '94 as mere neutrals were quick to deliver their collective judgement. Did we not like that.

# ON WITH THE SHOW
## CHICAGO, 17 JUNE 1994

In July 1988 an unprecedented result made football traditionalists shudder. It was USA 10 Brazil 2. Not such a shock as it sounds, for that was the decisive vote by which FIFA elected America hosts for the 1994 World Cup. It meant that the greatest show on earth pitched camp in a nation that lacked a professional football league, insisted on calling the game 'soccer', and routinely employed terms such as 'shutout', 'net minder', 'violation zone' and 'head shot'. Sceptics predicted 'the worst World Cup of all time'.

Determined to prove the doubters wrong, America set their stall out early doors. They planned the glitziest and most star-studded opening ceremony ever. If they could get that right it would set the tone for the rest of the tournament. Football was showbiz, after all, and nobody did showbiz like America.

On 17 June 1994, all eyes were on the Soldier Field Stadium, Chicago. There were 63,000 inside and a billion watching on television. First up was the Latino singer Jon Secada. Or at least he should have been up. A rising trapdoor set to elevate him dramatically onto the stage got jammed. Secada stumbled, dislocating a shoulder, but carried on like a trooper. He delivered the national anthem, the very symbol of American achievement itself, with just his head and shoulders poking through the hole in the stage.

Secada may have fallen flat on his face metaphorically, but another star bit the dust literally. Chat-show queen Oprah Winfrey went full length as she dismounted the stage. The USA's showcase opening wasn't going well. But no matter. These were mere B-listers. Top of the bill was superstar pop diva Diana Ross. The former Supreme would surely live up to her name.

Dressed in a bright-red trouser suit and sporting a huge poodle perm, she couldn't be missed. Nor could the climactic penalty she was set up to score to declare the World Cup open. From just a few yards out and with a gaping goal to aim at, nothing had been left to chance. Youngsters even formed a funnel-shaped guard of honour to guide Miss Ross to her target.

But miss she did, somehow contriving to slew the ball wide as the goalkeeper made a spectacularly choreographed wrong-way dive and the goalposts split asunder, supposedly parted by the ferocity of the unerring shot. There was no second chance. The USA had flunked under the full gaze of the football world.

The World Cup's most glaring missed chance gave newspaper editors a field day: MISS DIANA ROSS, AIN'T NO GOALPOSTS WIDE ENOUGH and MISKICKIN SUPREME were three of the many punning headlines. All the prophets of doom said 'I told you so' and waited for the tournament to go belly up.

Yet strangely they were as wide of the mark as the Ross spot kick. USA '94 broke all previous attendance and TV records and was universally acclaimed as a great World Cup. When it climaxed with the first ever penalty shoot-out in a final, it seemed to vindicate the increasingly Americanised approach to the game.

But when Italy's Roberto Baggio gifted the trophy to Brazil via a terrible penalty miss of his own, one die-hard British journalist couldn't resist a shot of his own: 'The fifteenth World Cup ended exactly as it began – with a risible penalty miss by a highly paid and vastly overrated superstar.'

# *TRULY TRAGIC*

## PASADENA, 22 JUNE 1994

Colombia's expectations were sky-high ahead of USA '94. They were unbeaten in their six qualifying games, including two victories over Argentina. The most astonishing was their 5–0 win in Buenos Aires. Form like that made them popular with the tipsters. The great Pelé pronounced them favourites to lift the trophy.

But Pelé had also once predicted that 'an African nation will win the World Cup before the twentieth century is out'. Strangely, nobody ever reminds him how wrong he was. As a clairvoyant, Pelé wasn't so great. Despite the huge bets piled on Colombia to triumph, they underperformed in a big way. In their opening game they lost 3–1 to Romania at the Rose Bowl in Pasadena.

Next up were the hosts, the USA, at the same venue. If Colombia lost that one, they were out. In the 34th minute John Harkes sent a teasing centre across the back of the Colombian defence. Their normally assured central defender, Andrés Escobar, snaked out a long leg and diverted it firmly past his own goalkeeper.

'What a tragedy for the Colombian defence,' said one English commentator.

Colombia lost 2–1, and, despite beating Switzerland in the last group game, they returned home to face a bitterly disappointed nation. Although devastated by his error, Escobar put on a brave face. 'This is football. Life goes on,' he told reporters. In the ultra-seedy world of the Colombian game, Andrés Escobar was a rare nice guy. They called him 'El Caballero' ('The Gentleman').

What happened next was a massive shock. On 2 July, ten days after his 'tragic' own goal, 27-year-old Escobar was shot dead in a restaurant car park while out with his fiancée in his home town of Medellín. After a brief confrontation with three men and a woman, twelve bullets were pumped into his body from close range. Witnesses said the killer hissed, 'Thanks for the own goal' as he did the deed. One hundred thousand lined the streets for Escobar's funeral.

Much conjectural media coverage followed the sensational killing. A popular line was that a 'heartbroken and enraged fan' had exacted revenge on the hapless scorer of 'the goal that dare not speak its name'. The full truth was never discovered, but the assassination had much more to do with drug cartels and betting syndicates than genuine football supportership. Medellín has a truly dangerous reputation. The writer who called it *una ciudad con cuerpo* (a city with body) was a sinister punster.

Humberto Munoz Castro, a chauffeur to a local millionaire, was arrested for the shooting. He was said to be a *sicario*, a hit man, acting for wealthy drug barons whose syndicates had bet $20 million on Colombia's beating the USA. On 30 June 1995 Castro was sentenced to 43 years and 5 months in prison.

The statue of Andrés Escobar at Medellín's stadium commemorates both 'El Caballero' and a fleeting 34th minute error in a football match. 'What a tragedy for the Colombian defence' had proved to be both the biggest overstatement and greatest understatement in commentating history.

# ROGER AND OUT

## PALO ALTO, 28 JUNE 1994

Part of the World Cup's charm is that its 'moments' can happen when they're least expected and in the most 'inappropriate' of places.

Take the Stanford Stadium in Palo Alto, California. Situated next to the famous university in the heart of the Silicon Valley, it's barely a quarter-back pass from San Francisco Bay. Hardly a hotbed of 'association football'. Yet on 28 June 1994 it witnessed three records that are likely to remain unbroken for ever.

But who's to say the eighty thousand 'soccer' fans gathered there didn't deserve it? For this was nothing more than a 'dead' first-round group game between a newly independent Russia and the 'Indomitable Lions' of Cameroon. Neither side could progress further in the tournament. Yet two men separated by age, creed and colour chose this supremely insignificant moment of USA '94 to write their names in history.

Russia's Oleg Salenko had played just six internationals before this one, which was to be only his third and indeed final appearance in a World Cup match. A legend he wasn't. All of which made his unprecedented feat of scoring five times in sixty minutes a pretty good way to sign off.

Never mind that one was a penalty and two were described as 'soft'. The 24-year-old native of St Petersburg had undeniably become the only player ever to 'go nap' (score five) in a World Cup game.

Although Cameroon offered scant resistance throughout the humbling 6–1 reversal, the BBC website reporter who labelled Salenko's achievement 'a shallow and meaningless feat' was surely being churlish. Not as deep and meaningful as being a BBC website reporter, evidently.

189

That's the perennial oddity of this game. In terms of media coverage, Salenko took a back-row seat to a man on the losing side. An older and wiser man, it has to be said. In fact at 42 years and 39 days, Cameroon's Roger Milla was *the* oldest player ever to appear in a World Cup match. That's Record Number Two.

The miraculous veteran grabbed the headlines because he was already a cult figure. Born Albert Roger Miller (changed to Milla because 'it sounded more African') in Yaoundé in May 1952, he won the African Player of the Year award in 1976 when Oleg Salenko was only seven years old.

Six years later, having made his name in the French league with Monaco, he was in the Cameroon side who made their World Cup debut at Spain '82. 'The Indomitable Lions' were eliminated but remained unbeaten, a feat that made the wider world take African football seriously for the first time. And Milla, with his gap-toothed grin, round jovial face and bouncy gait, was the charismatic star of the show.

Little did anyone know then that the thirty-year-old, already the granddad of the side, was only warming up. In 1987 he 'hung up his boots' and moved to Réunion Island in the Indian Ocean for what he thought would be a peaceful retirement. But when Cameroon again qualified – this time for Italia '90 – the country's president telephoned Milla personally and pleaded for him to make 'one last appearance'. How could he refuse?

Cameroon reached the quarter-finals and the old man of 38 lit up the tournament. All his five appearances were as substitute, and a brace of match-winning goals in each of two vital games earned him the inevitable title 'supersub'. Each strike was celebrated with Milla's trademark *makossa* dance around the corner flag, since imitated around the world. Everybody said what a fitting end it was to a remarkable career.

What did they know? Four years later, Milla turned up for USA '94. That's where we came in. And you've guessed it. When the 42-year-old 'supersub' came on for the second half against Russia, he took just two minutes to score Cameroon's consolation goal. Milla became the oldest player ever to score in a finals match. That's Record Number Three.

This time it really was 'Roger and out'. Salenko and Milla shook hands at the final whistle, never to appear on the World Cup stage again. Both men had given their nonplussed American audience a record-breaking day to remember.

# DON'T MENTION THE BALL
## WATERLOO, 26 APRIL 1996

There was something 'not quite cricket' about the climax to the 1966 World Cup final at Wembley. England paraded the trophy on a glorious lap of honour. Germany paraded the ball on an inglorious lap of dishonour.

According to British tradition the iconic amber orb should have been given to the hat-trick hero Geoff Hurst. According to German tradition, whoever grabbed it first at the final whistle could sneak it out of the country and covet it for ever in an 'I've got it and you've not' kind of way.

The shifty ball lifter was the German midfielder Helmut Haller, scorer of the game's first goal. It was tucked under his arm even as he shook hands with Her Majesty the Queen. It took thirty years for His Majesty Geoff Hurst to get it back. Haller finally met his Waterloo on 26 April 1996, but only after the most remarkable ball tussle in football history.

Back in 1966, no one really complained. Football memorabilia was no big deal. Haller gave the ball to his son Jürgen for his fifth birthday. Over twenty years later, after it had been signed by Pelé, Eusébio and other 'greats', it was languishing almost forgotten in Jürgen's cellar. But when England was made host of the 1996 European Championships, the magazine *Total Football* suggested the 1966 ball should 'come home'.

The *Sun* and the *Mirror* both began 'get Hursty's ball back' campaigns. Much wartime imagery was called upon. 'Don't mention the ball' was a favourite. The Hallers seemed bemused by the whole thing. 'It rolled towards me at the end. I picked it up. So how could I steal it?' said Helmut. 'We'll listen to offers,' said Jürgen. Soon the two tabloids were in a war of their own. It would be a massive scoop to land the relic of '66.

192

Investigative journalists were dispatched to Augsburg to track the Hallers down. Countless gold diggers leaped on the bandwagon. At least thirty 'authentic' match balls were offered to the press. The *Observer* ran a wicked headline in response – HALLER HAS GOT ONLY ONE BALL.

In the end, the *Mirror* were first to clinch a deal. Helmut would come to London to collect £70,000 in cash, which had been put up by the Virgin boss Richard Branson in conjunction with Eurostar. The ball would come separately with Jürgen into Stansted airport. From there a helicopter would take it to a secret location, where Hurst would be waiting. *Mirror* photographers would get the money shot, then whisk the ball to another shoot with Branson at Waterloo Station, where it would go on display during Euro '96.

The plot unfolded like that of the best spy thrillers. A posse of *Sun* desperadoes constantly trailed the *Mirror* men to try to steal a photo of the ball. Or even the ball itself. There were blankets over heads, dummy packages in locked boots, dark glasses, clandestine meetings, car chases, informers and huge telescopic lenses. Geoff Hurst was booked into a posh Hertfordshire hotel under the pseudonym Albert Hall. At one point in the chase he took refuge in a Little Chef café.

The *Mirror* eventually won the day and the ball touched down on Friday, 26 April. By teatime it was at Waterloo Station. Hurst, Branson and Helmut Haller were photographed for the next day's paper. The *Mirror* headline was triumphant: THEY THINK IT'S ALL OVER – IT'S HIS NOW! The *Sun* headline smacked of sour grapes: THE GREEDIEST KRAUTS ON EARTH. *The Times* added balance, calmly reporting that 'the recovery of this item of mystical significance has finally brought an end to the "Thirty Years War".'

The crazy weekend continued. Haller overindulged at an Italian restaurant and spent Saturday morning wandering around London nursing a massive hangover. Geoff Hurst met up with the German goalkeeper Hans Tilkowski to recreate his 1966 Wembley hat trick (at the ground of Hatfield Heath FC!). The *Sun* demanded 'the greedy krauts' give their £70,000 to charity, which they eventually did – allegedly.

After its roller-coaster journey, the holy relic of '66 found a permanent home in the National Football Museum at Preston North End's Deepdale ground. Anyone handling it must wear white gloves. The precious autographs have faded to nothing because Richard Branson displayed the ball at Waterloo Station in the full glare of the sun. Few Germans make the trip to Preston to see it.

The full story of the world's most celebrated ball is skilfully told in Peter Allen's *An Amber Glow*, a book of some ninety thousand words. Never let it be said that a football is a mere 'bag of wind'.

# *UP THE EXISTENTIALISTS*

## TALLINN, 9 OCTOBER 1996

The existentialist philosopher Jean-Paul Sartre was a master at stating the obvious: 'In a football match, everything is complicated by the presence of the opposite team.' If there were no opposition, then victory would be a foregone conclusion. But had the canny Frenchman lived to follow Scotland during their 1998 World Cup qualifying campaign, he might have thought again. For on 9 October 1996 they spectacularly demolished his theory.

The mild-mannered Scotland manager, Craig Brown, took his team to Tallinn for the Group 4 qualifying match against Estonia in a relaxed frame of mind. Having just beaten Latvia 2–0 in Riga on 5 October, Scotland felt confident. Only when Scottish officials saw the floodlights in the Kadriorg Stadium did Brown see red.

In preparation for the 6.45 p.m. kick-off, Estonian officials had arranged for temporary floodlighting to be brought from Finland. But the lights were mounted on lorries and stood much below the usual height. So Scotland complained to FIFA that their goalkeeper might be dazzled when dealing with crosses.

Not wishing a Scottish keeper to be any more embarrassed by inswinging corners than was customary, FIFA responded positively. At 9 a.m. on the morning of the game they announced that the kick-off would be brought forward from 6.45 p.m. to 3 p.m. Scotland's backup team immediately went into overdrive to inform their travelling fans. After a routine trawl of the bars of Tallinn, the clans were soon gathered for the early start.

But the Estonian officials had other ideas. Concerned about getting the security staff into the stadium at short notice, they gave no official word of their acceptance. There were their fans to consider too. Most were at work during the day. Apart from that, the team hotel was eighty kilometres (fifty miles) from the ground. Everything would be too much of a rush. And what about the television contract? That was all arranged for a 6.45 p.m. kick-off.

Scotland arrived right on cue. Just before three o'clock John Collins led out the team to a throaty roar from their supporters followed by a hastily composed chant: 'One team in Tallinn, there's only one team in Tallinn.' Estonia had failed to show.

The referee, Miroslav Radoman of Yugoslavia, sensibly dispensed with the tossing of the coin lest Collins should call wrongly and a state of impasse arise.

Scotland lined up, Radoman blew the whistle, and Billy Dodds tapped the ball to Collins. Radoman blew again. The match was over in three seconds.

Tosh McKinlay punched the air and raised his hands to the Scottish fans as they chanted, 'Easy, easy.' Scotland took the existentialist view. They considered they had won the game by default, as a FIFA directive stated that a team would win 3–0 if the opposition failed to turn up.

But Estonia did turn up. The team bus arrived at the Kadriorg Stadium at 5 p.m. The side claimed they were ready to play in accordance with the original schedule. Estonia's coach Tarmo Ruutli later made his point for the media by standing, arms folded, on the floodlit pitch impatiently 'waiting for Scotland to arrive'. FIFA were faced with a dilemma.

Acting with the speed and efficiency for which they are renowned, they came to a decision nearly a month later. On 7 November the World Cup organising committee decided that Estonia and Scotland should replay the tie on neutral ground. Although the Scots felt they were being punished for something that was no fault of their own, there was no option but to accede to FIFA's dictate.

Even with eleven players against none, Scotland had failed to win the game.

The two sides finally met on 11 February 1997 in Monaco. The kick-off that had originally been brought forward by three and three-quarter hours had now been delayed by four months and two days. Some Scottish fans turned up with miners' lamps atop their heads in mock tribute to the floodlight farce in Tallinn.

It was almost inevitable that the Estonia goalkeeper Mart Poom would keep a clean sheet. The game finished 0–0 and Scotland were so dire they were booed off the field by their own fans.

FIFA were spared a major backlash only because Scotland eventually finished second in the group to qualify for France '98. Alas, they failed to win a game there despite turning up at the right time for all three of their fixtures. None of the Scottish fans shouted 'Up the Existentialists', but most agreed it was essential to be philosophical when following Scotland at the World Cup.

# THE ROAD TO DAMASCUS
## DAMASCUS, 2 JUNE 1997

According to biblical tradition, men 'see the light' on the road to Damascus. When Jesus spoke to the sceptical Saul, he understood in a flash the meaning of everything. He changed his name to Paul. It was a life-changing experience.

Nearly two thousand years later, the Maldives football team trod the road to Damascus. They'd probably have settled for something similar. They certainly experienced an 'eye opener'. But were their lives changed for the better? Probably not.

The qualifying rounds for the 1998 World Cup in France produced several records. A hundred and seventy-four countries, more than ever before, decided to enter. Many were World Cup virgins, among them the island republic of the Maldives.

As the minnows prepared to travel to Syria, chosen as venue for the initial Asian Zone qualifiers, the world's press reeled out the sort of interesting factoids that painted a sympathetic view of the islanders: 'Their players will on average be six inches shorter than their opponents. Many learned their skills as children using a coconut for a ball. Finding pitches to play on is very difficult as 99.6 per cent of the island archipelago is officially classed as water.' A faintly colonial message, but clear in its tone. Don't expect too much, and do be kind to the little chaps.

Their opening game was against Iran in Damascus on 2 June 1997. After it, Clive White of the *Daily Telegraph* wrote in his report: 'Next year's World Cup in France will decide which country has the globe's greatest team, but discovering the worst has proved simpler. It is surely the Maldives.'

That was hardly the gentle touch, but understandable in the circumstances. Iran won the game 17–0. It was the highest score in 67 years of World Cup competition. Karim Bagheri, later to move to Charlton Athletic, bagged seven. The Maldives players' lack of height may have been a factor. Ten of the goals were headers.

Nine days later the teams met again, this time on Iranian territory in Tehran. And again Clive White reached for his acid-dipped pen: 'The Maldivian eleven walked triumphantly off the field, heads held high. They had only lost 9–0.' The Maldives' stature had swiftly been diminished to laughable proportions.

That may have had something to do with the results of their other group matches, all crammed into the space of eleven nightmarish days to save on travelling. Against Syria they were consistent, losing 12–0 on both occasions. Against the most misspelled World Cup competitors of all time, Kyrgyzstan, they improved beyond measure. They kept the score down to 3–0 in the first game and 6–0 in their final fixture as the curtain blessedly fell on an eventful campaign.

The final table made the Maldives all-time record breakers. Six straight defeats, no goals scored, and a negative goal difference of 59, which has never been 'beaten'. American Samoa were later to come close from a fixture schedule of just four games (see 'Scoring for Fun') but the Maldives still shade it.

Bravely the side's Bolivian coach Romulo Cortez faced the press. His succinct comments suggested that he and his boys had indeed seen the light on the road to Damascus: 'Half my team wanted to quit after the first game. I'm afraid we are not quite ready for this kind of competition.'

The islanders' performances have since improved, while other nations have suffered traumas of their own. But most football followers would still say the worst team in World Cup history is the Maldives. Clive White told them so.

# A TERRIBLE LOSER

## BAGHDAD, 6 JUNE 1997

Iraq's first World Cup appearance was at Mexico '86. Although they lost all their three games, they fully expected the experience to provide a platform for future success. It seemed all they needed was that extra bit of motivation.

The man brought in to provide it was Uday Hussein, the eldest son of the Iraqi leader Saddam Hussein. He was appointed president of the Iraqi Football Association in 1987. The 23-year-old enjoyed football in the same way he enjoyed fast cars, loose women, expensive Italian suits and huge Cuban cigars. There were no half-measures. His father gave him a simple brief – win.

But Uday's first experience at the helm was a bitter one. Iraq were eliminated from the Italia '90 qualifying tournament by a single point. Nor did their luck improve four years later. They narrowly failed to qualify for USA '94 after last-day results conspired cruelly against them. Aside from the football issue, losing face to their political enemy America was a huge blow. Defeat was becoming harder to bear with each passing campaign.

Iraq plummeted to 140th in the FIFA world rankings. Uday made it clear that qualifying for France '98 wasn't just desirable – it was compulsory.

Even before the 'do or die' campaign had begun, persistent rumours suggested that the FA chief's 'motivational methods' could be unconventional. The players were said to have been routinely tortured and humiliated. Uday was already a convicted murderer, so the allegations were patently plausible. A further insight into his character was afforded by a chilling remark from one of his bodyguards: 'Uday is very much like Saddam, but not quite as nice.'

Fear of losing can do strange things to footballers. On 23 May 1997 Iraq began their qualifying quest with a 6–2 away win against Pakistan. It seemed the 'encouragement' had hit the mark. But Pakistan later showed how truly weak they were by losing 7–0 to Kazakhstan. With only three teams in the group, the crunch fixtures were obviously those between Iraq and Kazakhstan.

Kazakhstan came to Baghdad on 6 June 1997. A crowd of twenty thousand saw Iraq go ahead after only two minutes. The scene was set for a glorious triumph. At least until Kazakhstan scored either side of the break. Iraq lost the game 2–1.

The post-match fallout makes Western motivational techniques look tame. Forget Alex Ferguson's red-hot scoldings. The man they call 'the Hairdryer' is a breath of fresh air compared with Uday Hussein.

According to the testimony of two Iraqi players who have since defected to the West, several of the most culpable losers were transported to the notorious Radwaniya prison. After having their heads shaved as a mark of shame they were dragged across gravel paths until their backs were raw. Then they were made to immerse themselves in vats of raw sewage. It made sure the wounds would become infected.

Perhaps worst of all for footballers was the ancient torture known as *falaka* – that's being repeatedly beaten on the soles of the feet until the victim is barely able to walk. Several of the players endured that dubious pleasure. In Uday Hussein's 'coaching manual' it was meant to instil pride.

Strangely, it didn't work. Iraq were still in with an outside chance of qualifying for France '98 when they travelled to Kazakhstan for the return fixture. But a side utterly broken of its spirit lost 3–1. Iraq's dream of a second World Cup finals appearance was over.

Naturally the torture allegations were denied by the Hussein regime. A FIFA delegation swiftly dispatched to Baghdad to find evidence came up with nothing. The only players they were permitted to speak to had already been 'briefed' by Uday. But respected Iraqi internationals later spoke out.

London-based Sharar Haydar was adamant: 'Believe me absolutely. The torture happened.'

Iraq's quest for a share of the ultimate World Cup experience is no longer in the hands of Uday Hussein. Football's most terrible loser died on 22 July 2003 after a shoot-out with American troops in Mosul.

Bernd Stange, a German coach, in heading Iraq's 2006 World Cup qualifying campaign, had a difficult task on his hands. Much of his coaching had to be done by telephone because he feared walking the streets of Baghdad. But at least the feet of his players were spared further abuse. The Iraqi side continued to lose more than they won, but they certainly didn't pay quite so dearly.

# WE SHALL NOT BE MOVED
## ABERDEEN, 6 SEPTEMBER 1997

Football is a resilient sport. It takes something truly extraordinary to bring the game to a grinding halt. Such as what happened at 4 a.m. on Sunday, 31 August 1997. Within a week, football had stopped in its tracks.

At 3 o'clock on Saturday, 6 September, the Pittodrie Stadium in Aberdeen lay empty when it should have been full to the rafters for the Scotland-versus-Belarus World Cup qualifying game. With Scotland on the brink of securing a place at France '98, no foreseeable circumstance could have prevented the Tartan Army from urging their side to what they hoped would be one more valuable win in a tight group. But the death of a fairytale princess is not foreseeable.

When Diana, Princess of Wales, was killed in a car crash in Paris, ordinary service was not resumed for quite some time. As sections of the British population entered (some would say bizarrely) a state of unprecedented shock, Prime Minister Tony Blair sensed instinctively that the funeral date, Saturday, 6 September, must be a day of national mourning.

That naturally included sport and entertainment. All scheduled English League games were immediately cancelled. So too the five race meetings. Theatres lowered their curtains. Even TV commercials involving indelicate references to 'princesses' or 'fast cars' were pulled. Businesses closed until the funeral was over, most opening at 2 o'clock on Saturday afternoon.

So it wasn't really so strange that Pittodrie lay silent. The real oddity was the bitter battle that took place *before* the game was called off. For the hard-bitten Scottish FA was fully intent on a 'business as usual' stance.

203

The *Daily Telegraph* sounded the first note of disquiet on the Wednesday before the funeral – SOCCER GAME GOES AHEAD is quite an unusual headline when you think about it. The Scottish Football Association chief executive, Jim Farry, refused to be moved: 'We've consulted with FIFA and they say we can go ahead, so long as we have the usual marks of respect such as a minute's silence, black armbands and half-mast flags.' The candlelight-vigil brigades wailed their disapproval – 'can' is one thing; 'will' is another.

A spokesperson from the Lord Chamberlain's Office made things worse: 'The match doesn't conflict directly with the morning funeral, so there's no protocol problem.' Then they added an unfortunate aside: 'Life goes on.'

That prompted a massive public outcry. The demand for cancellation was overwhelming. And huge numbers of complainants were Scotland fans. The Scottish FA, apparently believing that antiroyalist sentiment was taken as read north of the border, had severely miscalculated the mood of a nation. Scotland's captain, Gary McAllister – caught between two camps – only muddied the waters: 'I think it's good for the match to go ahead. It gives us an opportunity to convey our feelings.'

Striker Ally McCoist didn't agree: 'I'll pull out if we play.' As anger mounted, calls were made for Jim 'Hardheart' Farry to resign. Tony Blair joined the chorus as he wiped another tear from his eye. Barely had the prime minister got the onion back in his pocket than the Scottish secretary Donald Dewar labelled the decision to play 'unbelievably disrespectful'. Belarus swiftly agreed to a rescheduling. Jim Farry relented and called the game off.

As a becalmed British nation nodded sage approval, the oddest thing of all happened. The game kicked off the very next day almost as if nothing had happened. Same teams, same spectators, same crude chants, same late tackles, same unseemly spitting – but on Sunday, not Saturday. So that was all right, then. The crowd went home deliriously happy as Scotland won 4–1 and went on to qualify for France '98.

This is a great story for the cynics, and one that divides opinion. Graham Sharpe, in his book *Final Whistle*, was quick to point out that most shops and businesses had opened for trade at 2 p.m. 'It was possible to shop at supermarkets, visit theme parks, buy a Big Mac or purchase a lottery ticket, but not possible to watch, play in, or bet on a football match.'

An unprecedented level of moral outrage, nationwide hype and indignation may have forced Scottish football to tip its cap to a princess, but Sharpe arguably had a point.

Which is exactly what Scotland had after a disastrous showing at France '98. No wins and one point. They finished bottom of the group and came home early. It was 'Scotland the grave' all over again.

# WHAT MIGHT HAVE BEEN
## MARSEILLE, 15 JUNE 1998

On the surface, there was nothing at all remarkable about England's opening game at France '98. Glenn Hoddle's side played Tunisia at the Vélodrome in Marseille on 15 June. Alan Shearer scored just before half-time. Paul Scholes made the game safe a minute from the final whistle. England were moderate. Tunisia were poor. A 2–0 win was fair enough. Three points were in the bag.

But this was one of those games in which fringe events made the news. Three stories of the odd variety emerged – one light-hearted, one disgraceful and the other downright chilling. In fact the final one added a new dimension to the World Cup that will stay with it for ever.

I'll start with the frivolous. Glenn Hoddle and Alan Shearer conducted what appeared to be a very odd television interview after the game. Both men spoke well, but only Hoddle was shown in shot. All Shearer's comments emerged from a disembodied source off screen. It looked like a pretty bad case of rank bad camera work.

Only later did the real reason emerge. In the background behind Shearer was a huge MARSEILLE sign. Shearer's head hid the M and the ILLE was out of shot. Showing great professionalism, either the cameraman or a studio vision mixer had chosen to spare Shearer's blushes. Most fans except those of Newcastle United rather wish he hadn't.

Now the disgraceful. No such propriety was observed by hundreds of England fans who had travelled to France without tickets. Down on the beaches of the Côte d'Azur, rear quarters were bared, bellies flaunted and huge quantities of beer consumed. It was almost bound to get even uglier, and did. The night before the game, national and international news channels broadcast pictures of England fans engaging in what looked like open warfare against police, rival fans and even among themselves.

The violence continued for seven hours. Bottles and chairs were thrown. There were several stabbings. Innocent tourists caught up in the mayhem were terrified. There were nearly a hundred arrests and fifty injuries. It was the most public display of fan violence in World Cup history. And it carried the 'Made in England' label.

The *Mirror* front page headline blasted, A BLOODY DISGRACE. And some journalists blamed the newspaper's rival for fuelling the fire. A *Guardian* editorial pointed the finger: 'The start of the trouble coincided with the arrival of a double-decker bus, sponsored by the *Sun,* playing the national anthem and handing out bowler hats.' As for the Tunisian national anthem, many England fans both at the game and watching on giant screens roundly booed it. The entire affair was one side of the World Cup that no genuine fan had ever wished to witness.

Yet here is the really strange thing. That violence might have paled into insignificance but for events in Belgium three months earlier. This is the chilling story of the trio. It concerns a man who was passionate about football, but who would stop at nothing to achieve his fanatical ends. It seems like a distasteful pun to say he was an Arsenal fan. But he was of sorts. His name is Osama Bin Laden.

In early 1994 the Saudi Arabian-born leader of the terrorist group Al-Qaeda spent three months in London, visiting his supporters and meeting bankers. During his stay Bin Laden went to Highbury four times to watch Arsenal. He bought his sons gifts from the club shop. He was a loving father with a passion for football.

But, because he understood football, he also realised its potential as a terrorist target. Few hits could be bigger than one made at a World Cup. And the 1998 World Cup included his two biggest Western enemies, the USA and England.

Little publicity has ever been given to the plot that was hatched. The authorities didn't wish to scaremonger. But, when police finally uncovered it barely two weeks before the 1998 World Cup began, those in the know heaved a huge sigh of relief.

The police operation first began in earnest in Belgium. On 3 March 1998 they raided a house in Brussels and arrested seven members of an Algerian terrorist group thought to be linked to Bin Laden's Al-Qaeda. Having extracted 'sensitive intelligence', they launched dozens of raids on further suspects' homes on 26 May. No one can be certain that the plan really would have been effected, but it was a sensational one.

David Beckham and the England team were to have been massacred on the pitch during the Tunisia game, using biological weapons. Another group of terrorists were to simultaneously burst into the hotel where the American players would be watching the game on television and murder them. Even though the plot failed, it made FIFA very nervous indeed.

As it was, Osama Bin Laden eventually pulled off the attack we now know as 9/11. The strike on the twin towers of the World Trade Center in New York was devastating. Football might so easily have been first. Taken in conjunction with the near-miss at the 1998 World Cup, the New York tragedy changed the face of football's premier tournament for ever.

For the 2002 World Cup in Japan and South Korea, antiterrorist measures were given renewed priority. The opening game paired champions France with rank outsiders Senegal. The Africans pulled off a major shock by winning the game 1–0. The multitalented French side exited the tournament after three games without a single win or goal to their credit. Senegal amazingly advanced to the quarter-final, where only a cruel 'Golden Goal' defeat against Turkey put them out. The word 'shock' was much used in analysing the topsy-turvy fortunes of France and Senegal.

But the real shock of the 2002 World Cup was what lay largely unseen. The *Daily Mail* lifted the lid a few days before the tournament began:

Anti-aircraft missiles will be deployed inside the Seoul football stadium when France kicks off the World Cup on Friday. The operation will also include fighter jets and helicopters patrolling the skies. Military forces across South Korea are on high alert with submarines and warships off the coast to thwart a maritime attack. All flights within a six mile radius of stadiums hosting games have been banned from two hours before kick-off until an hour afterwards.

By comparison, the previous World Cup seemed almost tranquil. But the events surrounding the England-versus-Tunisia clash in Marseille had sounded an early warning. The game's premier competition acquired a permanent new dimension at a stroke.

England's shamed fans and Shearer's comical interview may have received the wider airing, but the real story in the South of France on 15 June 1998 was the one that *didn't* happen. It's to be hoped that 'World Cup' and 'terrorist attack' never do make the headlines together.

# A FEAST OF FOOTBALL

## BORDEAUX, 23 JUNE 1998

Nothing is quite like 'being there'. Watching a World Cup at home on television just isn't the same. The extra ingredient enjoyed by the travelling fans is what the Irish call 'the *craic*' – which basically means having a great time of it no matter what's happened on the field. Lovers of the *piste* have their *après ski*. Devotees of the *mondial* have their *après match*.

In a post-tournament analysis of France '98, one highly qualified football sociologist explained the phenomenon: 'Fans who travel to a World Cup experience an opportunity for cross-cultural referencing and the diverse sampling of local and national ethnicities and ethnological behaviour on a scale seldom afforded them in any other walk of life.' I think what he meant was 'meet the locals, have a drink, chat up some Brazilians, drink, eat, chat up some Italians, eat, drink, be sick, moan about the referee, chat up some Scandinavians, drink, eat, drink, and come back broke'.

Strangely, the most common complaint from returning fans is that the chat-up subjects never seem particularly receptive. Which leaves food and drink as the prime activities. That being the case, Scotland fans were fortunate indeed to be allocated Bordeaux for one of their group games. Even if they came back early, the *expérience gastronomique* would be unsurpassed. I quote from my guidebook:

> There is little more alluring than a glass of Bordeaux. Centuries of blending mastery, combined with a unique terrain and climate, give birth to a refinement of equilibrium of a highly enticing nature. Nor should we forget the other half of the gastronomic experience. Of all the local

210

specialities none surpasses the renowned *sauce bordelaise* made with red wine, marrow-based brown stock, shallots and seasonings, which marries particularly well with *entrecôte*, especially one grilled over the fragrant trimmings of a freshly pruned vine.

On 10 June 1998 Scotland lost 2–0 to Brazil in Paris. Six days later in Bordeaux, they drew 1–1 with Norway. On 23 June, still in with an excellent chance of progressing to the second round, they travelled to St Étienne and were soundly trounced 3–0 by Morocco. Scotland's unenviable but legendary record of never advancing beyond the first round of a single World Cup was duly preserved.

Naturally the Tartan Army were disappointed, but by no means devastated. Many drowned their sorrows in the customary manner, among them a group of ten based in Bordeaux who decided to push the boat out. Their bill came to £1,400, so they must have eaten well. Not perhaps the finest wines or the very best Michelin-starred restaurant at a mere £140 a head, but a decent blow-out all the same. Good enough to be reported in the British press, at any rate:

Ten Scotland fans following their side in Bordeaux for the World Cup have spent £600 on a takeaway order of lager and curry which they telephoned through to the Eye of the Tiger restaurant in Bournemouth. They then spent a further £800 on a charter flight to deliver it to Bordeaux.

For the first time in this book I believe I'm speechless. So I'll leave the last word to the restaurant boss Mustafa Aolad: 'It was such a good order we'd like to have delivered free, but unfortunately it was beyond our usual five-mile radius. We all support Scotland now.'

# NOT NATURAL

## PARIS, 26 JUNE 1998

When a book called *Footballers' Haircuts* made the 2003 bestseller lists, it confirmed what the fans have known for years: without the bizarre world of football coiffure, the game would be far less entertaining than it is.

Early individuality at the World Cup owed more to accidents of nature than fashion. When Billy Wright paraded his 'ice-cream quiff' at Brazil 1950, it was just the way it grew. Bobby Charlton's famously pointless 'comb-over' was born of desperate necessity and misplaced vanity. Martin Peters had a choirboy cut on his first birthday and stuck with it.

But it all changed once Paul 'der Afro' Breitner introduced fashion sense to the 1974 World Cup. The German full-back's 'big' statement not only inspired a tribute song to his amazing thatch, but encouraged others to follow his lead – evidently a poodle's lead, judging by Kevin Keegan's ludicrous perm. Then came Chris Waddle's dodgy mullet, David Beckham's much-maligned Mohawk and David Seaman's 'you'd never imagine it from the way I speak' ponytail.

Overseas players particularly excelled themselves. The plugged-into-an-electric-socket look of Colombia's Carlos Valderrama was the most voluminous of all time. Coby Jones of the USA took inspiration from a floor mop. Taribo West's bright-green pigtails earned a stern rebuke from the Nigerian culture minister: 'Our youths copy our footballers,' said Otunba Runshewe, 'but the players seem to forget that braids embrace a sense of homosexuality in the developing world, and we certainly don't want that.'

He ought to have been thankful that such expressions of individuality are generally the province of lone males with egos bigger than their brains. Imagine if an entire team was dumb enough to have a bad-hair day *en masse*. But of course no manager would ever sanction it. Apart from Anghel Iordanescu of Romania.

His side's France '98 World Cup experience started normally enough with a 1–0 Group G victory against Colombia, who were captained by Valderrama. Maybe his bouncy curls gave the Romanians odd ideas, because, after beating England 2–1 in Toulouse, they celebrated their guaranteed passage into the next phase in a very strange manner indeed. It certainly wasn't natural.

For their final group game against Tunisia at the Stade de France on 26 June, the entire Romanian team went peroxide-blond – except the goalkeeper, who was bald. He was kept company by Coach Iordanescu, who shaved his own head in moral support. No odder-looking team has ever competed at a World Cup.

'This is a bonding exercise and lucky charm to carry us all the way to the final,' explained Iordanescu. But, after struggling to a feeble 1–1 draw against Tunisia, Romania's team of clones were beaten 1–0 by Croatia in the knockout stage. A twice-taken penalty by Davor Suker sent them home wondering why they'd ever agreed to the hare-brained scheme in the first place.

Dark as nature intended, they had won two. After turning to the bottle, they won none. Everyone outside the Romanian camp observed that blonds didn't have more fun, but they were definitely very dumb.

# THE X FACTOR
## ST ÉTIENNE, 30 JUNE 1998

Who knows the secret factor that makes a World Cup winner? England in '66. West Germany in '74. Argentina in '78. 'The hosts always win!' I hear you cry.

Brazil at Mexico '70. The Germans again at Italia '90. So much for that 'Eureka!' moment.

Don't ask me why, but as France '98 beckoned I had very good vibes about England. As 10 June drew closer, the feeling grew. By the day before the big kick-off I pretty much believed that Glenn Hoddle's boys would be lifting the trophy on 12 July – even without Paul Gascoigne, controversially dropped from the squad. No matter that the biggest number of countries ever would be competing – 32 teams increased from 24 – the cream always rises to the top. Numbers don't count in football.

But 'Big Jim' down at my local disagreed: 'It's all in the numbers. Let me show you an equation.' That clinched it. After close scrutiny and three pints, I felt it in my water that 1998 was definitely England's year:

**The Theory of World Cup Fortunes According to Big Jim**
Brazil winners in 1970 and 1994      $1{,}970 + 1{,}994 = 3{,}964$
Argentina winners in 1978 and 1986      $1{,}978 + 1{,}986 = 3{,}964$
West Germany winners in 1974 and 1990 $1{,}974 + 1{,}990 = 3{,}964$
England winners in 1966 and '$x$'      $1{,}966 + {}$'$x$'$ = 3{,}964$

So '$x$' must equal 1,998. England therefore winners in 1998.

'QED', as we seldom say in football.

The theory certainly stood some repeating. It served me admirably around the hostelries of Derby as England progressed to the second-round knockout stage. Then came the game against Argentina in St Étienne on 30 June, when, as we too often say in football, 'England lost on penalties'. First a miss from Paul Ince, then the crucial fifth spot kick from David 'I've never taken one before' Batty. His feeble effort was beaten away by the Argentine keeper Carlos Roa. Another dream cruelly shattered. So much for the numbers game.

But 'Big Jim' remained upbeat: 'Fickle creatures, numbers,' he said, 'always apt to be unpredictable.' Especially where superstition's concerned. Look at what Paul Gascoigne said before the finals: "I've got this thing about the Number 4. I don't know why 4 – my favourite used to be 5 and then 7. Then I got this thing about 13, where nothing would be done in 4s because 4 and 9 are 13. I've no idea where 9 comes from. I got it into my head because 9 and 4 are 13. That's the same as 6 and 7. I can't bear to see them together because that's 13 again. So, when I go out onto the park, I won't go out 6th or 7th. Nor 4th. It'll be either 5th or 8th".'

But 5 and 8 are 13, Gazza. And what were the shirt numbers of Ince, Batty and Roa? They were 4, 8 and 1, which make 13. It was obvious England's fate was in the numbers all along.

# *NO WAY BACK*

## LONDON, 2 FEBRUARY 1999

Glenn Hoddle succeeded Terry Venables as England manager in the summer of 1996. He guided England to the 1998 World Cup, where they lost to Argentina on penalties in the second round. In terms of results, his reign was unremarkable. But his dethronement was anything but. No national manager has been sacked in more bizarre circumstances.

The seeds of the story began in 1976, when Hoddle was a seventeen-year-old prodigy at Tottenham Hotspur. It was then, while carrying a niggling hamstring injury, that he first met Eileen Drewery, the mother of his girlfriend Michelle. Eileen claimed to be a gifted practitioner of 'remote healing'. Glenn's injury cleared up immediately. He became a believer in faith healing from that day.

Ten years later, while on holiday in Israel, Hoddle had another revelatory experience. He became a born-again Christian. Eileen praised his conversion, for her powers too were God-given. His faith should have had no real bearing on his football. The two were separate issues. But, when Hoddle became England manager, he decided he needed support. And it was to his long-term mentor, Eileen Drewery, that he turned.

The former Essex pub landlady became part of the England set-up. Hoddle encouraged his players to use her services. Later, he insisted on it. The England manager seemed increasingly to rely on Drewery for fitness reports. Journalists speculated that she was instrumental in his team selection. The tabloid headline writers were quick to spot that 'Hodd' rhymed with 'odd'.

Some of Drewery's claims were truly bizarre. On 11 October 1997, England played Italy away in their last World Cup

216

qualifier. England needed only a draw to clinch their place at France '98. With the score at 0–0 very late in the game, England's Ian Wright missed a golden opportunity to snatch victory. Glenn's 'guru' claimed she had willed Wright to hit the woodwork, which he did, as she thought a late winner might provoke crowd trouble. Fortunately for Eileen, Italy didn't score a last-second winner of their own. No wonder the press began a concerted 'Hoddle out' campaign.

As it was, the England manager laid it on a plate. Barely had his side returned from their France '98 disappointment than Hoddle's *World Cup Story* was published. The book smacked of profiteering from failure. Moreover, it betrayed many confidences between Hoddle and his players. And pages 49–55 were devoted entirely to singing the praises of Eileen Drewery. It was one more nail in Hoddle's coffin.

As pressure mounted for the oddball England coach to be dismissed, the final straw came following an interview he did for *The Times* at the end of January 1999. Hoddle spoke candidly about success, failure and the role of the fates: 'You and I have been physically given two hands and two legs and half-decent brains. Some people have not been born like that. And it's for a reason. The karma is working from another lifetime. What you sow you reap.'

In an age of political correctness, Hoddle didn't stand a chance. Lobbyists for the disabled community demanded his sacking for the 'insulting implication that disability is a punishment for previous misdeeds'. Hoddle admitted his belief in reincarnation but insisted he'd been grossly misquoted.

Every man and his dog seemed to have an opinion. The *Church Times* ran a leader article supporting the England manager. The Indian magazine *Maharajah* suggested Hoddle should become India's national coach. Opinion in England divided the nation. Then, crucially, Prime Minister Tony Blair was asked an unusual question on television: 'Should the England manager be sacked?' The master of spin took only a moment to compute how the Hoddle affair might affect his own popularity: 'Yes, on balance I believe he should go.'

And that was it. Glenn Hoddle became the only England manager to be effectively sacked by a prime minister. And the first to be dismissed for reasons of faith. On 2 February 1999 he was called to the FA headquarters at Lancaster Gate and the deed was swiftly done. Strangely, he didn't say 'I'll be back.'

# *RIP, SIR ALF*

## IPSWICH, 28 APRIL 1999

From the vantage point of today's dewy-eyed 'book of condolence' world, it seems strange indeed that the only man ever to manage England to a World Cup triumph was never truly popular with the football public at large. Alf Ramsey didn't come over as a man of the people. He could appear aloof. They said he was a prude and a killjoy. Too proper by far. He was both cruelly mocked and fiercely maligned for what his harshest critics called 'a terse correctness born of downright snobbery'. What a strange way to treat a winner!

Only when Sir Alf Ramsey died in an Ipswich nursing home on Wednesday, 28 April 1999, aged 79, did football realise what it had lost. But then it was too late.

Alfred Ernest Ramsey was born in Dagenham, Essex, on 22 January 1920, the son of a grocer with Romany roots. He played for Portsmouth, Southampton and Tottenham Hotspur. He captained England. He was a deep-thinking, precise and ultra-cool right-back nicknamed 'The General'.

He became manager of unfashionable Ipswich Town in 1955. In 1962 they won the League Championship. He was appointed England manager the same year and won them the World Cup in 1966, just as he said he would. When Geoff Hurst's decisive hat-trick goal billowed the Wembley net, the England bench went wild – except Alf, who sat impassively and told trainer Harold Shepherdson to 'sit down and behave yourself'.

The aloofness may have been a cover for a deep-seated lack of confidence. Alf felt inferior to the FA 'suits' he habitually referred to as 'those people'. He tried gamely to gentrify his Essex accent, but what came out wasn't quite right. The dropped 'g' and missing 'h', the clipped military tone and his famous 'most certainly' catchphrase were all good fodder for his critics.

But at heart Alf *was* a man of the people. England's 1966 right-back George Cohen tells a great anecdote about the celebration banquet at the Royal Garden Hotel in Kensington on the night England won the World Cup. I hope it's true, because it shows the human side to the real Ramsey, which few ever witnessed.

An overbearing waiter seems particularly keen that England's triumphant manager should have some *petits pois*. Alf turns to look at him with an icy stare. The eyebrows are bushy, his lips barely parted at all. Think a villainous Gerry Anderson puppet and you're not far off.

Alf has had one more drink than he's accustomed to. He is happy. Alf has just won the World Cup for England. He is truly relaxed for the first time in years. Alf addresses the white-coated waiter: 'I don't want no fuckin' peas.'

Of all the wonderful World Cup moments I've encountered while researching this book, that sublime double negative with dropped 'g' and profanity is up there with the very best. Alf is human after all. The players already knew that. He was a strict disciplinarian, but all of them respected him. That's one very good reason why England triumphed in 1966.

Plain old Alf became Sir Alf Ramsey in 1967. He suffered a stroke during the 1998 World Cup finals. He struggled with Alzheimer's disease. When he died, his former player Alan Mullery said simply, 'He was such a nice man. I don't think we will see another like him.'

Would England fans take that enigmatic and strangely unpopular winner back for just one more World Cup campaign? Most certainly.

# BRANDI PULLS IT OFF

## PASADENA, 10 JULY 1999

The event the die-hards thought they would never see first took place in 1991. The USA beat Norway 2–1 in China. But most of the world hardly knew it was on. The Brian Glanville school of thought still reigned. The acerbic football writer had once observed of the shameless participants that 'such an unnatural practice should be permitted, but only in private by consenting adults'.

When it happened for a second time in 1995, the affair was again low-key. Norway beat Germany 2–0 in Sweden. More football fans were aware of it this time, but most were inclined to agree with Ron Atkinson. The master chauvinist had earlier suggested that the players would be 'better off staying in the kitchen'.

But, when it was held for a third time in 1999, an amazing transformation occurred. Attendance records were smashed. Media coverage was unprecedented. The United States president, Bill Clinton, declared the final 'the best sporting event I have ever seen'. Brian Glanville and Ron Atkinson kept strangely quiet. The FIFA Women's World Cup had come of age.

Much of its newfound success was down to rampant promotion. The third Women's World Cup was hosted by the United States and the event was sufficiently well hyped for sponsors and TV companies to overcome their scepticism. The American squad were a gutsy group of girls. And the patriotic opening ceremony roused a nation.

Curiosity got the better of the American public. More than 600,000 tickets were sold. And, when the USA disposed of the highly fancied German and Brazilian sides to advance to the final, passing interest turned to genuine excitement. But, if the world media were to take notice, there had to be something more.

221

In the event, the American defender Brandi Chastain was to lay it on a plate.

The final was held in California's Pasadena Rose Bowl on 10 July 1999. The USA's opponents were China. The crowd of 90,185 was a world record for any women's sporting event. Yet the match itself failed to deliver. There wasn't even a hint of controversy. Isabel, the Peruvian referee, had little trouble controlling a dire defensive affair. Her French assistants, Nicole and Ghislaine, understood the offside rule perfectly. When the game finished 0–0 after extra time, many USA supporters were beginning to question whether 'soccer' really had what it takes. If ever a moment was tailor-made for a dramatic penalty shootout, this was it.

Cue local reporter: 'After a zip-zip tie in regulation and a total shutout in sudden death, we passed from double goose-egg territory into shootout country. China kicked two straight before USA netminder Briana Scurry dove left to bat out a shooting effort from Liu Ying. It stood 4–4 when Brandi Chastain entered the zone and strode straight to the mark to score high right past the left leap of a flailing Gao Hong. That was the killer strike which delivered the World Cup of Soccer Champions to the ecstatic United States squad before a packed stadium of whooping admirers and millions of soccer-mad TV viewers.'

Brandi Chastain did what any footballer would do in the circumstances. She whipped off her white Number 6 shirt, twirled it around her head and slid to her knees before being engulfed by a sea of glistening bodies. The photographer who got the best shot did very well out of it.

That a picture of a 31-year-old ponytailed blonde in a navy-blue sports bra should cause so much of a stir is quite frankly bizarre. But the Americans can be strangely prudish. The newspaper editors who ran with the Brandi shot were considered quite daring. And, when Chastain used the term 'Goddamn' in the post-match interview, middle America was further outraged, seeing it as blasphemy. Brandi became a media star overnight. In a moment of unscheduled spontaneity women's football had got the exposure it had craved for so long.

The victorious team held a victory parade through Disneyland the next day. The shirtless image was networked around the globe. Poster sales boomed. All great fun, but there's a disquieting element of incongruity in the fact that it should have taken an image of a girl in a bra to give the Women's World Cup the lift it needed. Brandi Chastain seemed uncomfortably conscious of that. While acutely aware that she had become famous for the wrong reasons, the offending garment was just too valuable to cast aside completely. Her inevitable book was titled *It's Not About the Bra*. Which sort of suggests it is.

Even members of the Glanville and Atkinson fan club have been forced to accept that women's football is here to stay. And the female World Cup seems set to follow the same oddity-strewn path as its male equivalent. The 2003 tournament should have been played in China but was transferred to the USA following the outbreak of the SARS virus. The final had a strangely familiar feel to it. Sweden were beaten 2–1 via a cruel 'Golden Goal' from the Germans.

China did host the 2007 tournament, at which Germany became the first team to successfully defend a women's world crown. Again the tally of oddities was healthily bolstered. In their opening game the German girls defeated Argentina 11-0 – a record for the Women's World Cup. And their 2-0 victory over Brazil in the final set another mark – Germany completed the entire tournament without conceding a goal.

That the Women's World Cup will go from strength to strength is assured. The FIFA president, Sepp Blatter, predicted as much at USA '99. Shortly before 'Brandi's Final' he declared that 'the future of football is feminine'. Spectator and media interest will certainly grow apace – but will football embrace the feminine touch to the ultimate degree? Only when female players compete alongside men in 'the' World Cup will the journey be complete. That really would be a story – even for *The World Cup's Strangest Moments*.

# *A STIFF DECISION*

## BLOEMFONTEIN, 22 APRIL 2000

When the first World Cup was held in Uruguay in 1930, FIFA's top brass virtually pleaded for participants. But, even after vigorous lobbying, only thirteen teams bothered to turn up.

Seventy-two years later, the goalposts had shifted somewhat. A staggering 195 countries were desperate to compete at the seventeenth World Cup in Japan and South Korea in 2002. But now FIFA made them sweat. Only 32 were allowed.

The upshot of this numerical conundrum was a multi-tiered stage of qualifying games, which was quite mind-boggling in its conception. In some parts of the world, the qualifying tournament began in March 2000 with a preliminary phase, progressed through first-round knockout qualifiers, on to second-round group qualifiers, into the zone finals and then the interzone play-offs. Somewhere along the way I believe there was a round robin.

The system made for some odd games. The Republic of Ireland clinched their finals place only by beating Iran over two legs in the Asian–European final play-off stage. Both Honduras and Trinidad and Tobago negotiated a tortuous run of 22 qualifying games and still missed out on a trip to the finals. There is no such thing as a nice simple system where FIFA are concerned.

All of which means that every fixture counts, even those that the mainstream football nations might consider to be 'quaint'. Take South Africa versus Lesotho, which was played in Bloemfontein on 22 April 2000. South Africa required only a draw to see them progress one step nearer the finals. Lesotho needed a win by three clear goals to avoid being eliminated.

The high stakes made both sides unduly sensitive to all the issues surrounding the game, not least the appointment of a suitable referee. Not only must he be neutral, but also completely immune to any attempts at bribery. Ideally his great-grandmother must never have set foot in either South Africa or Lesotho, and on no account must he be susceptible to black magic.

After careful consideration FIFA selected the Zambian official Boxen Chinagu. Nothing about him seemed in the least bit controversial. As it was, the game proved easy to control. An eager home crowd of eighteen thousand saw Shaun Bartlett score the only goal in a 1–0 win for South Africa. Already 2–0 down from the first leg, Lesotho knew their World Cup trail was at an end. Everybody agreed the match was admirably handled by the Zambian referee. In fact Boxen Chinagu had an exceptionally quiet game. Not least because he wasn't there. The referee's name was Aaron Nkole.

Boxen Chinagu had simply failed to turn up, although, in fairness, his excuse was a reasonable one: Boxen Chinagu was dead. Zambian officials informed squirming FIFA executives that he'd perished in a road accident before the kick-off – six months before the kick-off, to be exact. FIFA are called upon to make many stiff decisions. Asking a dead referee to take charge of a vital World Cup qualifying game wasn't one of their best.

As for South Africa, they did make it all the way to South Korea, but went home after the opening group games with just a single win against Slovenia to their credit. Considering all the trials and tribulations of the qualifying route, they later greeted the announcement that their country had been chosen by FIFA to hold the 2010 World Cup with more than a little joy. Hosts are not required to qualify.

# *SCORING FOR FUN*
## COFFS HARBOUR, 11 APRIL 2001

Football statisticians would be very dull people indeed if records were never broken. That's why the 'statto' types are particularly thankful for those games in which the brave minnows swim with the bigger fish. Something unusual is always likely to happen.

Take the World Cup qualifying game between Fiji and New Zealand on 16 August 1981. Fiji lost it 13–0, which was a record defeat for a World Cup match. But the score provoked a sense of disquiet in the statisticians' camp. Eyewitnesses told of the Fijians drinking copious quantities of brandy in their hotel bar shortly before kick-off. That surely rendered the score a one-off freak. It was too much too soon. As football became ever more sophisticated, it seemed the age of the joke result would pass quietly into obscurity. The statisticians were worried that their conversations might become boring.

But they needn't have been. Almost twenty years later, with an eye on the 2002 World Cup in Japan and South Korea, the Pacific Islanders of Guam entered the qualifiers for the very first time. Few teams break records on their debut, but Guam didn't disappoint. On 24 November 2000 in Tabris, they were beaten 19–0 by Iran.

Hardened statisticians wept with joy at the World Cup record they thought they'd never see. All but the true obsessives, who bewailed the fact that it still didn't beat the all-time Full International record. That belonged to Kuwait 20 Bhutan 0, which stood from 14 February 2000. It seemed the 'St Valentine's Day Massacre' held an unassailable place in football history.

But amazingly that reckoned without Tonga. They also fancied a trip to the 2002 World Cup. On 9 April 2001, less than six months after the Guam debacle, the Tongans faced Australia at

Coffs Harbour, New South Wales, in the Oceania Zone qualifiers. Australia discovered that day why the Kingdom of Tonga is known as 'The Friendly Isles'. The 'Socceroos' ran out winners 22–0.

With both a World Cup and Full International record falling at a stroke, even some of the statisticians were heard to say 'this is getting ridiculous'. Again the pessimists said 'that's safe for all time', but the real experts weren't so sure. They'd been studying the group results.

Remarkably, Tonga had already won a game, beating the Polynesian Islanders Samoa 1–0. Obviously the Samoans were dire. But they in turn had already beaten their near neighbours, American Samoa, by a whacking margin of 8–0. That made the American Samoans much worse than dire.

Just two days after Tonga's undignified stuffing, the theory was put to the test. When Australia entertained American Samoa on 11 April 2001, the Coffs Harbour terrace wags were already talking about 'getting the calculators out'. For ten minutes the joke looked weak, but then the floodgates opened. The fifteen-minute half-time break proved the longest spell without a goal.

The urge to list the times is irresistible – 10, 12, 13, 14, 17, 19, 21, 23, 25, 27, 29, 32, 33, 37, 42, 45, 50, 51, 55, 56, 58, 60, 65, 66, 78, 80, 81, 84, 85, 88, 89. Despite keeping it tight between the 66th and 78th minutes, the visitors were simply overwhelmed. The game finished Australia 31 American Samoa 0. It would be grossly unfair to mention the name of the goalkeeper, Nicky Salapu.

If there's such a state as statisticians' nirvana, the number crunchers attained it that day. Then Seventh Heaven and Cloud Nine quickly followed as they realised that the Aussie striker Archie Thompson had added two more records to their books. His personal tally of 13 goals beat both the World Cup record (7) and the Full International record (10) for a single game.

The post-match analysis produced two of the great interviews of all time. Aussie coach Frank Farina refused to get carried away: 'We don't really look at the opposition. We concentrate on our own game, and it's been working quite well for us lately.'

American Samoa's team manager Tony Langkilde refused to contemplate suicide: 'We're here as part of a learning process. We're FIFA members and have a right to play. We're not too downhearted. We have to build from here. Our players' average age was just eighteen. The only way is forward.'

I suspect he may be right. And there the World Cup high-score trail must surely end. Not that the anoraks will let the subject lie. For what is arguably the strangest 'stat' of all is that American Samoa's group record of 'Played 4, lost 4, no goals scored, and 57 conceded' is not the worst of all time. For that you must look elsewhere in this book (see 'The Road to Damascus').

# BACK FROM THE DEAD
## FREETOWN, 21 APRIL 2001

Let's be honest. For the majority of the African nations, the World Cup qualifying competition is more important than the real thing. Just getting to the finals is everything. Anything extra is a bonus. Even the star-studded 'Super Eagles' of Nigeria knew that. Having made it to both USA '94 and France '98, they were determined to complete a hat trick by playing at the 2002 World Cup. What's more, the Nigerian nation demanded it.

But, approaching the halfway mark of their qualifying campaign, the dead certs were in deep crisis. In a group of five Nigeria lay third behind unfancied Liberia and lowly Sudan. Second favourites Ghana were hot on their tails. The sole no-hopers were Sierra Leone, the one side from 25 African hopefuls not to have registered a win in the 2002 qualifiers. Only one team would qualify from the group.

If Nigeria were to kick-start a revival, their next game provided a perfect opportunity. Sierra Leone were their opponents. Even away in Freetown that was surely a banker. But some of Nigeria's more superstitious fans were nervous. They blamed the unbelievably bad run on a hoodoo. According to them, the spirit of a former Nigerian captain was restless.

Sam 'Zagallo' Opone last played in a World Cup qualifier in October 1969. Thirty years later, living in the southern town of Aladja and largely forgotten, he suffered a stroke, which left him paralysed. As was the way in a nation renowned for its 'traditional medicine', he went to a witch doctor. Europe calls them complementary therapists. But Blacky Awommi was off form. The 'magic sponge' proved ineffective.

The medicine man became concerned for his reputation. Claiming he was owed money for his services, he withdrew treatment only to see his patient expire before the $1,200 bill could be settled. Understandably, Sam Opone's family were in no hurry to pay. So Blacky Awommi took remedial action. He refused to give up the corpse.

He kept Sam Opone's body for four months, right the way through Nigeria's nightmare patch. And, despite the best efforts of the Nigerian FA to secure the release of the ex-player, Blacky Awommi stood firm. As no doubt did the corpse. Blacky also threatened to use magic to kill Opone's son 'Lucky' unless the bill was settled.

Sinister threats apart, the 'Magic Sponger' also had a great eye for PR. Five days before Nigeria travelled to Sierra Leone for their 'turning point' game, his case got a nice write-up in the *Daily Champion*: 'Five months after my father's death I haven't seen his body,' said 'Lucky' Opone. 'We cannot afford this bill. But it has to be paid. Something must be done.'

The formbook suggested it was impossible for Nigeria to lose to Sierra Leone. Especially with the players they had. Joseph Yobo, Taribo West, Finidi George, Jay-Jay Okocha – each was a big star in Europe. Nigeria's Dutch coach Jo Bonfrère was so confident, he promised to resign if his side didn't win.

Freetown's National Stadium was packed on 21 April 2001. Most of the locals had come just to ogle at Nigeria. But on 26 minutes the home crowd erupted as local boy Mansarray Sidique put Sierra Leone one up. And the dead ducks of the group hung on for an 'impossible' 1–0 victory. It seemed Nigeria were cursed. Was Sam Opone's tortured spirit really queering their pitch?

The result caused a huge outcry. Now five points adrift of Liberia's 'Lone Stars', Nigeria's 2002 World Cup hopes lay in shreds. Coach Jo Bonfrère didn't resign, but instead was sacked. As for the highly paid Nigerian squad, they took the only course of action possible. Three days after their shameful loss they had a whip-round and paid Blacky Awommi's bill.

After Sam Opone's corpse was laid to rest and his spirit set free, Nigeria's fortunes changed completely. They beat Liberia 2–0, routed Sudan 4–0 in Khartoum and completed their fixtures in Lagos with a 3–0 victory against Ghana. Favourable results elsewhere saw them qualify for the 2002 World Cup by a single point.

Surprisingly the 'Super Eagles' didn't win a game in the finals. Maybe the journey back from the dead had been too emotionally exhausting. Sam 'Zagallo' Opone remains the only deceased footballer ever to 'participate' in a qualifying campaign.

# A HELL OF A LINE-UP

## ANTANANARIVO, 5 MAY 2001

It's ten minutes to kick-off on 5 May 2001 in Madagascar's bustling capital Antananarivo. The home side prepare to face Tunisia in a 2002 World Cup qualifying game.

Inside the Mahamasina Stadium an expectant crowd of 5,016 await the announcement of the teams. A small colony of ring-tailed lemurs has gathered to enjoy the fun. Any plans the Tunisian coach might have had to dissect the opposition line-up had been swiftly abandoned when the team sheet arrived. The Tannoy crackles into action. Here is the Madagascar side:

Raharison, Radafison, Rakotonbrabe, Radonamaha, Ratsimi-halona, Randriamarozaka, Randrianaivo, Randrianoelison, Razafindrakoto, Rasoanaivo and Ralison.

And to think we had a chuckle when Hoddle and Waddle played together for England. Maybe the Madagascar coach planned to beat Tunisia by a cunning process of disorientation. For good measure, his name was Randriambololona. 'Give us an R' was a popular chant in Madagascar. Naturally, the team played in red. But their subtly ironic nickname was 'Club M'.

If the referee was worried about the spectre of taking names, he didn't outwardly show it. Perhaps he had a long pencil. But it did seem a copout that no Madagascar players were booked in the first half, despite several robust challenges that seemed to warrant certain cards.

With the score at 0–0, and Madagascar still in with a remote chance of qualifying, Randriambololona decided to ring the changes. Radafison was replaced after 46 minutes, but even that didn't relieve the referee of his predicament. Twenty-three minutes into the second half he cautioned the unfortunate substitute, only to be told his name was Ralahajanahary. The hapless official is believed to have said 'Doh!'

The game was still goalless with eighteen minutes to go. Randriambololona decided on another change. Ralison was replaced to provide extra width. The man who gave it was Randrinanteneina. But, alas for Madagascar, the ruse failed. Two goals for Tunisia in the 85th and 90th minutes dashed even the mathematical chances of the islanders qualifying. There was only time for Randrianoelison to get himself booked, probably deliberately, before the gibbering referee ended the game.

Having overcome the hurdle of the most challenging team line-up of all time, Tunisia went on to qualify for the 2002 World Cup in Japan and South Korea, but failed to win a game. As for Madagascar's absence from the finals, commentators throughout the world heaved a collective sigh of relief.

# FANTASY FOOTBALL

## MUNICH, 1 SEPTEMBER 2001

When England and Germany were drawn together in the same group of the 2002 World Cup qualifiers, England fans feared the worst. Since their famous World Cup final triumph in 1966, England's key encounters with the Germans had so often ended in tears. The 3–2 defeat at Mexico '70, the semifinal loss at Italia '90 and another semifinal defeat at Euro '96 – each one was a bitter pill to swallow.

True to form, the qualifying campaign started disastrously. On 7 October 2000 England faced Germany at Wembley in their first game. The fixture carried added emotional significance because it was the last ever international played beneath the twin towers of the grand old stadium. Naturally, Germany spoiled the party. A David Seaman blunder handed the visitors a 1–0 win. Even the timing of the goal (thirteen minutes) smacked of mockery. The England manager Kevin Keegan resigned as a result. Wembley Stadium was demolished.

The return fixture was at the Olympic Stadium in Munich on Saturday, 1 September 2001. Germany stood top of Group 9. England could not afford to lose. But the Germans were unassailable on home territory, and England's new manager Sven-Göran Eriksson was still on trial. Yet again the entire English nation prepared for a night of torture. The sense of inevitability was palpable.

Sure enough, the nightmare continued. After only six minutes Carsten Jancker put Germany ahead. England fans vented their displeasure in rhyme. But then something happened that even a *Roy of the Rovers* scriptwriter might have baulked at. Sven's boys began to play fantasy football.

Michael Owen's equaliser came at the perfect payback time – on exactly thirteen minutes. Steven Gerrard put England 2–1 ahead on the stroke of half-time. Owen nabbed his second three minutes after the break. He completed a stunning hat trick eighteen minutes later. The clock showed 66 minutes. It was a timely tribute to Geoff Hurst, the last Englishman to net three against the Germans. Emile Heskey completed the rout with sixteen minutes left.

The German team looked an utter rabble. Oliver Kahn flapped around in goal like a distressed kipper. His teammates floundered in a sea of mediocrity they didn't have the stomach for. They prayed for the final whistle. Thousands of fans deserted the sinking ship long before the end. Britannia ruled the waves. George had slain the dragon. The scoreboard read DEUTSCHLAND 1 ENGLAND 5.

No England victory had been more of a surprise. England fans were just as stunned as the Germans. The *News of the World* milked it shamelessly: DON'T MENTION THE SCORE – BUT IT'S ENGLAND 5 GERMANY 1. Michael Owen declared himself 'in dreamland' and even the German greats were forced to concede some ground. Franz Beckenbauer grudgingly declared that he had 'never seen a better England team'. Karl-Heinz Rummenigge described the defeat as 'the worst in the entire history of German football'.

England and Germany both made it to the 2002 World Cup. England lost in the quarter-final to Brazil, who went on to beat Germany in the final. So both sides ended losers, but England retained the bragging rights. No one could tarnish the memory of that dreamlike Saturday in September 2001.

Cue Jürgen 'Bubble Burster' Klinsmann: 'We have to give England every acknowledgement for that wonderful 5–1 performance. But remember, it didn't happen in the finals.' There speaks the sort of man who enjoys telling children that Santa Claus doesn't exist. Still, it was good while it lasted.

# PHILATELY GOT THEM EVERYWHERE
## SAN MARINO, 1 APRIL 2002

It's been labelled 'The Postcard Republic' and 'The Italian Lilliput'. With a population of 28,000 and an area of just 23 square miles, it's all too easy to overlook the Republic of San Marino, the tiny landlocked enclave in Northern Italy just south of the Adriatic coastal resort of Rimini.

No wonder its official title is the Most Serene Republic of San Marino. Nothing much happens there. Apart from tourism, its most thriving industry is the production of its famously colourful postage stamps.

As for football, their 1–0 win over fellow microstate Liechtenstein in an April 2004 friendly was San Marino's first competitive victory in 73 years of trying. Their standard World Cup qualifying record is 'bottom of the group with no points'. So, let's face it, the odds on their making this book purely on football merit rated as pretty slim. So, instead, they fell back on philately. When the story broke on 1 April 2002, the date suggested a foolish and rather weak joke. But this one, like the gum on the back of Israel's World Cup stamps, is strictly kosher.

Their own football locker being bare, San Marino's postal authority opted to commemorate the 2002 World Cup with a set of six stamps honouring '*Le grandi vittorie della nationale Italiana.*' Sucking up to the big boy next door is always a sensible move.

The first stamp, marking Italy's World Cup final victory in Rome in 1934, proudly proclaimed the score in bold *azzurri* blue: 'Italy 4 Czechoslovakia 2'. A bit too bold, to be fair. The correct score was 2–1. The second stamp hailed Italy's second final win against Hungary at France '38. This time the score was printed as 1–0 when it was actually 4–2. A case of the Hungarian defence being better on paper than it was on the pitch.

236

Although the rest of the set was spot-on, news of the philatelic own-goal was swiftly posted to agencies all over the world. But despite their unwanted World Cup fame, the San Marino postal authority refused to be licked: 'We have printed 130,000 sets,' said an unflurried spokesman, 'but we shall not recall them. Italy did win both games, so at least we got that right.'

To a nation who lost 10–0 to Norway in a World Cup qualifier in November 1992, accurate scorekeeping has never been high on poor San Marino's agenda. With that in mind, I'll balance their philatelic shame with their one moment of genuine fame. Facing England in Bologna (even 'home' matches are played in Italy) on 17 November 1993 in a World Cup qualifying game, San Marino sensationally scored in 8.3 seconds after a dreadfully short back pass by Stuart Pearce was nicked into England's net by part-timer Davide Gualtieri.

San Marino lost the game 7–1, but remain in the record books for the quickest ever goal scored against England and the fastest in a World Cup qualifier.

That stunning strike also prompted the strangest ever start to a radio commentary. With Graham Taylor's England already doomed to sit out USA '94 at home, Jonathan Pearce went for the irony vote: 'Welcome to Bologna on Capital Gold for England versus San Marino with Tennent's Pilsner brewed with Czechoslovakian yeast for that extra Pilsner taste, and England are one down.'

Now that is worth a commemorative stamp.

# LESSONS IN JAPANESE
## SAITAMA, 2 JUNE 2002

The seventeenth World Cup had an odd look to it from the start. South Korea and Japan became the first co-hosts of the tournament. Even the shorthand title was clumsy – Japorea '02. But the exotic venue was a great hit with travelling supporters, who flocked to the 2002 World Cup seeking a whole new experience. Among them were the thousands of England fans who journeyed to Japan for the 'Group of Death' games against Sweden, Argentina and Nigeria.

But the pending invasion stirred a sense of disquiet in England's Football Association. Courtesy and moderation are important to the Japanese. Some members of England's 'Barmy Army' didn't know the meaning of the words.

That's why the overriding message in the official guidelines was 'make an effort'. It was especially noted that 'the Japanese will be delighted if you attempt their language'.

One particular supporter took this very much to heart. His confidence grew as he studied his phrasebook and realised that a number of English football words had been adopted by the Japanese. 'Penalty', 'corner' and 'offside' were exactly the same. '*Refuri*', '*kipa*' and '*hafu taimu*' were thinly adapted. A *boru* was meant to be kicked and the name of the *gemu* was '*sakka*'. And for post-match there was *biru*, *jin tonniku* and maybe even a *garufurendu*. He was a red-blooded male, after all.

Full of his newfound 'Japanese Made Easy' swagger, he decided to take the plunge. On the day of England's opening game against Sweden in Saitama, he visited a shop that printed slogans on T-shirts. He explained what he wanted. The nearest Japanese equivalent to ENGLAND ON TOUR – I LOVE JAPAN.

His efforts at bridging the language gulf seemed to work. Many knowing nods were elicited from the locals as he travelled to the game. Everywhere he went they smiled, some more overtly than others. The game against Sweden finished 1–1. Then England famously beat Argentina and drew against Nigeria. But, despite their advance to the second round, our language student wasn't happy.

No one had told him that the deferential modesty of the Japanese can be balanced by a wicked sense of humour. After being tipped off by a sympathetic translator, he quickly added a curt and exaggeratedly gruff '*no-sankyu*' to his growing repertoire. The T-shirt read GAY SUBMISSIVE ENGLISHMAN SEEKS MUSCULAR JAPANESE BOY.

# THE TWELFTH MAN

## INCHEON, 14 JUNE 2002

One of the most memorable things about the 2002 World Cup was the fervour displayed by the supporters of co-hosts South Korea. They seemed instinctively to know that 'fan' is merely a contraction of 'fanatic'.

They called themselves the 'Red Devils'. They worshipped their team via an uneasy combination of semi-militarised precision and wide-eyed innocence seldom seen in Europe or South America. More experienced fans cynically prepare for defeat even before it arrives. Generally speaking, it lessens the blow. But the 'Red Devils' were naïve. A young man named Lee certainly didn't know the drill. Not being prepared to accept defeat proved to be his downfall.

If you've anticipated a post-match suicide you've got it wrong. This was more novel. Like most of us, Lee had dreams of being on the pitch helping his heroes to victory. And, as South Korea prepared to face Portugal in their final Group D game, he knew they couldn't afford to lose. Defeat spelled elimination at the first hurdle, a fate no World Cup host had ever suffered in sixteen previous tournaments. That was unthinkable. Swept along by the mounting hysteria, Lee resolved to help his beloved South Korea win the match.

A few hours before the game kicked off in Incheon on Friday, 14 June, he went to the municipal beach in the southeastern city of Pusan. Before many witnesses, he bowed several times towards the sea, doused himself with paint thinner and set himself alight. He died from terrible burns on his way to hospital.

The translation of his suicide note revealed all:

I am choosing death because South Korea has far to go to compete with Latin American and European teams. So I will be a ghost, the 12th player on the pitch, and do my best for the team.

If he did get on, he must have had a decent game. After 27 minutes the Argentine referee Sanchez dismissed Portugal's star striker João Pinto. On 66 minutes he red-carded Beto. Was the twelfth man calling on celestial help? Spookily, the referee's first name was Angel.

With a two-man advantage South Korea scored the only goal of the game in the seventieth minute. Lee's dream had materialised. South Korea further surprised the watching world by progressing to the semifinals, where they lost 1–0 to Germany. But their phantom twelfth man never did see them lose.

Doctors later explained that Lee was suffering from 'a mental disorder aggravated by a mass psychosis surrounding Korea's role as World Cup hosts'. I believe his to be the first 'pre-victory suicide' in World Cup history, but 'post-defeat suicide' is more common. When Brazil lost 2–1 to their fierce rivals Uruguay in the 1950 final, 'several suicides' were reported by the press.

Even qualifying games have claimed victims. In Umuahia in March 2001, a Nigerian fan threatened to drink poison if his side didn't beat Ghana in Accra. After the 0–0 result he took a hearty swig from a bottle. 'Only after he started foaming at the mouth and died did we take him seriously,' said an unintentionally humorous witness.

In 1964 the Liverpool manager Bill Shankly drily referred to football as being 'much more important than life and death'. He never intended it to be taken literally. Sadly, the 'Red Devil' and his ilk took Shankly at his word.

# *JAFFA CAKES AND THAT*
## FARNHAM, 19 JUNE 2002

In the very early days of international football it was not unheard of for an England team to enjoy a full roast lunch in preparation for an afternoon game. A hearty feed was then considered to bolster a fellow's strength. Madness surely - how could they possibly have managed without a specialist dietician?

In 2002 the England manager Sven-Göran Eriksson, supported by a myriad of backroom staff, set out to demonstrate the utter folly of their long-dead counterparts. But the comedic episode that followed, shot through with huge dollops of absurdity, ended only in abject failure. Meat and two veg might have been better all along.

The madness began with a press release on 2 April. That was two months ahead of England's opening fixture against Sweden in the 2002 World Cup in Japan. Sadly, this woeful tale of 'overegging the pudding' wasn't an April Fools' hoax. David Beckham and the squad win the World Cup for England for the only time since 1966'.

After visiting Japan on a meticulously planned, all-expenses-paid fact-finding mission, England's food guru revealed his secret weapon. It would be jaffa cakes. Roger outlined his plans in a finely honed speech: 'Mostly it's sushi and noodles and stuff over there. I'll mainly use fish and local produce because they're great in Japan. But some vital things you just can't get. We'll be bringing our own jaffa cakes, baked beans and cereals like shredded wheat and that.'

The hopes of a nation ought to have surged afresh. Strangely, they didn't. The Delia Smith of the England camp pursued the point by fixating on the key part of the scientifically formulated diet and that: 'The thing with jaffa cakes is that they're high in carbohydrate, low in fat and a great store of energy. We'll use them before the game, and then in the refuelling process afterwards.'

By the start of May, the England manager also seemed convinced that the delicious combination of light sponge, dark chocolate and that smashing orangey bit in the middle would see 'Team Jaffa' sweep aside the likes of Brazil. Sven smiled knowingly as the McVitie's (the biscuit makers) press officer Sarah Goodfellow upped the ante: 'Jaffa cakes taste great and are full of mischief. That should give us the edge on the pitch.'

By the end of the first- and second-round matches, the jaffa supplies had eased England into a quarter-final clash with Brazil. And no one had accused them of being jammy. Then, on 19 June, two days before the monumental game, providential news came from afar. Twenty-four-year-old Jim Peacock from Farnham, Surrey, contacted the press: DAVID BECKHAM'S FACE FOUND ON JAFFA CAKE must be the weirdest World Cup headline of all time.

Jim was beside himself: 'I was about to put it in my mouth when I saw Becks staring back at me from the chocolate. I couldn't believe it.' McVitie's brand manager Lisa Wakely was quick to see an opportunity: 'We all know that jaffa cakes are England's secret weapon. This is a sign of victory for Friday's game.'

Friday's game is covered in the next story (see 'BBC Blue'). Suffice to say that by the end of it England supporters were united in a single thought. They knew exactly where the nutritionist and the Swede should stick their secret weapon. Sideways and that.

# BBC BLUE

## SHIZUOKA, 21 JUNE 2002

There are times for every supporter when genuine hope turns into such abject despair that a rational and objective view of events is simply impossible to summon up. That's why we have pundits, none of whom come more highly acclaimed than those from the BBC, that eloquent purveyor of impartial good taste in all matters sporting.

Friday, 21 June, proved a desperately bad day for England fans. After a comfortable 3–0 win against Denmark in the second round of the 2002 World Cup, most of the nation felt 'cautiously optimistic' as England prepared to face Brazil in the quarter-final. Manager Sven-Göran Eriksson was adamant that David Beckham had 'fully recovered' from a fractured second meta-tarsal. David Seaman was still 'England's number one'. Paul Scholes looked rock-solid. Men of such calibre were utterly to be relied upon.

When Liverpool's Michael Owen put England ahead on 23 minutes, cautious optimism turned to genuine expectation. Suddenly, a favourable semifinal clash with Turkey or Senegal looked a real possibility. That could mean Germany in the final. Thoughts rushed ahead to another 1966. This time Beckham, Seaman and Scholes would be the heroes.

With seconds to go to half-time, Beckham jumped exaggeratedly out of a tackle tight on the touchline, hoping the ball would run for an England throw-in (not protecting his foot, heaven forbid!). But Brazil kept it in. Scholes, thrown off his guard, missed the backup challenge. The ball was swiftly moved to Rivaldo, who levelled with a clinical finish on 46 minutes and 49 seconds.

Four minutes after the break, England conceded again. Ronaldinho's speculative free kick – half cross, half shot –

afforded David Seaman ample time to judge the ball's flight and pluck it from the air. But England's (soon to be deposed) number one seemed to be wearing concrete boots. The ball sailed into his top right corner.

When Ronaldinho was shown a red card just seven minutes later, an England comeback looked possible, but Brazil used every trick in the book to stifle the game. Eriksson's substitution of Michael Owen in the 79th minute finally signalled that England had lost the plot. They lost the game 2–1 and crashed out.

The collective shoulders of a nation sagged as never before. Irrational recriminations and the most outrageous profanities were hurled around with reckless abandon. It was time for the BBC to justify its licence money. Cue balanced rhetoric.

Gary 'The Queen Mother of Football' Lineker chaired the panel. Alan 'Diabolical Defending' Hansen led the pundits. Ian 'Wright Wright' Wright, a passionate former England striker, completed the mix. After the main broadcast was concluded, digital subscribers were invited to press the red button for extended analysis. The blue button would have been more appropriate.

Soon after the link began, the screen went blank and an orange box appeared showing a 'service disconnected' announcement. The pundits thought their satellite time had expired. But the sound stayed on for another ten minutes.

Lineker asked Hansen which match was on next: 'It's the fucking Krauts,' replied the Scot, before treating himself to a good laugh at England's expense as Ian Wright eloquently rationalised the action: 'Seaman was fucking five yards off his line, man. And what the fuck was Eriksson doing taking fucking Michael Owen off?'

More effing and blinding followed as Peter 'Every Other Word' Reid informally joined the discussion and Wright continued his tirade of abuse against England's sorry performance. Hansen, still apparently beside himself with glee at England's tragic demise, finally wound the proceedings up: 'Right, let's go down the pub. It's karaoke time for you boys.'

A po-faced spokesman for the BBC later apologised for the 'unfortunate technical fault which meant private banter and post-match repartee was inadvertently broadcast'. Lineker and the team were said to be mortified.

Strangely, there were virtually no viewer complaints. A nation devastated by defeat simply delivered its own measured verdict. Hansen was nothing but a Scottish ******. Wrighty was ******* spot-on. Reidy was ******* well right. And no one gave a **** about the BBC. It was a black day for England and a very blue one for the red-faced pundits.

## ONE FOR THE FUTURE

### FUKUOKA, 25 JUNE 2002

Everybody in Japan for the 2002 World Cup agreed on one thing: the local boy Nagoya showed astonishing promise. World-weary journalists waxed lyrical about 'economy of effort and graceful movement'. Commentators praised his 'uncanny 360-degree vision'. After just six years in football, Nagoya's ability was certainly remarkable. Shrewd scouts wrote 'one to watch' in their notebooks. He needed to be developed. He was only three feet tall.

Welcome to the sixth Robot World Cup ('RoboCup' for short) in Fukuoka, where Nagoya and his identical humanoid teammates emerged triumphant. But no dismissive jokes, please. While the human World Cup was being played elsewhere in Japan, the robots were planning a very serious future.

It was in 1993 that Professor Alan Mackworth from the University of British Columbia in Canada first mooted the possibility of robot football. The idea greatly appealed to the Japanese robotics expert Hiroaki Kitano. Before the scientific community could say R2-D2 and C-3P0 he was assembling a squad. The rest of the world responded in kind. So in 1997 Kitano launched RoboCup.

The players made great strides (if a little stiff at times) and the tournament became an annual event. By 2002, robots from 29 different countries were airing their skills before a total audience of nearly 120,000 spectators.

But let's not get carried away. I've seen the footage. Baby Tigers (Japan) against Dirty Dozen (Germany) looked remarkably like a contest between toasters on wheels. And those in the Four-Legged League ('Robomutts') appeared to spend most of the time sniffing each other's shorts. Essex Rovers (England) lost on penalties. Elvis from Sweden fell over and couldn't get up again. Even the giants of the Humanoid League were way off the pace.

But Hiroaki Kitano is a man not easily deterred. 'We have big plans,' he said. 'In 1997 the robots were mostly remote-controlled, and even the best could barely recognise a ball. Now they are completely autonomous and are able to seek possession and interact with their teammates.'

And he didn't stop there. Kitano has set out a mission statement for FIRA (Fédération Internationale de RoboCup Association), which is frightening in its simplicity: 'By 2050 FIRA will produce a team of fully autonomous humanoid robot soccer players which shall win a game complying with official FIFA rules against the reigning human World Cup soccer champions.'

Having seen the robots play, I am not inclined to shout 'Come on, you Humanoids' or 'Up the Bots' with any degree of confidence. Even England's Ray 'The Crab' Wilkins on a bad day played fewer sideways passes than Nagoya at his best. But that's just the sort of remark Hiroaki Kitano thrives on: 'Remember that the world's first electronic digital computer was developed only in 1947. Look at where we are now. In 1997 a computer called "Deep Blue" beat the world chess champion Garry Kasparov. All that in fifty years.'

That can't be denied. But chess is a game of intellect – one in which a blindfolded chimpanzee might challenge the average footballer with some degree of confidence. But football is all about physical movement. That's where the humanoid robots fall down, literally.

But again the RoboCup fraternity have an answer. Listen to Jong-Hwan Kim, president of FIRA: 'People scoff at their peril. The world is changing in unprecedented ways and with unimaginable speed. A robot age only dreamed about and depicted in science fiction will soon become a reality.'

I'll take a chance and scoff at my peril. The odds on a bunch of humanoids beating the winners of the 2050 World Cup are about the same as Wayne Rooney becoming a chess grand master.

# THE OTHER FINAL

## THIMPHU, 30 JUNE 2002

The first World Cup of the new millennium was a glittering multimillion-dollar extravaganza. On Sunday, 30 June, in the Yokohama Stadium, Japan, the two most successful teams in World Cup history fittingly met in the final. Brazil triumphed 2–0 over Germany, both goals coming from Ronaldo. The 'Samba Boys' had set a new record by winning all seven of their games. Brazil were indisputably the best team in the world.

Yet this was also a day for underdogs. Just a few hours earlier, but many miles away, another game had already been played to decide 'the worst team in the world'. A documentary about this otherworldly 'alternative fixture' was made by a Dutch film company. They called it *The Other Final*.

The match that has been called 'an antidote to all the commercial ills of big football' would never have occurred but for Holland's shock failure to qualify for the 2002 World Cup. It set filmmaker Johan Kramer pondering the plight of failure. What if the two *worst* teams in the world had their very own final? Blessed with FIFA's approval, Kramer was soon calling 'lights, camera, action' at the ultimate play-off.

Propping up the FIFA world rankings at 203 were Montserrat, from the Caribbean island famous for little more than its beautiful scenery and active volcanoes. National sport, cricket. Towering above them at a lofty 202 were Bhutan, representing the tiny and remote Himalayan Kingdom where men wear 'kilts', ancient Buddhist traditions reign, and football pitches are a luxury in themselves. National sport, archery.

Being patently the senior side, Bhutan were given home advantage. Poor Montserrat took five gruelling days to travel to the capital Thimphu. While seven of their players were being laid low by food poisoning en route, the Bhutanese calmly relaxed and sharpened their skills ready for the big game. When it came, the Chlanlimithang Stadium (altitude 7,500 feet) played host to a record crowd of 15,000, three times the entire population of Montserrat.

Fair play and enjoyment were the order of the day in the game dubbed 'Highlanders versus Islanders'. No sponsorship or advertising sullied the scene, and not a single call girl visited the hotel room of the English referee Steve Bennett. In true Corinthian spirit, schoolchildren were kitted out in the colours of both sides to make the cheering equal. And all tickets for the 'Shangri La final' were free. Everything was so laid back it wasn't so much high drama as high lama.

It proved to be no day for giant-killers. Cecil Park in the islanders' goal had a bad time as favourites Bhutan romped home 4–0 winners. So now it was official. Montserrat were 'the worst side in the world'. Not that Bhutan made too much of the bragging rights. True to the spirit of the game, the trophy was shared. After the presentation, both camps repaired to a local bar to watch their own 'other final', Germany versus Brazil.

All agreed the day was a great success. The former World Cup star Roberto Baggio, a devotee of the Buddhist faith, summed it up: 'This match showed the real spirit of football. It is a language which every nation, rich or poor, large or small, can speak. At a time when commercialism rules, here is an almost naïve project that puts pure love for the game above all else.'

As for the managers, not a single morsel of pizza was thrown. Even so, they were quick to copy the interview style of their professional counterparts. 'For the last four weeks we trained really hard, and the boys translated that into goals,' said Bhutan's Dutch coach, Aric Schanz. The Montserrat boss, William Lewis, was marginally less effusive: 'The altitude played a very big role.'

# LUCK OF THE IRISH

## YOKOHAMA, 30 JUNE 2002

When the Yokohama International Stadium in Japan staged the seventeenth World Cup final on 30 June 2002, there was nothing about the game itself that was in the least bit strange by 21st-century standards. Two teams played. One won. The other lost. A dog didn't score the winning goal.

So it was odd that Dr Peter O'Donoghue, one of the 2.5 billion worldwide TV audience, stared at the screen with such strange intensity. It was as if his entire reputation depended on it. Make no mistake, this was one anxious man.

And not without reason. Accompanied by much media hype, the sports studies lecturer from the University of Ulster had used a sophisticated computer model to predict the outcome of the final before the tournament had even started. And he had no desire to hear his students reciting an old Irish-Japanese proverb at his expense: 'Egg on face comes to him whose dick is too clever.'

The computer model left nothing to chance – none of the hunches based on years of experience that were favoured by mere supporters. It predicted that Brazil, universally regarded as one of the greatest sides in the world, and already four times winners, would lift the 2002 World Cup. Their final opponents would be Italy, who were also known as a team who could play a bit.

Before the tournament began Dr O'Donoghue spoke excitedly to BBC News: 'This is number crunching versus subjective judgement. The pundits have predicted Argentina to beat Italy in the final. But I'm confident. My model takes into account FIFA world ranking, distance travelled and rest between games. I've run the simulation two thousand times and it's definitely Brazil to beat Italy.'

So confident was Dr O'Donoghue that for the first time in his life he entered a betting shop. He placed £20 on that exact outcome. When both Italy and Brazil advanced from their groups to the knockout stage, things looked well on track. But the second round brought a slight glitch. Italy (FIFA ranking 6) lost 2–1 to South Korea (FIFA ranking 40). Some careless junior assistant must have under-tweaked the 'distance' factor.

Despite the £20 loss and much joyous sniping from his critics, it was with some relief that Dr O'Donoghue saw Brazil cruise to the final. Being Irish, he didn't even mind their knocking out England on the way. In any case, the computer had predicted England's elimination – by the French in the second round. Which would have been possible but for the fact that France (FIFA ranking 1) went out in Round One. The reigning World Cup holders failed to score a single goal in the tournament and even contrived to lose to Senegal (FIFA ranking 42).

Brazil faced Germany in the final. All was not lost. A win for Brazil would still guarantee the headline, COMPUTER PREDICTS WORLD CUP WINNER. That would be enough, especially as rival academics were already suffering 'egg on face' trauma. Warwick University's GARI (Glover Automated Results Indicator) had predicted an Argentina triumph by some margin. After they failed to get past the group stage, the computer's keeper Henry Stott tried damage limitation: 'We're far from perfect. In reality, the point of football is for us to marvel at the underlying chaos and unpredictability of the game.' Loose translation: 'My sophisticated model failed utterly. It's a funny old game, Brian.'

A German win in the final would also have left the yolk on Dr O'Donoghue. But Brazil saved his bacon. Ronaldo scored both goals in the 2–0 victory, which secured the Brazilians their fifth World Cup triumph.

Newspapers around the world duly paid homage to the computer clairvoyants. Dr. O'Donoghue fairly beamed with pride. Forget the Italy blip. And the £20. Wasn't it truly amazing that a computer had predicted Brazil as winners from a field of 32 teams? Or maybe it was just the luck of the Irish.

# SIX POINTS TO FIFA

## PARIS, 21 MAY 2004

At their Centennial Congress in Paris on Friday, 21 May 2004, FIFA handed six points to Cameroon that they had already 'lost'. And the qualifying competition didn't even begin until June.

Confused? So were Cameroon's upcoming opponents, Egypt, Ivory Coast, Libya, Sudan and Benin. What lay behind FIFA's latest bout of dithering ineptitude was a debate over the toughest question ever posed in the illustrious history of the World Cup: 'When are shirts and shorts not shirts and shorts?'

Cameroon's unduly narcissistic relationship with their natty green, red and yellow strip first hit the headlines at Italia '90. The fashion guru John Galliano labelled it 'a real cool look', and thousands of youngsters evidently agreed, as the manufacturers of Subbuteo were inundated by requests for team sets painted in the new colours. Extra recruits were taken on to meet demand.

Cameroon and their sponsors realised they could turn heads and empty wallets without actually winning football matches. In the 2002 African Cup of Nations in Mali, they plumped for grungy sleeveless shirts of the style worn in Australian Rules football. FIFA raised a paternal eyebrow and strictly forbade the wearing of 'vests' at the 2002 World Cup in Japan and South Korea. The 'Indomitable Lions' obeyed the dictate, but only by adding odd-looking 'temporary' sleeves. They were sailing ever closer to the wind.

It was a case of FIFA's authority versus Cameroon's exuberance, and the footballers recruited an unlikely ally. At the 2002 French Open, the tennis star Serena Williams played in a sleeveless green shirt, red shorts, yellow football socks and yellow and green trainers, a tribute dreamed up by her sponsor Puma, whom she shared with Cameroon: 'They're the greatest soccer team in Africa,' drooled the American, before admitting she couldn't name a single player.

The stand-off reached a head during the 2004 African Cup of Nations in Tunisia. In their opening match against Algeria on 25 January, Cameroon sported an all-in-one Lycra-style outfit branded the UniQT (Uni-kit), in which the shorts and shirts formed a single garment. For practicality and added fun, there were concealed zips on the shoulders and blood-red claw marks across the socks and ribcage.

FIFA spluttered loudly. They pointed to Law 4 of the Laws of Association Football. That specified 'shirts and shorts' as the sole acceptable attire. After much argument Cameroon were permitted to wear the offending article in the opening stages, but FIFA specifically forbade it for the quarter-final against Nigeria. When Cameroon openly defied the directive, they again stole the headlines, despite losing the game.

FIFA finally decided it was time to make an example of the fashion rebels. In Zurich on 16 April 2004 they docked Cameroon an automatic six points from their 2006 World Cup qualifying campaign, which was due to commence in June. They also levied a $154,000 fine. Now Cameroon spluttered. With thirty points up for grabs from ten games, a deduction of six was a considerable blow. Egypt and the others feigned sympathy but sniggered quietly as Cameroon planned an appeal.

To FIFA's credit they stuck to their guns, quickly dismissing the appeal with an iron fist. But only a few weeks later they began to toy with the velvet glove, as Cameroon's German lawyers threatened to take the case all the way to the Court of Arbitration for Sport. What's more, they issued a sinister threat: 'If necessary, we will be suing FIFA for substantial damages.'

The Confederation of African Football then presented a petition of support, which carried the signatures of all 52 African countries. When it came to the crunch, none of Cameroon's group rivals wanted to be seen as spoilsports. On 21 May 2004 Cameroon were given back their 'lost' six points by a FIFA legislature scared stiff of a legal humiliation.

'Do not see this as a U-turn,' urged the FIFA president Sepp Blatter. 'It is merely a pardon.' But everybody knew that football's world governing body had bottled it, lured into submission by a team of expensive German lawyers, pushy Puma marketing executives and influential African delegates.

Does that mean that a coach and horses has been driven through the 'shirts and shorts' rule? Who knows until someone puts it to the test again. And what other boundaries might be crossed? Anyone for playing in skins? Only one thing is certain: whenever Cameroon are playing, all eyes will be on their kit.

# A BROTHERLY CHAT

## ADELAIDE, 29 MAY 2004

Some questions in football are best left unasked. So here's a word of warning. Unless you have a great deal of time on your hands, never ask a trivia fiend about brothers playing in the World Cup. Read this instead. It's much quicker.

If ever you should ask the fateful question, the fevered response will generally begin with events in Adelaide on 29 May 2004. Australia beat New Zealand 1–0 in their opening qualifier for the 2006 World Cup. Included in the 'Socceroos' line-up was Max Vieri, born in Sydney but then playing for the Italian club Napoli. But his superstar brother Christian (of Inter Milan fame) had already played many times for Italy on account of being born in Bologna. They were the first brothers to play for different countries in World Cup games.

Once faced with such a revelation, you'll probably give a stock reply: 'That's strange. Two brothers both reaching the pinnacle of their sport must be quite unusual. It wasn't in the World Cup finals, though. *That* must be really rare.'

But in giving that nice polite response you have just committed a cardinal sin. You have given the anorak from hell what's known as an 'in'. The Monologue from Hell will go something like this: 'Not rare at all. Just think of England. There's Gary and Phil Neville. And Bobby and Jack Charlton when we won it in '66. The only other brothers to get winners' medals were Fritz and Ottmar Walter in 1954, both in the West German side that beat Hungary. And they were the only brothers to score in the same match – two apiece in the semifinal against Austria.

'But,' continues the Monologue, 'even they weren't the first brothers to play in a World Cup final. Juan and Mario Evaristo were in the Argentina side that lost to Uruguay in the very first final in 1930. Two other brothers from that World Cup have a claim to fame as well. Manuel and Felipe Rosas turned out for Mexico against France in the first World Cup game ever played. No one can beat that. Same as Willy and René van de Kerkhof for Holland in the 1978 final when they lost to Argentina. They were twins. And both of them scored in Round Two – Willy against Austria and René against West Germany. But each in the 82nd minute. How spooky is *that*?'

At this point it would be wisest not to answer but instead to quietly slip away to a 'prior engagement'. But almost certainly he'll be too quick for you (they're always male, by the way) and launch into Phase Two: 'Odd things seem to happen to brothers. Remember Cameroon in the first match of Italia '90 against Argentina? Kana Biyick got sent off and five minutes later Omam Biyick scored the winner. No brothers have done that before. Like the two Russians from 1982, the only goalkeeping brothers ever chosen for a World Cup squad. Viktor and Vyacheslav Chanov. Shame neither got a game.

'A really bizarre one was Luis and Mario Perez, the Mexican brothers. Luis played in the 1930 World Cup and Mario in 1950. Mario must have been an afterthought. Strange thing is, his son Mario junior played exactly twenty years later at Mexico '70. That's not brothers, though.

'Do managers count?' asks the Monologist. 'Zeze Moreira was in charge of Brazil at Switzerland '54 and his brother Aimore managed them at Chile '62, when they won it. There's a thought. I wonder if Fabio Capello has a brother. Wayne Rooney has. Wouldn't really be ready until 2014, though. Rooney might have shot it by then.'

This rambling moment of crisis is the ideal point to introduce what ought to be a neat line of closure: 'You've got an incredible knowledge. That must be all the brothers in World Cup history.' But that also would be futile. 'In' number two has just been delivered gift-wrapped on a plate: 'Not by a long way. What about Michael and Brian Laudrup for Denmark at France '98? I'll bring the list in next time I see you. And there are loads more in the qualifiers. Just think about that.'

My advice is don't. But our learned friend does have a point of sorts. Having one son playing in a World Cup would be enough for most parents to be proud of. That so many have had two is one of the more remarkable statistics to be found in the World Cup record books.

# BRING MAVIS ON

## VIENNA, 4 SEPTEMBER 2004

Many England internationals have suffered ignominious moments in the pursuit of World Cup glory, but none has matched the cruel ridicule heaped on one particular player after a 2006 World Cup qualifying game. Even before the match he was known as 'Calamity James'. After it he was the victim of every bad pun his critics could muster. And the distasteful incident led to the most remarkable few days in England's recent history.

The Manchester City goalkeeper David James had a reputation for costly errors. But, as England prepared to face Austria in Vienna on 4 September 2004, Sven-Göran Eriksson stuck by his man. But the fans were worried. This was England's first qualifying game for Germany 2006. A good start was vital.

Two-thirds of the way through the game all the anxiety seemed unfounded. Chelsea's Frank Lampard had put England ahead via a well-worked free kick after 24 minutes, and Liverpool's Steven Gerrard added a classy screamer twenty minutes into the second half. Even though David James had looked dodgy at times, England fans began to relax. Austria were ranked 89th in the world. A comeback looked unlikely.

Fans watching at home on television assumed an air of joviality. One of the Austrians was named Sick. The captain was Ivanschitz. Their coach was Hans Krankl. Much schoolboy tittering ensued. Newspaper editors were already toying with headlines: IT'S A WALTZ FOR ENGLAND, GOODNIGHT VIENNA, STRUDEL IN THE PARK FOR SVEN'S MEN, APFEL DO NICELY. A three-point opener couldn't be bettered.

A week may be a long time in politics, but nowhere near as long as three minutes in football. Happenings between the 71st and 73rd changed everything. First the Austrian substitute

Roland Kollman pulled one back with a Beckhamesque free kick, then Andreas Ivanschitz tried a speculative shot from outside the box. David James dived but it slithered under his body. As goalkeeping bloopers go, this one was a howler.

Austria hung on for the 2–2 draw and England forfeited two points that they'd already had in the bag. To say the English press reacted badly would be an understatement. The huge banner headlines, JESSIE and JAMES THE WORST, were almost kind compared with the ridicule heaped on James by the *Sun*. The unforgiving tabloid ran a mocking campaign suggesting a donkey could do better in goal than the calamitous custodian.

But then it went further. They actually found a donkey, stuck it in goal, and rolled shots at it until the hapless creature stubbornly flicked one away with its hind legs. Soon Mavis the donkey was a media star. The *Sun* ran the photo under the headline ASS MORE LIKE IT. A pair of donkey ears was superimposed on a picture of the England keeper. The caption read, '*Sun* donkey goalie saves shot James couldn't'.

The hysteria might have died down quickly had England's second qualifying game not been scheduled for four days later. They faced Poland in Chorzów on 8 September. Would Sven stick with James? The *Sun* decided to give him a little help by asking its readers to vote on their 'Eeyore the Jury' telephone hotline. The result was a landslide: 95 per cent voted for Mavis to replace James in goal against Poland. Sven-Göran Eriksson duly dropped him from the side.

Did Sven take notice of the *Sun* readers? Had he had the donkey watched? No one will ever know. But the spectacle of a donkey making a first ever World Cup appearance was cleverly averted by drafting in the Spurs keeper Paul Robinson. England beat Poland 2–1. Robinson had a fine game. The qualification campaign was back on track.

And that should have been that. But, instead of letting the result do the talking, the England players used their mouths – or not, as the case may be. After the game they sent the press to Coventry as a protest for their shameful treatment of James. 'Our lips are sealed,' they chorused, at least in mind.

Taking a vow of silence might have seemed a good idea at the time, but it only angered the press afresh. David Lacey of the *Guardian* really let rip: 'Beckham and his fellow conspirators stalked off to the team coach with lips pursed and noses aloft like Roedean schoolgirls ignoring jeering ragamuffins.' It was left to an FA spokesman to splutter a feeble explanation that the players' feelings had been 'severely hurt'.

The 'Mavis the donkey' saga was one of the oddest in World Cup history. But that a simple goalkeeping error should have escalated to such a degree probably says more about the *Sun* and the egos of highly paid footballers than it does about the World Cup itself.

Amid all the vitriol, two observations are worth repeating. Brian Reade in the *Mirror* put the player protest into perspective: 'If anyone was going to go on strike over such an outrageous slur on their colleagues it should have been the animals at Chester Zoo.' And he was joined by the American journalist Ben Knight: 'Mavis the donkey is far more qualified to edit the *Sun* than she is to tend goal for England.'

But the fallout is difficult to ignore. A Google internet search for 'Donkey "David James"' scores 4,690 hits. A search for 'the excellent goalkeeping of David James' returns a big fat zero. The only amazing thing is that not a single critic suggested that the man deposed by a donkey should be put out to grass at the Irish club Bray Wanderers. Even the *Sun* missed that one.

# ONCE UPON A TIME
## VADUZ, 9 OCTOBER 2004

Surprise results are fairly commonplace in World Cup qualifying games. Genuine shocks rather less so. But the true rarities, the ones that really upset the apple cart, carry the scarcest tag of all. Even the most hyperbolic football writer knows that 'fairy tale' has to be reserved for the truly unexpected. Like the astonishing five days experienced by Liechtenstein in October 2004.

Much about the independent principality of Liechtenstein is unusual. Its population of only 33,000 is smaller than the ground capacities of many of the international sides the country have played football against. Its one prison could barely hold a World Cup squad – 22 criminals and it's full. There are only eleven towns and no such thing as the Liechtenstein League. Its seven football clubs play in the Swiss League. Their top international scorer is 'Super' Mario Frick. At the last count his all-time haul was a princely seven.

The territory is sandwiched between Austria and Switzerland. Its capital Vaduz is dominated by a sixteenth-century castle perched high in the Alps. Every year on National Day the sovereign invites the entire population of the country into his garden for a glass of wine. Exactly the right setting for a football fairy tale, but statistics suggested that making one happen was an impossible dream.

Liechtenstein first competed in the World Cup qualifiers in 1998. An aggregate loss of 16–1 against Romania was just one of the humiliating reverses they suffered. The worst was an 11–1 home bashing by Macedonia. Things were little better in 2002. In fact Liechtenstein had established such a reputation as a joke side that they became the subject of a humorous travel book.

*Stamping Grounds* saw the author Charlie Connelly following the team's progress throughout the 2002 World Cup qualifiers. The thrust of the affectionate but irreverent tome was that he wanted to see Liechtenstein win just one game. But much was against them. Most of their players were part-time. Their star sweeper had to miss a match to bring in his wine harvest. Alas, the brave assortment of bankers, postmen and sundry artisans lost every game and failed to score a single goal. Connelly's book became a bestseller. Liechtenstein became football's celebrity fall guys.

Not that they were deterred. They entered the qualifying competition for Germany 2006 hoping for an improvement. But their start suggested another clean sweep of defeats. In August 2004 they lost 2–1 at home to Estonia and the following month were beaten 7–0 in Bratislava by Slovakia. And the fixtures made uncomfortable reading. The next visitors to Vaduz were Portugal, the star-studded runners-up in the 2004 European Championships.

Betting men might have put their mortgage on a Portuguese win. In four previous games against Liechtenstein, the aggregate score stood 28–0. Portugal were ranked eighth in the world. Liechtenstein languished at 151st. In more than sixty inter-nationals Liechtenstein had registered only one win in a competitive fixture – against Azerbaijan in 1998. Most damning of all, they had lost against the Faroe Islands and San Marino, two super-minnows. Portugal had won both their qualifying games so far without conceding a goal. The prospects looked grim.

The game against Portugal took place at the Rheinpark in Vaduz on 9 October 2004. The Portuguese cruised into a 2–0 lead in 39 minutes. The second goal was an own goal. The referee's name was Panic. Liechtenstein might well have done.

No one knows what was said at half-time, but by the 78th minute the score stood at 2–2. And there it stayed. A draw might not seem such a fairy-tale result, but in truth it was one of the biggest shocks ever recorded in international football.

The Portuguese press were unforgiving. The daily tabloid *Correio de Manha* ran the headline NATIONAL TEAM

263

HUMILIATED. The sports daily *A Bola* preferred THE JOKE OF EUROPE. The *Record* opted for A RIDICULOUS TEAM. The criticism certainly stung the Portuguese into action. Four days later they hammered Russia 7–0, a result that further emphasised the enormity of the shock draw in Vaduz.

Liechtenstein might have basked in their unaccustomed glory, but they too had another qualifier to play in the week ahead. On 13 October they faced fellow no-hopers Luxembourg away. To universal rejoicing, Liechtenstein's newfound form continued as they triumphed 4–0. It was their first ever away victory and their only World Cup qualifying win to date. But it was a mere aberration. They have since lapsed back into losing ways.

There is no explanation for two such 'out-of-the-blue' results. It's what makes football such a dramatic game. Liechtenstein's mixed bag of minor professionals and part-timers may never qualify for a World Cup. Portugal's highly paid superstars could one day win the tournament. And years from now the misty-eyed elders of Vaduz will relate their once-upon-a-time tales of a magical week.

Football's wags are no longer able to use Liechtenstein as the butt of their jokes. A revised edition of Charlie Connelly's *Stamping Grounds* seems like a good bet.

# ONE GREEN BOTTLE

## RIO DE JANEIRO, 19 JANUARY 2005

On Wednesday, 19 January 2005, the news agency Reuters issued a story from Rio de Janeiro concerning a dispute between age-old rivals Brazil and Argentina. There was nothing strange about yet another petty squabble. Except this wasn't 'another' incident at all. The match it concerned took place fifteen years earlier.

On 24 June 1990 Brazil met Argentina in the second-round knockout phase of Italia '90 at the Stadio Delle Alpi ('Alpine Stadium') in Turin. After dominating the game completely without scoring, Brazil lost to an 81st-minute strike from Caniggia following a neat pass by Maradona. Two minutes later the frustrated Brazilian captain Ricardo Gomes was sent off. Yet again Brazil had been 'done' by Argentina. But for once it seemed like a perfectly honest victory.

That was until two days after the game. Then Brazil's left-back Branco claimed he had been drugged by a spiked water bottle 'generously' handed to him by the Argentine medical team midway through the second half. He said it made him 'dizzy and uncoordinated' for the rest of the game. The Brazilian camp claimed the incident affected the result.

All Brazil remained convinced there had been skulduggery, although nothing was ever proved. But in December 2004 new evidence came out of the blue. Diego Maradona, who was by then past caring, admitted on a television show that the allegations were correct. The Argentine FA responded by suggesting, 'Maradona was not in control of his senses.' But both the Brazilian and Argentine press found the lead irresistible.

The Buenos Aires magazine *Veintetres* asked Carlos Bilardo, the Argentine manager at Italia '90, for a straight answer. But his reply was ambiguous: 'I'm not saying it didn't happen.' That was enough for Brazil to reopen the case in a big way. 'This has proved what we have always known,' said Marco Teixeira, secretary of the Brazilian Football Confederation. 'We shall prepare a full dossier for FIFA.'

The reawakened dispute sent Brazil fans searching through their old videos for another look at the incident. An Argentinian player was fouled and stayed down. The physio and water boy ran on. The heat was stifling. One of the Argentinians picked up a green bottle and began to drink, only quickly to spit out the contents after being alerted by the physio. The player then drank from a clear bottle instead, and the (specially prepared?) green bottle was handed to Brazil's Branco as 'a friendly gesture'. He took a hearty swig.

Several more Argentine players are said to have admitted the ruse. According to Maradona the bottle contained Rohypnol (the 'date-rape drug'), a relaxant in small doses but otherwise a strong sedative: 'This wasn't gamesmanship,' fumed Sebastiao Lazaroni, Brazil's manager at the time. 'This was a very dirty trick. Fifteen years or fifteen days doesn't matter. We want action.' Argentina's water boy Galindez, the guilty cocktail waiter, was prepared to give it to him: 'He can come outside any time he wants. I'm ready.'

The result will stand. For once FIFA are largely powerless. Brazil and Argentina will keep on arguing the toss. We will ponder whether there is really such a thing as a kind gesture in World Cup competition, and whether football hatchets are ever truly buried. And Branco should be wondering what on earth made him drink from that one green bottle in the first place. Maybe the heat had already got to him before Argentina did.

# THE THING FROM TRING

## STUTTGART, 22 JUNE 2006

The Hertfordshire market town of Tring is not famous for much. Numbering referee Graham Poll among its 'most famous sons' probably says it all. So when the vastly experienced official was appointed the only British referee at the 2006 World Cup in Germany, he had every reason to walk tall in his home town. Indeed bookmakers considered him a fair bet to be given charge of the World Cup final itself – provided he didn't make a major blunder.

Yet no sooner were the Group matches over than Poll was named one of 14 referees to be sent home. That he did in fact make that 'major blunder' could be judged by a glance at any of the newspaper headlines following the Australia v Croatia game in Stuttgart on 22 June. The British tabloids were merciless. GRAHAM'S THREE CARD TRICK was one of the kindest. POLL LOST THE PLOT less so. But the bluntest of all was reserved for the *Sun* – which poetically dubbed the hapless official THE THING FROM TRING.

Yet it had all started so well – Poll refereed his first two games without undue controversy. Then came the final Group F match which proved crucial in deciding which of Australia or Croatia would progress with Brazil to the next stage. A draw would clinch it for Australia – Croatia needed the win.

Perhaps the kick-off was a portent of things to come – Poll blew to start the game then called back the bemused players to set the ball rolling again. Nor were the team line-ups particularly helpful to him. The Australian side included the rather Croatian-sounding Kalac, Grella, Sterjovski and Viduka. And Croatia fielded several players born in Australia who spoke English with authentic Aussie accents. If Poll planned any bookings he needed to be on the ball.

But thereby lay his downfall. After 61 minutes he brandished a yellow card to Croatia's number 3 Josip Simunic. And after 89 minutes - with the score precariously poised at 2-2 – he again showed Simunic a yellow. But as the defender turned to leave the field for an early bath, he looked back only to realise that Poll had failed to show the obligatory red card – Simunic played on.

Fortunately for Poll, in the few minutes remaining, the Croatians narrowly failed to score the goal that would have put Australia out. And only at the final whistle, when Simunic vociferously alerted Poll to his error, did the flustered referee brandish a third yellow card followed at last by the red.

Poll later gave a lame explanation. When booking Simunic initially he had mistakenly noted down the name of the Australian number 3 instead, so he later believed the second Simunic booking to be his first. It seems the small matter of a glaring difference in shirt colour had been overlooked.

That is how Josip Simunic became only the second player in World Cup finals history to be shown three yellow cards (see 'The Whistle Blower' for the first, again involving Australia) and why 'the thing from Tring' was dispatched home a forlorn figure of fun instead of a man in triumph.

Poll declared himself devastated at such a fundamental error, immediately announcing that he would never referee a finals game again – as if he would have. He did resume control of Premiership games, but his three-card aberration provided the fans with heaven-sent ammunition. Wherever he appeared, chants from both sets of fans rang loud in his ears: 'Three cards and he lost the plot' – 'Graham Graham show us a red' – 'He's forever showing yellow' – 'Get your cards out for the lads' – and many more not suitable for a book like this one.

It soon proved more than he could stand. At the age of only 43 – with seven potential years still ahead – Poll hung up his whistle for good. His final game in a career spanning 1,544 matches was the Derby County v West Bromwich Albion Championship play-off at Wembley on 28 May 2007.

How tragic that one silly error should curtail the career of the man who will be lastingly remembered as 'three card Poll'. Yet strangely many in football who had suffered his whistle to their cost were united in a common reaction – it couldn't have happened to a nicer chap.

# CARDS FOR EVERY OCCASION
## NUREMBERG, 25 JUNE 2006

This story concerns two games played forty-four years apart at Chile '62 and Germany '06. Yet they are curiously connected. Each was a violent contest given the epithet 'battle'. And but for the chastening circumstances of the first, the colourful record set at the second could never have happened.

The key to the link is English referee Ken Aston. His torrid time at Chile '62 led him subsequently to change the face of football for all time. And his innovative thinking unwittingly enabled a new World Cup record to be established at Germany '06. Ken's nightmare occurred on 2 June 1962 when World Cup hosts Chile beat Italy 2-0 (see 'The Battle of Santiago') in a bruising encounter described in subsequent literature as 'the most brutal game ever seen'. After extreme ill-discipline had reigned for the entire ninety minutes, a visibly shaken Aston was escorted from the pitch by armed police. He never took charge of a World Cup match again.

But his experience that dark day had a lasting influence on football's future. The lunging tackles and flailing arms, and his utter feeling of helplessness in the midst of battle, preyed on poor Ken's mind. He mused to himself afterwards – how could referees be given absolute control?

The answer came to him in a flash four years later. His 'Eureka!' moment followed the England v Argentina Quarter-Final at Wembley in 1966 (see 'Animals'). As Ken explained, that fiery game brought the ugly memories of Santiago flooding back:

> 'Nothing had changed by 1966. The Argentines wouldn't respond to the German referee. It was sheer chaos. Then next day the officials announced that both Bobby and

Jack Charlton had been cautioned during the match, but neither player knew. That set me thinking about a signalling system. I was driving home in my MG when the traffic lights changed, so I slowed down and stopped. I didn't question the decision. So I thought that's it. Yellow for 'take it easy', red for 'stop'. That's what football needs.'

The day Ken Aston saw the light added a new dimension to football's lexicon. When his 'red and yellow cards' were introduced to the world at Mexico '70, he and FIFA were convinced that 'disciplinary mayhem' would be a phrase quickly consigned to the game's history.

Initially it seemed to work. Russia's Evgueni Lovchev was the first player to be 'shown yellow'. It came in the opening match against Mexico. But there it stopped. The players dutifully obeyed the Aston Highway Code. Not a single red was seen at Mexico '70.

But four years later the 'amber-gambling' began. At West Germany '74, in a match against the hosts, Chile's Carlos Caszely became the World Cup's first 'red-carded' player when he kicked out at Bertie Vogts. It was the moment Aston's Utopian dream ended. Players and referees have never looked back.

And by Germany '06 the dream had reached nightmare proportions. A staggering 373 cards were shown during the tournament – 345 yellow and 28 red – a World Cup Finals record. Blessedly, Ken Aston MBE wasn't there to witness the abuse of his invention by both players and officials. He died in 2001 aged 86. Not surprisingly, there were some notable individual performances by referees. Indeed the most extreme came in the second match of this sorry saga – the 'card-fest' fiasco between Portugal and Holland on 25 June 2006 in Nuremberg. The Second Round clash was controlled by the Russian referee Valentin Ivanov - the word 'controlled' employed only in its loosest sense.

In the time-honoured fashion the contest was dubbed 'The Battle of Nuremberg'. But it was also tagged 'the dirtiest game of all time' – and Ivanov's antics made it 'official'. His 16 yellow cards equalled the previous World Cup record set by Spanish referee Antonio Nieto at Japorea '02. But Ivanov also brandished four reds which took his overall tally to 20. That's how a 44-year-old teacher from Moscow – in his last big game before retiring – set an all-time carding record for a finals match.

Yet although the game finished nine-a-side and was certainly robust, it was no 'Battle of Santiago'. Maniche – scorer of Portugal's goal in a narrow 1-0 win – shrugged it off as 'not a violent match'. The truth was that Ivanov used his red and yellow ammunition recklessly, needlessly imposing himself at every juncture. In his own defence he claimed to have merely followed the FIFA guidelines on fair play, but admitted 'it was my toughest match'.

His critics' words were less understated. 'Diabolical', 'farcical' and 'ludicrous' led the way. Most controversial of all, FIFA president Sepp Blatter joined in the condemnation, suggesting Ivanov's performance was 'not at the level of the players', and that 'there could have been a yellow card for the referee'.

In the wake of Ivanov's bizarre performance, it seems likely that his record will never be surpassed on such a big stage. It used to be the overbearing Welshman Clive 'The Book' Thomas (see 'The Whistle-Blower') who was regularly voted the most incompetent World Cup referee of all time. Thanks to an out of control Russian ego and the bright ideas of Ken Aston four decades earlier, the new man in power is Valentin 'The Card' Ivanov.

# *SWISS MISS*

## COLOGNE, 26 JUNE 2006

The legendary Liverpool manager Bill Shankly once called football 'a simple game made complicated by people who should know better'. A key tenet of his theory was that clean sheets breed success. For Shankly understood an old football truism. It remains impossible to lose a game if you never concede a goal – except via the lottery of penalties.

Ahead of Germany '06 Switzerland's manager Kobi Kuhn might have pondered this, for in seven previous World Cup finals appearances the Swiss had failed to keep a single clean sheet in 22 games. And they had never won the tournament. Kuhn was no Bill Shankly – but like the down-to-earth Scot he was a profound thinker and rather a sage. He hadn't reached the age of 62 without knowing the value of a solid defence. Something had to change.

Having qualified for Germany '06 with a bright young squad, he impressed on his dutiful players the fundamental importance of that elusive clean sheet. Drawn in Group G with France, Togo and South Korea, chances of Switzerland making progress looked reasonable. Things started well. On 13 June in Stuttgart they drew 0-0 with their big brother neighbours France. To the travelling Swiss army that was a moral victory. Next came Togo in Dortmund on 19 June – another shut-out saw Switzerland emerge 2-0 victors over a side experiencing 'turmoil in the camp'. Then in Hanover on 23 June the first phase of the job was neatly completed by a 2-0 win over South Korea.

The 'keep it tight' philosophy had proved its worth. Three clean sheets saw Switzerland top their group with 7 points – two victories and one draw. Now they had to face Ukraine in the Round of 16. No complicated tactical plans were necessary – the wily old Kuhn simply called for more of the same.

And he got it too. On 26 June in Cologne his boys had again held out when 90 minutes expired. But here the clean sheet theory began to reveal its most obvious flaw – for no Swiss player had managed to score either. Yet still they stuck doggedly to the doctrine. In extra time Ukraine were again kept at bay – but ominously the Swiss attack once more drew a blank. After 120 minutes the 0-0 stalemate reigned – and so to the lottery.

The penalties were concluded swiftly. The Eastern Europeans held their nerve to convert three of their first four spot-kicks, while Streller, Barnetta and Cabanas all missed for Switzerland. No more action was necessary – the Swiss players left the field wondering where the plan had failed. Some shed floods of tears. Like a belief in Santa Claus cruelly shattered, the clean sheet myth had been tragically exposed to once-innocent youngsters.

Switzerland had played 390 minutes without their goal once being breached, yet found themselves out of the tournament. The feat – if that it was – earned them an unenviable record. Switzerland became the first team in history to be knocked out of a FIFA World Cup without letting in a single goal.

Both the team and supporters took heart from this. When the squad flew into Zurich, over 1,000 turned up to welcome back 'their heroes'. Manager Kuhn remained philosophical – 'The recognition from our fans is the most positive thing. Let's forget the penalties and remember our clean sheets. We will keep on building'. The SWISS ON A ROLL headlines had been fun while they lasted. But the enduring legacy of a 2006 World Cup exit on penalties alone was the much more poignant SWISS MISS.

# BEST FRENCH BUTTER

## BERLIN, 9 JULY 2006

As a football spectacle the 2006 World Cup Final between Italy and France at the Olympic Stadium in Berlin proved disappointing. France went ahead via a Zinedine Zidane penalty after 6 minutes. Twelve minutes later Italy equalised through Marco Materazzi, whose trip had earlier cost his side the penalty. The rest of the game proved surprisingly turgid, the score remaining 1-1 even after extra time. The subsequent penalty shoot-out was won 5-3 by Italy, who despite the tameness of the contest joyously celebrated their fourth World Cup triumph.

Yet strangely the subdued final provided one of the most remarkable moments in the whole of World Cup history. And curiously it involved the scoring duo Zidane and Materazzi, with the superstar Frenchman stealing the headlines.

Before the World Cup began, 34-year-old Zidane had affirmed his intent to retire at the end of his last game in the tournament. That placed him under closer scrutiny than even he was used to – everybody was curious to see what Zidane's final act as a player would be.

The watching world found out 5 minutes into the second period of extra-time.

Shortly after a brief tussle when Zidane yanked Materazzi's shirt, words between the pair were exchanged. Play continued, and the spat appeared to be over as both players progressed upfield to resume their positions. But when Zidane was a few yards ahead, he rounded on Materazzi, lowered his head in the manner of a maddened bull or peevish goat and butted the Italian square in the chest, knocking him backwards clean off his feet.

Once alerted to the assault by his fourth official, the Argentine referee had no choice but to dismiss Zidane from the field – the

Frenchman departed to a shameful 'early bath', literally the final 'head-bowed' moment in a glittering but controversial career. Why he had done it nobody knew. Zidane – born in Marseille to Algerian parents – implied that Materazzi had insulted both his mother and his sister. Materazzi strenuously denied the allegation. Sections of the media called in 'expert' lip-readers for enlightenment, but their findings were strangely diverse. According to BBC News, Materazzi had called Zidane 'a liar' before bidding him 'an ugly death to you and your family'. But another source came up with the pithier 'you're the son of a terrorist whore'.

None but the two players will ever know the truth. But whatever the provocation, the Zidane response was widely considered inexcusable, particularly as FIFA had chosen the 2006 tournament to launch a special initiative on 'fair play'. But thereby hangs the final curious twist in a bizarre tale. Zinedine Zidane won the coveted 'Golden Ball' award for the 2006 World Cup's 'best player'. He was also elected to the 23-man squad for the tournament's 'All Star Team' – voted for by FIFA's own 'technical study group'.

Perhaps even Zidane felt a pang of shame. He later issued an apology, but qualified it with the resonant phrase 'je ne regrette rien' – 'I regret nothing'.

Did that include being excluded from the penalty shoot-out when his country needed him most? No one was brave enough to ask without body armour!

# BERT'S POSTHUMOUS FEAT
## ZURICH, 10 NOVEMBER 2006

It was the inimitable Brian Clough – 'the best manager England never had' – who sagely pointed out that 'it only takes a second to score a goal'. So it should be perfectly possible to score a hat-trick in three seconds. Well no actually, but we know what the great man meant. In fact the fastest hat-trick in World Cup Finals history was at Spain '82 when Hungary substitute Laszlo Kiss bagged a remarkable treble in just seven minutes against a hapless Paraguay (see 'Kissed Goodbye').

But most hat-tricks take a little longer. Or in the case of Bert Patenaude of the United States a lot longer. Arguably 76 years – for that was how long it took for Bert's hotly-disputed hat-trick to be officially recognised.

The saga of this long-running oddity begins in Uruguay at the first FIFA World Cup in 1930 – and ends in the offices of FIFA in Zurich in 2006. First the unequivocal facts – that in Montevideo on 19 July 1930 Argentina had thrashed Mexico 6-3 helped by a cast-iron treble from Guillermo Stabile. The undisputed feat earned Stabile a place in the record books as the scorer of the first hat-trick in World Cup history. And there he remained, apparently unassailable for all time – until Bert Patenaude ghosted in from the dead to displace him.

Bertram 'Bert' Albert Patenaude was born in Fall River, Massachusetts, United States on 4 November 1909. When he died in 1974 on his 65th birthday his world football credentials were unremarkable. But Bert passed to the great dressing room in the sky certain that a place in World Cup history had been unfairly denied him, for he always claimed that on 17 July 1930 he had scored a hat-trick of his own – two days before Stabile bagged the famous 'first'.

277

In his own version of events the historic feat was achieved when United States beat Paraguay 3-0 in the inaugural World Cup. Bert opened the scoring in the 10th minute and also notched the final goal in the 50th minute. And by his own account he had netted the middle goal after 15 minutes.

Yet for some reason – later cited as a minor deflection – Bert had not been officially credited with that second goal. One source gave it the US player Tom Florie and another tagged it an own goal by Paraguay's Aurelio Gonzalez. Bert's all-important strike had been air-brushed from football history. So for years he remained officially the scorer of a paltry brace rather than a celebrated triple. But when Patenaude was inducted into the US Soccer Hall of Fame in 1971 the matter re-surfaced. When interviewed Patenaude stuck to his story – well who wouldn't?

Yet nothing would have changed but for a group of dogged statisticians unearthing the original sources. First they checked the 1930 World Cup report submitted to the United States Football Association by manager Alfred Cummings – it credited Patenaude with all three goals. Then they found three survivors of the game who backed Bert to the hilt. Some 1930 newspaper reports were equally convincing – the Argentina daily *La Prensa* not only gave Bert the hat-trick, but issued diagrams of how the goals were scored.

That was enough for the stats gurus to press the case. The all-powerful FIFA authorities were approached. Having rather more urgent matters to consider, the case proved a slow burner. But finally a decision was made. On 10 November 2006 poor Guillermo Stabile was stripped of his honour in favour of his US rival.

So that is how Bert Patenaude finally secured World Cup immortality and found his way into the *Guinness World Records Book* to boot. He will remain forever the scorer of the World Cup's first hat-trick. And at a lingering 76 years the one that took longest to complete – now what might Brian Clough have made of that?

# *WWW.YOUMISSED.COM*

## GLASGOW, 11 OCTOBER 2008

Before 'action replays' a player could miss an open goal and consign it to oblivion after a few beers. But if television rendered refuge from such howlers more difficult, the internet has since made escape impossible. Which is why Scottish international striker Chris Iwelumo must have wished he had played in another era, for his 'worst miss of all time' has been viewed online by chortling millions the world over.

Born to a Nigerian father and Scottish mother, the vagaries of eligibility enabled Scotland manager George Burley to give the Wolverhampton Wanderers striker his big international chance. Iwelumo had always expected his full Scottish debut to be memorable – but in rather a different way.

Hampden Park on 11 October 2008 was no place for the faint-hearted. Scotland faced Norway in a key 2010 World Cup qualifier. Although only Scotland's third game, a win might well have set the tone for a triumphant campaign. As it was, the spoils were shared in a no-score draw – and in the final event Scotland narrowly failed to qualify for South Africa 2010.

After 57 minutes Iwelumo came on as a substitute. His recurring nightmare moment arrived all too soon. In the 64th minute a perfect ball delivered square into the box from the left evaded the despairing sprawl of Norway's keeper at the near post. Scotland's debutant had timed his run to perfection. When the ball arrived at his feet Iwelumo was three yards from the goal line, central between the posts, with no keeper to beat. And the goal is eight yards wide. Surely any touch would do.

There are many epithets applied to such chances – 'gilt-edged', 'on a plate', 'absolute sitter', 'tap in', 'nailed on certainty', 'open goal' – yet none does justice to an opportunity which has entered football folklore simply as 'Iwelumo's miss'.

Perhaps he was contemplating his goal celebration even as he made contact. We will never know – but at the biggest moment of his career he somehow contrived to play the ball back high across the face of goal inches wide of the near post. Could his grandmother have scored? Without a doubt – and blindfolded too.

The Scottish fans clutched their heads in mass disbelief. Iwelumo looked stunned, sickened and embarrassed in equal part. And when the miss was shown on the stadium's big screen, an audible gasp filled the Hampden air.

No sooner had the misdeed been perpetrated than the pundits dubbed the spurned chance the 'greatest miss of all time' – so great in fact that the radio commentary duo of Alan Rough and Ewen Cameron had initially celebrated a goal. When they realised their error they delivered in unison the most comedic 'ooooh noooo' ever to grace the airwaves – worth a listen in its own right.

Although quickly supported by manager Burley and the Scottish squad, Iwelumo remained inconsolable. He confessed to 'days of torture and sleepless nights' and to watching replays of the chance over and over again.

And he wasn't the only one. Once the blooper was posted on the internet the fun really started. Cumulative viewings ran well into the millions worldwide – still rising. Nor is a single viewing enough – at the next click of the mouse he must surely score. Except he never does and never will.

Poor Chris Iwelumo isn't the first player to endure trial by internet. But none in World Cup history has suffered so cruelly. If only he had put it 'in' the net, he'd have spared himself so much ridicule 'on' the net. But he didn't, and his nightmare will recur *ad infinitum*. In the harsh world of e-football there is no hiding place. Lest we forget – it's 'Iwelumo's Miss' on www.youtube.com.

# THE BEARDED WONDER
## WEMBLEY, 14 OCTOBER 2009

The final whistle of *The World Cup's Strangest Moments* is almost upon us, although a Frenchman made a late successful bid to grasp the last page with both hands – or was it one hand twice? – so it is time in this penultimate story to take stock from an England perspective. At Germany 2006 England were eliminated on penalties by Portugal in the Quarter Final. Manager Sven-Göran Eriksson was shown the door and replaced by his assistant Steve McClaren. In November 2007 he too was dismissed after England failed to qualify for Euro 2008. The FA then turned to the former Italian international Fabio Capello, only the second non-Englishman to manage the national side. His first challenge was clear – to qualify for the 2010 World Cup in South Africa.

Cue what is arguably the most unbelievable climax to any match in *The World Cup's Strangest Moments*. England were robbed in the last second of the final qualifying game after a freak goal was wrongly allowed to stand by a Portuguese referee. His assistant, distracted by a fox which had strayed onto the Wembley pitch, had failed to raise a flag for a clear offside. The strike on goal hit the creature a glancing blow. The ball deflected away from the England keeper's futile dive to nestle in the net. The fox bit captain John Terry as it fled the scene. Terry floored the referee. England had failed to qualify.

All gloriously untrue! Yet the reality was almost as strange as the imagined nightmare. England won nine of their ten qualifying games, securing the prize with a 5-1 victory against erstwhile bogey side Croatia. They qualified with two games to spare, the first time any England manager had achieved that feat. Capello's side had scored 34 goals and conceded only 6. No major controversy had dogged the campaign. No hard luck stories. England fans and even the media were truly chilled for the first time in years. South Africa beckoned.

As a consequence England's final qualifying game has no right to make it into this book. On 14 October 2009 a Wembley crowd of 76,897 witnessed an academic 3-0 victory over Belarus. So relaxed was the occasion that the biggest talking point during the game was the luxuriant new beard of substitute David Beckham. When he entered the action after 58 minutes to earn his 115th cap, it brought the biggest cheer of the night.

But therein lays the twist. For it was after the final whistle that Beckham really hit the news. His former Manchester United team-mate Steve Bruce, manager of Sunderland, seemed instinctively to know that a strange story was required – and he obliged with a corker.

Bruce was working as a television pundit for ITV. It was his job to elect a 'man of the match'. He chose David Beckham. That he had played only 32 minutes, hadn't scored, or performed even a minor miracle, did not seem to unduly worry the besotted pundit – the 'bearded wonder' got the award and that was that.

With little much else to write about, the tabloid press yelled 'outrage'. Didn't Peter Crouch score twice? One paper labelled Bruce's decision 'grotesque'. The *Daily Mail* ranted: 'Beckham mania descended into certifiable lunacy when he was named man of a match in which he made a lesser contribution than the ball boys.' Even manager Capello made a rare joke – 'It is like Barack Obama getting the Nobel Peace Prize'. There was more to that jest than met the casual eye – only days earlier the rookie US president had won the Nobel Peace Prize!

After Steve Bruce had finished spluttering his lame justification –'one of his passes was magnificent' – all thoughts turned to South Africa 2010. On 4 December 2009 the draw was made in Cape Town. No one dropped the balls. All went smoothly – England nabbed what was considered a 'comfortable' Group C with USA, Algeria and Slovenia. And on that slender hope, fans of the 'Three Lions' dared to dream of the only World

Cup Final victory since 1966. The Sun newspaper set the tone by spelling out the word 'EASY' in their headline – England, Algeria, Slovenia, Yanks. Over the pond the *Los Angeles Times* labelled *The Sun* 'scurrilous'. The fun had already started.

# FINISHING TOUCHES
## PARIS, 18 NOVEMBER 2009

The finishing touches to the *World Cup's Strangest Moments* had been scheduled to be applied by the previous story. The 'Bearded Wonder' David Beckham had secured 'by a whisker' his last-page rights. The floundering pundit Steve Bruce had proved a perfect court jester. England were South Africa-bound. Surely nothing between that and the big kick-off in June 2010 could top it.

But the enigmatic Frenchman Thierry Henry had other ideas. At the eleventh hour the Barcelona striker delivered a *coup de grace* which added his own final and wicked touch to the World Cup build-up. It not only wrested the closing pages away from 'Becks' and 'Brucie'– it also left a Republic of Ireland camp suffused with rage, and the world's media analysing a contro-versial and crucial goal like few before it.

Here are the facts. After both nations finished second in their respective qualifying groups, Republic of Ireland and France met in a two-legged play-off to decide who would be boarding that plane to South Africa come summer 2010. In Dublin on 14 November 2009 France won the first leg 1-0. Ireland's prospects looked bleak.

But in the return only four days later at the Stade de France, the Republic quickly levelled via Robbie Keane on 32 minutes. At both full time and early in extra time the 1-1 aggregate prevailed. The lottery of penalties loomed. Unfashionable underdogs Ireland had a real chance of advancing to the 19th FIFA World Cup at the expense of their super-chic French opponents.

But then it happened. As the first period of extra time ticked away, a French free-kick delivered diagonally into the box appeared to have eluded everyone. But ghosting in at the far post was Henry. His first touch prevented the ball from going out of play. His second controlled it. And a final prod into the six-yard area enabled the inrushing William Gallas to bundle the ball over the line. The strike eased the French 2-1 ahead on aggregate, and so it remained. It was the goal that sent France to South Africa at Ireland's expense.

Yet something strange happened in the French press. The expected acclamations of 'Bravo Henry' and 'Vive la France' failed to materialise. Nor did the rest of the world receive the victory with anything but contempt. In Ireland itself the mood was darker than even the blackest Guinness.

And for a simple reason. The Irish had been roundly cheated. For the first two deft touches of Henry's vital assist had clearly been made with the Frenchman's hand! The Republic's players knew it. Henry admitted it. Millions of television viewers saw the cast-iron evidence within seconds of the incident. Even the pitch-side backroom staff had access to TV replays. Yet the Swedish referee Martin Hansson and both of his assistants appeared not to have noticed the infringement at all.

Not since Diego Maradona's infamous 'Hand of God' strike at Mexico 1986 had any goal attracted such universal attention. The mass media speedily dubbed the incident the 'Hand of Henry'. One journalist preferred 'Le Hand of God'. A less politically-correct one coined the 'Hand of Frog'. And in the pubs of Ireland the preferred phrase is one I am unable to repeat here.

Suffice to say that Henry in many quarters was accused of being a common cheat – and this a player who had on previous occasions declared himself quite a paragon of virtue. Yet now, although quickly admitting his 'guilt', Henry offered little in the way of remorse or apology. Instead, merely blaming the officials for missing the offence, he took refuge behind a convenient mantra – 'I am not the referee'.

In France the former World Cup winner Bixente Lizarazu – in his role as pundit - summed up the national mood: 'We are going to the World Cup, but we go to the locker room with our heads bowed. It was not something to be proud of. I shall not be going to the victory party.'

In Britain the *Daily Telegraph* allowed their columnist to really let rip, albeit with a bizarre metaphor: 'A win is a win, but the manner of it means Henry's halo didn't just slip, it fell right off, and is now being used as a toilet for the dog on a string of a Parisian tramp.' Strong words indeed.

As for the Irish, the mood swung between a seething sense of injustice and a resigned acceptance that 'the big teams always get the decisions'. A half-hearted request by the Football Association of Ireland for the game to be replayed was quickly rebuffed by FIFA. As was a (surely tongue-in-cheek) suggestion that Ireland be allowed to go to South Africa as the World Cup's 33rd team.

In the event, FIFA conducted 'an investigation' into the controversy which was no more than a PR exercise. And on 18 January 2010 their 'official statement' declared the 'Hand of Henry' affair effectively closed: 'Handling the ball could not be regarded as a serious infringement. There is no legal foundation to consider the case further.' No punishment was delivered.

So that is how France plundered their ticket to South Africa. But there my narrative must pass into the realms of conjecture. As I finish writing, the 2010 World Cup results, like those of all the future tournaments, are known to no one.

But more strange incidents are guaranteed. There will be skulduggery and drama for sure. Referees will lose it. Fans will perform bizarre rituals. More underdogs will have their day. With a bit of luck there might be a mass brawl of mascots. Or strangeness of a darker hue could yet cast its shadow across football's biggest stage. The World Cup is a prime target for terrorist attack.

Fabio Capello may make another joke. Pelé will doubtless hedge his bets by sagely predicting that 'an African nation will win the World Cup by the year 3,000'. Some hapless pundit will say the f-word on air. At least one player at every tournament will be sent home in disgrace. Scotland will one day reach the second phase. Thierry Henry will concede the 'handball' penalty that sends France crashing out. The moon may be made of cheese. And England – not Germany – will win the World Cup Final on penalties.

# SELECTED SOURCES

## BOOKS

Allen, Peter, *An Amber Glow: The Story of England's World Cup-winning Football*, Mainstream, 2000

Ballard, John & Suff, Paul, *The Dictionary of Football*, Boxtree, 1999

Camkin, John, *World Cup 1958*, Rupert Hart-Davis, 1958

Connelly, Charlie, *Stamping Grounds: Liechtenstein's World Cup Odyssey*, Little, Brown, 2002

Evans, Philip, *World Cup '90*, Hodder and Stoughton, 1990

Freddi, Cris, *Complete Book of the World Cup 2002*, HarperCollinsWillow, 2002

Glanville, Brian, *World Cup*, Robert Hale, 1958

Harris, Harry, *Hoddle's England: The road to France*, HarperCollinsWillow, 1998

Hoddle, Glenn, *My 1998 World Cup Story*, André Deutsch, 1998

Hurst, Geoff, *1966 And All That: My Autobiography*, Headline, 2001

Jones, Ken, *Jules Rimet Still Gleaming? England at the World Cup*, Virgin, 2003

Mayes, Harold, *World Cup Report 1966*, Heinemann, 1967

McColl, Graham, *England: The Alf Ramsey Years*, Chameleon, 1998

McColl, Graham, *Scotland in the World Cup Finals*, Chameleon, 1998

Miller, David, *The World Cup 1970*, Heinemann, 1970

Morrison, Ian, *The World Cup: A Complete Record*, Breedon Books, 1990

Pickering, David, *The Cassell Soccer Companion*, Cassell, 1998

Powell, Jeff, *Bobby Moore*, Robson Books, 1998

Robinson, John, *Soccer: The World Cup 1930–2006*, Soccer Books, 2006

Rollin, Jack, *England's World Cup Triumph*, Davies Books, 1966

Rollin, Jack, *Soccer Shorts*, Guinness Publishing, 1988

Saunders, Donald, *World Cup 1962*, Heinemann, 1962

Seddon, Peter, *A Football Compendium*, British Library, 1999

Seddon, Peter, *Football Talk*, Robson Books, 2004

Sharpe, Graham, *The Book of Bizarre Football*, Robson Books, 2002

Sharpe, Graham, *The Final Whistle*, Robson Books, 2001

Shaw, Phil, *The Book of Football Quotations*, Ebury Press, 2003

Shirley, Simon, *France 1998, The World Cup: A Definitive History and Guide*, Janus, 1998

Tibballs, Geoff, *Great Sporting Eccentrics*, Robson Books, 1998.

Ward, Andrew, *Football's Strangest Matches*, Robson Books, 1999.

Winkworth, Stephen, *Famous Sporting Fiascos*, The Bodley Head, 1982

## WEBSITES

www.planetworldcup.com

www.fifa.com

www.worldcup2010southafrica.com

www.uefa.com

www.wsc.co.uk

www.fourfourtwo.com

www.worldscoccer.com

www.worldcupyears.com

www.worldcupblog.com

www.ufwc.co.uk

www.expertfootball.com

www.worldcupweb.com

www.guardian.co.uk

www.telegraph.co.uk

www.timesonline.co.uk

www.dailymail.co.uk

www.thesun.co.uk

www.mirrorfootball.co.uk

www.express.co.uk

www.newsoftheworld.co.uk

www.philosophyfootball.com

www.soccerpost.com

www.thefa.com

www.englandfc.com